The Bib Sac Reader

Dr. G. W. Peters

The Bib Sac Reader

Commemorating Fifty Years of Publication
by Dallas Theological Seminary
1934-1983

edited by
John F. Walvoord
Roy B. Zuck

WITHDRAWN

MOODY PRESS
CHICAGO

© 1983 by
DALLAS THEOLOGICAL SEMINARY

Scripture quotations from the *New American Standard
Bible*, © 1960, 1962, 1963, 1968, 1971, 1972, 1973,
1975, and 1977 by The Lockman Foundation, are used
by permission.

Library of Congress Cataloging in Publication Data

Main entry under title:

The Bib sac reader.

Includes bibliograpical references.
 1. Bible—Criticism, interpretation, etc.—Addresses,
essays, lectures. 2. Theology—Addresses, essays, lectures. I. Walvoord, John F. II. Zuck, Roy B. III. Dallas
Theological Seminary. IV. Bibliotheca sacra (Andover,
Mass.: 1876)
BS540.B42 1983   230'.044   82-18843

ISBN: 0-8024-0459-6

1 2 3 4 5 Printing/BC/Year 87 86 85 84 83 82

Printed in the United States of America

Preface

The year 1983 marks the fiftieth year that Dallas Theological Seminary has published *Bibliotheca Sacra*. This volume has been compiled to celebrate that significant anniversary date. Dallas Seminary assumed the publication of this journal in 1934.

Bibliotheca Sacra, however, has been in continuous publication since 1843. Thus with the October 1982 issue, 140 years of publication were completed. (The January 1983 number is volume 140, not 141, because the numbering system began with the second year of publication.)

The founder of *Bibliotheca Sacra*, which means "Sacred Liberty," was Edward Robinson of New York City. It has the distinction of being the oldest continuously published theological journal in the Western Hemisphere. In addition its circulation is among the largest of theological journals.

These eight persons have served as editors of the journal:

Edward Robinson (1843)
Bela Bates Edwards (1844-51)
Edwards Amasa Park (1852-83)
George Frederick Wright (1884-1921)
Melvin Grove Kyle (1922-33)
Rollin T. Chafer (1934-40)
Lewis Sperry Chafer (1940-52)
John F. Walvoord (1952-)

In 1963 the book *The Truth for Today: Bibliotheca Sacra Reader* was published by Moody Press to commemorate Dallas Seminary's publishing of this journal from 1934 to 1963. That book included chapters selected and reprinted from those thirty years of publication. Now this volume, *The Bib Sac Reader*, is a compilation of twenty-one carefully selected articles from issues in the last decade. These include articles on theological, biblical, and ministerial subjects, written by Dallas Theological Seminary faculty members and other outstanding evangelical theologians and scholars. These chapters, it is believed, are representative of the excellent standards maintained by *Bibliotheca Sacra* through its many years of publishing ministry.

Table of Contents

*Indicates date when the article appeared in *Bibliotheca Sacra.*

Theological Studies

1

Some Important Aspects of Biblical Inerrancy

Charles C. Ryrie

Harold Lindsell's significant book *The Battle for the Bible*[1] has itself provoked a battle! The importance of that book lies in at least three areas: theology, history, and prediction. Inspiration and inerrancy, which underlie the doctrine of the authority of the Bible, are basic to theology. Lindsell's studies in history relative to what has happened to denominations and schools that compromised inerrancy provide significant perspective on the contemporary ecclesiastical scene. And those same historical observations give a basis for predicting what may happen to other groups in the future.

The reactions to the book have been almost as interesting and significant as the book itself. Some agreed wholeheartedly with its theses and warnings.[2] Others, named in the book, have challenged the charge that they have departed from a belief in inerrancy. To accomplish this, however, they have (a) substituted the word *infallible* or *inspired* for the word *inerrant*, or (b) qualified *inerrancy* by eliminating accuracy from its meaning, or (c) redefined it by allowing it to mean that there can be errors in nonsoteriological areas of biblical revelation.[3] Still others, while claiming to hold the view of inerrancy stated in the book, bemoan the furor and division it has

Charles C. Ryrie
A.B., Haverford College; Th.M., Th.D., Dallas Theological Seminary; Ph.D., Edinburgh University
Professor and Chairman, Department of Systematic Theology
Dallas Theological Seminary

generated.⁴ Either they consider inerrancy not to be the high priority doctrine Lindsell judges it to be, or they assume that divisions are to be avoided at all costs.

One should recognize that Lindsell does not claim that inerrancy is *the* watershed doctrine of the Christian faith, but he insists that to be properly called an evangelical one must hold to that doctrine. This has probably grated most on those who do not hold inerrancy but who want the label *evangelical*. However, agreement or disagreement with Lindsell's or anyone else's definition of the term *evangelical* must never obscure the fact that inerrancy is a crucial doctrine whose importance must not be eclipsed in the name of Christian unity or by the sleight of hand of redefinition.

INERRANCY AND THE TRUTHFULNESS OF GOD

A standard deductive argument for inerrancy is this: God is true (Rom. 3:4); the Scriptures were breathed out by God (2 Tim. 3:16); therefore the Scriptures are true (since they came from the breath of God, who is true). This is not to imply that those who deny or adjust the meaning of inerrancy deny that God is true; rather they point out that because God used fallible men, it is to be expected that what those men produced (the Bible) contains errors.

Logic alone could lead to either conclusion, but the Scriptures in 2 Peter 1:21 indicate which is correct.

English translations obscure the important parallelism in 2 Peter 1:21. Literally it reads, "For prophecy was not borne (or brought) by the will of man at any time, but men spoke from God, being borne (or brought) by the Holy Spirit." "Prophecy" here may refer to the entire Scriptures or just to the prophetic portions, but in either case the use of the same verb to contrast the will of man and the work of God is striking. Man's will, including his will to make mistakes, did not bring the Scriptures; rather, the Holy Spirit who is perfect and who bore the human writers along, brought man the Scriptures.

> It was through the instrumentality of men who "spake from him." More specifically, it was through an operation of the Holy Ghost on these men which is described as "bearing" them. The term here used is a very specific one. It is not to be confounded with guiding, or directing, or controlling, or even leading in the

full sense of that word. It goes beyond all such terms, in assigning the effect produced specifically to the active agent. What is "borne" is taken up by the "bearer," and conveyed by the "bearer's" power, not its own, to the "bearer's" goal, not its own. The men who spoke from God are here declared, therefore, to have been taken up by the Holy Spirit and brought by His power to the goal of His choosing. The things which they spoke under this operation of the Spirit were therefore His things, not theirs.[5]

And God is true.

Admittedly, one can affirm the truthfulness of God and deny the truthfulness of the Bible, but this does not accord with the evidence of 2 Peter 1:21.[6]

SUBJECTIVISM AND LIMITED INERRANCY

Limited inerrancy means either (a) that inerrancy does not require Cape Kennedy standards of accuracy (and thus may include errors by ordinary mortals' standards), or (b) that inerrancy is limited to parts of the Bible that pertain to its saving message (and thus other parts may and do in fact contain errors). In either case one can scarcely escape the conclusion that limited inerrancy is a synonym (deliberately less conspicuous?) for errancy.

However, the limited inerrancy (= errancy) view inherently contains certain perplexing problems. One is the apparent conclusion that errors can teach truth. Hubbard, for example, states that one has a false view of the sufficiency of the Bible when "we claim it to be inerrant on the basis of minute details of chronology, geography, history, or cosmology."[7] Yet he affirms that "every part of Scripture is God-given" and that all parts have significance as they contribute to the whole which is "the infallible rule."[8] Undoubtedly the rejoinder to this conclusion would be that erroneous statements do not teach truth, but they do not hinder the communication of truth, particularly in revealing the truth about salvation. It would seem, however, to require more faith to believe that God-permitted errors do not affect the teaching of the Bible than to believe that God-guarded authors were kept from writing errors.

This leads to a second area of confusion. How can one be sure that the soteriological content of the Bible is without error? Ray Summers, after citing several examples of contradictions in the Bible, concludes: "I confess the infallibility and inerrancy of the Scriptures in accomplishing God's purpose for them—to give man the revelation of God in His redemptive love through Jesus Christ."[9] But how can he have confidence that the doctrine of redemptive love is true? His attempt to distinguish "historical accuracy" (which he does not hold to fully) from "doctrinal integrity" (which he does hold) is a false dichotomy. For all doctrinal integrity has to be based on historical accuracy. If there are historical inaccuracies, however minute, then one can have no guarantee of doctrinal integrity. Or to claim historical accuracy in statements regarding salvation and to deny it in other areas is a subjective distinction which is only as valid as the authority of the person who makes it.

This leads to a third problem. If, as limited inerrantists (= errantists) hold, there are areas of biblical truth which do not have to be inerrant, could one not expect to find agreement as to what those areas are or some criteria by which to determine such areas? But each writer seems to have his own list. Mickelson elaborates on Matthew 27:9 and says there are "hundreds of examples like this one."[10] Beegle lists Jude 14; Jude 9; 2 Kings 15:27; 2 Kings 18:1; Genesis 5; Acts 7:4; Acts 7:15-16; Galatians 3:17; Mark 14:30, 72; 1 Corinthians 3:19; and 2 Samuel 24:1 (cf. 1 Chron. 21:1).[11] Fuller is troubled by Matthew 13:31-32 and problems in Acts 7.[12] Mounce cites 2 Chronicles 4:2; Numbers 25:9 (cf. 1 Cor. 10:8); Mark 2:26; and Matthew 22:42 (cf. Luke 20:41) as examples of "a kind of inerrancy that falls short of perfect conformity to what was actually said" and of problems to which only "highly fanciful" explanations could be given.[13] Granted these writers are not attempting to give exhaustive lists, but what are the criteria for determining areas in which errors are immaterial? Or more important, what or who decides the boundary lines between the territory of permissible errancy and the territory of necessary inerrancy? These questions remind one of a similar problem which those who deny eternal security have. They agree that sin causes one to lose his salvation, but there is little agreement as to which specific sins would do this. The morass of subjectivism is composed of the quicksand of uncertainty.

AUGUSTINE AND INERRANCY

The history of a doctrine is almost always a worthwhile study. But one must ask, worthwhile for what purpose? Proponents and opponents of inerrancy usually investigate the history of that doctrine. Proponents seek to show inerrancy is not a new concept, but that the contemporary understanding of inerrancy is in accord with what has been taught in the past. Opponents insist that the modern definition of inerrancy is more rigid than the historical one.

Rogers, for example, labors to show that the divines of the church taught the principle of accommodation, or that the thoughts of the writers of Scripture were more important than the words (thus undermining verbal inspiration and inerrancy), or that the authority of Scripture is derived from the saving knowledge of Christ or the inner witness of the Spirit.[14] Rogers's goal is to try to show that the Fathers did not consider the "bare word of Scripture" to be authoritative in and of itself, since such teaching would demand inerrancy as its necessary corollary. His historical research leads him to conclude that "it is no doubt possible to define the meaning of biblical inerrancy according to the Bible's saving purpose and taking into account the human forms through which God condescended to reveal himself. Inerrancy thus defined could be heartily affirmed by those in the Augustinian tradition" (in contrast to Aristotelian notions which impose, in the tradition of Princeton theology, "notions of accuracy" on the Bible itself).[15]

Rogers's conclusions do not square with the facts. For one thing, the use of the word *accommodation* by some of the church divines does not mean they believed in an errant text. They simply meant that God condescended to speak in language so that man could understand.[16]

For another thing, Augustine did not connect inerrancy merely with the Bible's saving purpose, but with errorlessness. He clearly stated the following:

> Most disastrous consequences must follow upon our believing that anything false is found in the sacred books: that is to say that the men by whom the Scripture has been given to us and committed to writing, did not put down in these books anything false. If you once admit into such a high sanctuary of authority one false statement, there will not be left a single sentence of those books, which, if appearing to any one difficult in practice

or hard to believe, may not by the same fatal rule be explained away as a statement, in which, intentionally, the author declared what was not true.[17]

While it is true that Augustine did stress the religious, moral, and soteriological aim of Scripture, it is equally evident that he taught that the historical facts of the Bible were absolutely trustworthy.[18]

The Label *Evangelical*

The reactions to Lindsell's challenge as to whether a person can truly be an evangelical if he denies biblical inerrancy are perhaps more significant than the challenge itself. To be fair, Lindsell's critics should acknowledge that he recognizes that a person can be a Christian without holding to inerrancy.[19] But because the term *evangelical* has traditionally been defined as including a belief in the authority of the Bible, and because he insists that limited inerrancy effectually denies full authority, he concludes that one who holds limited inerrancy cannot truly be an evangelical.

Almost every definition of *evangelical* includes a statement concerning belief in the authority of Scripture. The question is whether limited or partial inerrancy (= partial errancy) can qualify as holding to the authority of the Bible. How can one escape the conclusion that limited inerrancy or partial errancy places a limitation on authority, since those passages which contain errors, however few or many, have either no authority or diluted authority or misleading authority, all of which adds up to some limitation of authority? By contrast, it is difficult to escape the conclusion that total inerrancy means unrestricted authority.

Those who deplore this kind of logic fear that it will lead to divisions in the church. They are right. It will, and it has. But who divided from whom? This idea that inerrancy is limited only to soteriological matters is new, and this is what has divided contemporary evangelicals (even before Lindsell's book). Even Clark Pinnock, who deplores these divisions, acknowledges that he has "deep misgivings" about where partial errancy has led Paul K. Jewett, because Pinnock recognizes that Jewett writes now from a liberal rather than a firmly evangelical theological methodology.[20]

Gerald T. Sheppard, of Union Theological Seminary, New

York, is not so charitable. He labels the methodology represented by Jewett as neoorthodox[21] and observes that Fuller Theological Seminary "has orchestrated a media campaign to defend the evangelical status of the seminary."[22] Further, he declares that Fuller Seminary demonstrates "a serious inconsistency in distinguishing evangelicalism from neo-orthodoxy" because "Barth, Brunner, Cullmann, and Eichrodt provide more attractive models at Fuller for an 'evangelical' approach to Scripture" than do Strong, Hodge, and Warfield.[23]

While it cannot be denied that insistence on total inerrancy leads to divisions, neither can it be denied that limited inerrancy (= partial errancy) leads to a nonevangelical view of the Bible. Can, then, limited inerrancy be truly or at least fully evangelical?

DOCETISM, EBIONISM, AND INERRANCY

Docetism, a first-century heresy, taught that Christ did not actually become flesh but only appeared as a man, thus robbing Him of genuine humanity. Though Docetism was a Christological error, an analogy has been drawn between it and the doctrine of inspiration which allegedly overemphasizes the divine authorship of the Scriptures to the neglect of its "humanness." Divine superintendence to the extent of producing an errorless Bible is said to be a Docetic view of inspiration. Barth made this charge,[24] and more recently so also did Berkouwer.[25] Jewett, too, regards the unlimited inerrancy view (which he links with mechanical dictation) as an example of the ancient heresy of Docetism, concluding that a balanced view of inspiration which recognizes fully the humanity of the writers does not require inerrancy.[26]

But if it be true (which it is not) that those who hold total inerrancy are espousing a heresy akin to Docetism, then it is equally true that those who hold partial inerrancy (= errancy) support a doctrine analogous to Ebionism. Ebionites denied the deity of Christ, regarding Him rather as the natural son of Joseph and Mary who was elected Son of God (not eternal) at His baptism. Though Jesus was a great prophet and higher than the archangels, He was not divine. If inerrancy is like Docetism, then errancy, albeit limited, is like Ebionism, since the humanity of the Bible permits errors in it. Thompson comments, "Real men living in the real world engaged in real struggle as spokesmen for God stand behind the words they inscribed. Certainly the Holy Spirit inspired, directed and taught them. But did He guarantee that their essays would never contain a single mistake?"[27] Thompson then answers no to his question and adds that he does not "regard the doctrine of inerrancy helpful or relevant."[28]

Though Docetism and Ebionism were heretical views of the person of Christ, there is an orthodox doctrine, namely, that He is fully God and sinless man united in one person forever. He was never less than God nor on any occasion a sinning man. At the Incarnation deity was joined with perfect humanity without diminishing the divine or involving the humanity in sin.

Likewise, the Bible is the product of the superintendence of God over human authors without involving error. This does not mean passivity on the part of the human authors nor does it mean freedom for them to include erroneous statements. It means using them in research (Luke 1:1-4), permitting them to express intense feeling (Rom. 9:1-3), transmitting direct revelation (Deut. 9:10), giving authoritative commands (1 Cor. 7:10), expressing opinions (1 Cor. 7:40), but always guided and guarded by the Holy Spirit (2 Pet. 1:21) so that the product can be said to have been breathed out by God (2 Tim. 3:16).

Because of this wedding of divine and human activity to produce inerrant autographs, the minute details of the Bible can be relied on. The Lord Jesus certainly relied on those details. When charged with blasphemy, He defended Himself on the basis of a single word from a rather "run-of-the-mill" passage (John 10:34 quoting Ps. 82:6).[29]

> Jesus puts all His emphasis on the exact word used. The argument would fall to the ground if any other word for "judge" had been employed. Yet Jesus not only appeals to the word, but says in connection with it that Scripture cannot be broken. The term "broken" is not defined.... But it is perfectly intelligible. It means that Scripture cannot be emptied of its force by being shown to be erroneous.[30]

To acknowledge the divine-human authorship of the Bible resulting in its total inerrancy is analogous to the orthodox doctrine of the person of Christ. And that doctrine of inerrant inspiration is affirmed by the way the Lord assigned authority to the minutiae of the text, which He could not have done had He held to so-called *limited* inerrancy.

The current discussion over inerrancy is highly significant and should never be relegated to the category of something only theologians speculate about. One's view of inerrancy does affect one's doctrine of inspiration, and that in turn is bound to affect the concept of the authority of the Bible which is basic to the interpretation and application of its message.

NOTES

1. Harold Lindsell, *The Battle for the Bible* (Grand Rapids: Zondervan, 1976).
2. See the author's review in *Bibliotheca Sacra* 133(October-December 1976):356-57.
3. See Jack Rogers, ed., *Biblical Authority* (Waco, Tex.: Word, 1977); "Evangelicals on Inerrancy," *Christianity Today*, 18 June 1976, p. 17; Robert Mounce, "Does the Bible Contain Errors?" *Eternity*, August 1976, pp. 49, 51.
4. See Clark H. Pinnock's review of Lindsell's book in *Eternity*, June 1976, pp. 40-41.
5. Benjamin Breckinridge Warfield, *The Inspiration and Authority of the Bible* (Philadelphia: Presbyterian and Reformed, 1948), p. 137.
6. David Hubbard's remark seems incongruous: "We seem to learn nothing from 2 Peter about the definition of inerrancy which dominates the current debate" ("The Current Tensions: Is There a Way Out?" in Rogers, p. 175).
7. Ibid., p. 168.
8. Ibid., p. 171.
9. Ray Summers, "How God Said It, Part II," *Baptist Standard*, 4 February, 1970, p. 12.
10. Berkeley Mickelsen, "The Bible's Own Approach to Authority," in Rogers, p. 86.
11. Dewey M. Beegle, *Scripture, Tradition, and Infallibility* (Grand Rapids: Eerdmans, 1973), pp. 175-97.
12. Daniel P. Fuller, "Evangelicalism and Biblical Inerrancy," mimeographed (Pasadena, Calif.: Fuller Theological Seminary, 1966), pp. 18-19.
13. Robert H. Mounce, "Clues to Understanding Biblical Accuracy," *Eternity*, June 1966, p. 18.
14. Jack Rogers, "The Church Doctrine of Biblical Authority," in Rogers, pp. 20-34.
15. Ibid., p. 45.
16. Geoffrey W. Bromiley, "The Church Doctrine of Inspiration," in Carl F. H. Henry, ed., *Revelation and the Bible* (Grand Rapids: Baker, 1958), p. 210.
17. Augustine, *Epistula* 28. 3. Evidently the "domino" idea did not originate with Lindsell!
18. A. D. R. Polman, *The Word of God According to St. Augustine*, trans. A. J. Pomerans (Grand Rapids: Eerdmans, 1961), pp. 52-63.
19. Lindsell, p. 210.

20. Clark Pinnock, "Three Views of the Bible in Contemporary Theology," in Rogers, p. 70.
21. Gerald T. Sheppard, "Biblical Hermeneutics: The Academic Language of Evangelical Identity," *Union Seminary Quarterly Review* 32(Winter 1977):94, n. 33.
22. Ibid., p. 89.
23. Ibid., pp. 89-90.
24. Cf. J. K. S. Reid, *The Authority of Scripture* (New York: Harper & Brothers, 1957), p. 218.
25. G. C. Berkouwer, *Holy Scripture* (Grand Rapids: Eerdmans, 1975), p. 18.
26. Paul K. Jewett, "Bulletin, Systematic Theology 1—The Doctrine of Scripture: The Divine Word in Human Words," mimeographed (Pasadena, Calif.: Fuller Theological Seminary, 1978), pp. 4-5.
27. Fred P. Thompson, Jr., "The Wrong War," *United Evangelical Action*, Winter 1976, p. 10. Thompson also labels the inerrancy view as "a species of literary docetism."
28. Ibid.
29. Leon Morris, *Commentary on the Gospel of John* (Grand Rapids: Eerdmans, 1971), p. 526.
30. Ibid., p. 527. See also Matthew 22:32, 45.

2

The Doctrine of Miracles

John A. Witmer

Affirmation of belief in miracles is an essential part of the theological commitment of biblical, historic Christianity. It is inseparably joined to the biblical doctrine of God as Creator and Ruler of all things. Miracles are woven into the fabric of Scripture, and belief in them is a concomitant of the historic Christian doctrine of the Bible as God's Word to men. C. S. Lewis rightly calls Christianity "... the story of a great Miracle."[1]

REACTIONS TO MIRACLES

This historic Christian affirmation of belief in miracles faces two differing reactions in contemporary thought. The first is bemused silence which grows out of the fact that the word *miracle* is used in such loose ways today that it has been robbed of much of its historic meaning. For example, *Miracle on Thirty-Fourth Street* is a fantasy for youth by Valentine Davies,[2] but it serves to identify the word *miracle* for many with the imaginary world of fiction and myth. Miracles, many believe, like the adventures of Hercules and Sinbad the sailor, never take place in real life. Others think of *miracles* as unusual human exploits—what Hesse calls "the remarkable,

John A. Witmer
A.B., Wheaton College; M.A., M.S.L.S., East Texas State University;
Th.M., Th.D., Dallas Theological Seminary
Director of the Library
Assistant Professor of Systematic Theology
Dallas Theological Seminary

unpredictable, coincidental, nature of the events." She points out that in most such cases "there would probably not be any implication of a divine or providential act in the events described."[3]

Still another use of the word *miracle* is found in the popular radio and television evangelist's challenge to his audience, "Expect a miracle today." In this case, a "divine or providential act" is implied, because the challenge is frequently coupled with the evangelist's promise, "Something good is going to happen to you." Here miracles are equated with the providential blessings of life. The implication is that miracles occur day after day in the lives of the evangelist and his associates and anyone who responds to his challenge. Little wonder that when historic Christians' belief in miracles is proclaimed people wonder what is meant.

DENIAL OF MIRACLES

The second response to the Christian affirmation of belief in miracles is the dogmatic denial of the possibility of miracles. This is made by the person, whether professedly religious or not, who in reality embraces a philosophy of naturalism. In his judgment, nature is supreme and nothing can conceivably interrupt its steady operation—not even God. As Einstein said, "the idea of a Being who interferes with the sequence of events in the world is absolutely impossible."[4]

Such a denial of miracles is frequently thought to be scientific. For example, Van Buren declares, "The idea of the empirical intervention of a supernatural 'God' in the world of men has been ruled out by the influence of modern science in our thinking."[5] It is not scientific, however, but rather metaphysical, the result of the person's philosophy or beliefs, not of the facts of science.

Underlying such dogmatic denial of miracles is the acceptance of the uniformity of nature and its operation in orderly fashion according to the laws of nature. This concept began with the laws of motion of Isaac Newton, whose mechanical physics was applied to nature by LaPlace. As a result "the whole process of nature is unique and rigidly determined."[6] Such a point of view is expressed in David Hume's definition of a miracle as "*a transgression of a law of nature by a particular volition of the Deity or by the interposition of some invisible agent.*"[7] Elsewhere Hume explains, "A miracle is a violation of the laws of nature; and as a firm and unalterable experience has established these laws, the proof against a miracle, from the very nature of the fact, is as entire as any argument from experience can possibly be imagined."[8] For many Hume succeeded in eliminating miracles by definition. Who would possess the temerity to give credence to something identified as a "transgression" and a "violation" of such an inviolable entity as "the laws of nature"?

Ironically, in the twentieth century the mechanistic view of the universe based on Newton's laws of motion has been largely abandoned in favor of the quantum theory. This considers the universe "in essence indeterministic"[9] and its laws merely statistical in nature, "that is, they do not determine occurrences of single events, but only proportions in large classes of events."[10] In other words science itself has now ruled out the point of view which for so long eliminated the possibility of miracles by definition. The new theories of science, however, are no friendlier to the recognition of miracles than the old. Furthermore, "undoubtedly a great deal of popular reaction to the notion of miracle is still conditioned by this view,"[11] that is, the Newtonian. But at least the point has been made that the uniformity of nature is a metaphysical assumption of science, part of its theoretical framework, not of its factual evidence. This is what Christians have argued all along.

THE CHRISTIAN POINT OF VIEW

The Christian position is not that the universe is capricious and erratic. Christians expect the sun to rise in the east tomorrow as it always has, just as everyone else does. Christians recognize that this world is a cosmos, an orderly system, not a chaos. More than that, Christians agree that the regularity of the universe is observable by men and expressible in principles or laws. As a result, Christians do not deny the existence of what are called the laws of nature. Nor do they think that the occurrence of miracles destroys these laws or makes them inoperative. What Christians reject is the idea that the universe is a self-contained, closed system with laws that are inviolable. Such a view is a metaphysical concept related to a philosophical system such as deism, materialism, or naturalism. Such a position rules out God and His relationship to the world and to men as believed by Christians on the basis of the biblical revelation.

The Christian position is that God is the self-existent Creator of all things (Gen. 1:1; Isa. 44:24; Acts 14:15; Eph. 3:9). But for Christians God is more than a cosmic watchmaker who has brought into being a giant machine that continues to run its prescribed course without intervention, even by its Creator. That is the view of deism, which accepts the transcendence of God over the world as Creator but denies His immanence. On the basis of biblical witness Christians believe that God is also the self-existent Sustainer and Governor of all things (Acts 14:16-17; 17:24-28). The eternal Son of God, who became incarnate as the Lord Jesus Christ, is described as "upholding all things by the word of his power" (Heb. 1:3).* He is the one in whom "all things consist" (Col. 1:17). As a result, the regularity of the universe that men call the laws of nature is in reality the normal pattern of the cosmos-sustaining power of God; for as Paul says, "God is not the author of confusion" (1 Cor. 14:33; cf. v. 40).

At this point the extreme on the other side of the Christian position demands consideration. In contrast to the scientific, rationalistic denial of the possibility of miracles, this romantic, mystical view insists that "all is a miracle." Voltaire continues, "The stupendous order of nature, the revolution of a hundred millions of worlds around a million of suns, the activity of light, the life of animals; all are grand and perpetual miracles."[12] In a similar vein, Walt Whitman exclaims,

> To me every hour of the light and dark is a miracle,
> Every cubic inch of space is a miracle.[13]

According to this view, if God is acknowledged at all, He is related to nature so closely that He is equated with it. This is pantheism, which denies the transcendence of God and stresses His immanence in the world to the point of identity. Such a view eliminates miracles as effectively as their denial does. By making the whole course of nature miraculous, no place is left for that which is truly miraculous according to the meaning of the word itself. As C. S. Lewis says in speaking about the normal course of nature, "A miracle is by definition

---

*All Scripture quotations in this article, except those noted otherwise, are from the King James Version.

an exception."[14] A miracle is a special application of the power of God to accomplish an unusual event.

As a result, the Christian position on God's relationship to the world involves a third point. The living God is not only the self-existent Creator and Sustainer of all things but also the Sovereign Ruler who is executing an eternal plan in His creation for the greater glory of His own Name (Rom. 11:33-36; Eph. 1:3-14; 3:11). All men need to learn the lesson that God taught Nebuchadnezzar "that the most High ruleth in the kingdom of men, and giveth it to whomsoever he will" (Dan. 4:18, 25, 34-35). In the carrying out of His program God from time to time steps into the normal course of nature and of history in extraordinary deeds. Such deeds are miracles and are a logical and necessary part of the biblical, Christian faith in God. As D. E. Trueblood wrote, "If the world is really the medium of God's personal action, miracle is wholly normal."[15]

For the biblical Christian, miracles are not expendable; they are not incidental but an essential part of his theistic world view. Miracles are a benchmark of historic biblical Christianity and distinguish it from its counterfeits. C. S. Lewis explains: "The popular 'religion' excludes miracles because it excludes the 'living God' of Christianity and believes instead in a kind of God who obviously would not do miracles, or indeed anything else."[16] Elsewhere he elaborates, "But in Christianity, the more we understand what God it is who is said to be present and the purpose for which He is said to have appeared, the more credible the miracles become. This is why we seldom find the Christian miracles denied except by those who have abandoned some part of the Christian doctrine."[17] Belief in miracles can serve as a touchstone of genuine Christian faith.

A PROPER DEFINITION

In developing an accurate definition of a miracle in accord with Scripture the first point is that a miracle is an extraordinary work of God, an exercise of supernatural divine power. As such it produces amazement, if not fear, in its observers. For example, as Israel stood at the shore of the Red Sea with the host of Pharaoh in pursuit, Moses said, "Fear ye not, stand still, and see the salvation of the LORD, which he will shew to you today" (Exod. 14:13) and, in the words of Rahab, "the LORD dried up the water of the Red sea for you" (Josh. 2:10). In connection with one of the miracles of the Lord Jesus the gospel records, "And they were all amazed at the mighty power of God" (Luke 9:43). In performing miracles God usually worked through chosen men as His agents, but what was done was recognized as ultimately the work of God (Acts 2:22; 19:11). Booth emphasizes this point in his definition of a miracle as "an observable phenomenon effected directly or indirectly by supernatural power."[18]

In a proper understanding of miracles it is also important to recognize that a miracle is a revelatory event. Because of their astounding character, miracles are a "special revelation of the presence of God."[19] But they also are related to the revelation of God's purposes and His program in the world by identifying God's servants as His messengers. Nicodemus told Jesus, "Rabbi, we know that thou art a teacher come from God: for no man can do these miracles that thou doest, except God be with him" (John 3:2).

A study of the Hebrew and Greek words used in connection with the miracles of Scripture helps in understanding the nature of these special events and in formulating a definition. On the basis of the four Greek words, all of which are translated in English by the word *miracle* at times in the New Testament, Thiessen defines a miracle as "a unique and extraordinary event awakening wonder ($\tau\acute{\epsilon}\rho\alpha\varsigma$), wrought by divine power ($\delta\acute{\upsilon}\nu\alpha\mu\iota\varsigma$), accomplishing some practical and benevolent work ($\acute{\epsilon}\rho\gamma o\nu$), and authenticating a messenger and his message as from God ($\sigma\eta\mu\epsilon\widehat{\iota}o\nu$)."[20] Such a biblical definition aids in distinguishing genuine miracles from the spurious and the satanic ones.

MIRACLES IN THE BIBLE

Since miracles relate to the revelation of God and His communication and execution of His program in the world, their focal point is the Lord Jesus Christ, the incarnate Son of God. Lewis says, "The central miracle asserted by Christians is the incarnation. They say that God became Man. Every other miracle prepares for this, exhibits this, or results from this." He calls the incarnation "the Grand Miracle."[21] Jesus' birth was indeed a miracle—conceived by the Holy Spirit in the womb of the virgin Mary (Luke 1:35). He was the supreme miracle worker (John 20:30-31). The Lord Jesus Christ is the miracle Person—God "manifest in the flesh" (1 Tim. 3:16). His miraculous resurrection (Acts 2:24; 1 Cor. 15:4) is the guarantee of victory over sin and death (1 Cor. 15:54-57) and of the miracle life to all who trust in Him (2 Cor. 5:17).

Although miracles cluster around the Lord Jesus Christ like steel shavings to a magnet, they are found throughout the Bible. However, even a casual reading of Scripture reveals that miracles occur with greater frequency at special times. Israel's deliverance from Egypt and entrance into Canaan provided one great concentration of miracles. So did the ministries of Elijah and Elisha when God sought to stem the tide of apostasy among His people. Related to the earthly life and miracles of Jesus are the miracles of the apostolic church. As Lewis explains, "God does not shake miracles into Nature at random as if from a pepper-caster. They come on great occasions: they are found at the great ganglions of history—not of political or social history, but of spiritual history which cannot be fully known by men."[22]

A form of miracle which cannot be overlooked is prophecy. For a human being to predict in detail what will occur in the future, near or far, and have it take place requires supernatural revelation and supernatural action. Prophecy looms large in the Bible. Chafer states that "over one-fourth of the books of the Bible are avowedly prophetic, and, in the actual text of all the Scriptures, at least one-fifth was prediction at the time it was written."[23] Furthermore, as Chafer states, "A portion of the Bible prediction has now been fulfilled, and . . . its fulfillment has been . . . precisely as predicted."[24] Hume does not accept the possibility of prophecy any more than that of miracles, but he recognizes the logical conclusion that "all prophecies are real miracles."[25]

From time to time in the Bible miraculous things were done by others than the servants of God. Examples are "the magicians of Egypt" (Exod. 7:11, 22), Simon the sorcerer of Samaria (Acts 8:9-11), Bar-Jesus or "Elymas the sorcerer" (Acts 13:6, 8), and the "seven sons of Sceva" (Acts 19:13-14). Some of these spectacles are mere trickery, spurious miracles. Others of them are truly supernatural events, but satanic in origin and power, not divine. Remember that the devil showed the Lord Jesus "all the kingdoms of the world in a moment of time" (Luke 4:5) and is able to transform himself "into an

angel of light" (2 Cor. 11:14). Satan's great miracle worker
will be the man of sin of the great Tribulation whose presence
is "after the working of Satan with all power and signs and
lying wonders" (2 Thess. 2:9). Christians should not be
deceived by satanically-inspired miracles; they should remember that his power, although superhuman, is finite, and
his conqueror is the Lord Jesus Christ. God's final miracles
are yet to come with the rapture of the church, the establishment of the Messiah's kingdom, and the creation of new heavens and a new earth.

MIRACLES TODAY

Since miracles in the Bible are tied to God's special revelation of Himself and of His program, centering in the Lord Jesus
Christ as God incarnate, "who was delivered for our offences,
and was raised again for our justification" (Rom. 4:25), miracles in the biblical pattern do not occur today. The gift of miracles provided by God for the apostolic church (1 Cor. 12:28-
29) is undoubtedly among those temporary gifts of the Holy
Spirit that passed away with the apostles. Just as God has
spoken climactically "in his Son" (Heb. 1:2, ASV),* so He has
acted in revelatory miracles.

This does not mean that God is not at work supernatu-
rally in the world today. A supernatural work of God takes
place each time another human being is regenerated by the
Holy Spirit (2 Cor. 5:17). Many times regeneration is followed
by almost immediate extraordinary transformation of personality and life-style that is truly miraculous. Furthermore, in
answer to believing prayer by His children, God provides
many things that defy human explanation—healings that are
medically inexplicable, deliverances from danger that seem
impossible, and provision of money, food, clothing, or shelter
from untraceable sources. Many believers can therefore testify, "Thou art the God that doest wonders" (Ps. 77:14). Christians properly call such mighty works of God *miracles*, but
they are in a different class from the miracles of Scripture.

Christians affirm their belief in miracles because of the
witness of the Bible as God's infallible message to men. John

American Standard Version.

Peterson summed up Christian faith in miracles best in these words from his song, "I believe in miracles, for I believe in God."

NOTES

1. C. S. Lewis, *Miracles* (New York: Macmillan, 1947), p. 83.
2. Valentine Davies, *Miracle on Thirty-Fourth Street* (New York: Harcourt Brace Jovanovich, 1967).
3. Mary Hesse, "Miracles and the Laws of Nature," in C. F. D. Moule, ed., *Miracles* (London: A. R. Mowbray & Co., 1965), p. 35.
4. Albert Einstein, "The Meeting Place of Science and Religion," in Edward H. Cotton, ed., *Has Science Discovered God?* (Freeport, N.Y.: Books for Libraries, 1931), p. 101.
5. Paul Van Buren, *The Secular Meaning of the Gospel* (New York: Macmillan, 1963), p. 100.
6. Hesse, p. 39.
7. David Hume, *An Enquiry Concerning Human Understanding* (LaSalle, Ill.: Open Court, 1955), p. 127, n. 1.
8. Ibid., p. 126.
9. Hesse, p. 38.
10. Ibid., p. 37.
11. Ibid.
12. *The Works of Voltaire: A Contemporary Version,* Philosophical Dictionary, 22 vols. (New York: Albert A. Knopf, 1927), 6:22.
13. Walt Whitman, "Miracles," in *Leaves of Grass* (Philadelphia: David McKay, 1900), p. 428.
14. Lewis, p. 56.
15. D. Elton Trueblood, *The Logic of Belief,* 2d ed. (New York: Harper & Brothers, 1942), p. 276.
16. Lewis, p. 99.
17. Ibid., p. 160.
18. John Louis Booth, "The Purpose of Miracles" (Th.D. diss., Dallas Theological Seminary, 1965), p. 8.
19. Henry C. Theissen, *Introductory Lectures in Systematic Theology* (Grand Rapids: Eerdmans, 1949), p. 36.
20. Henry C. Theissen, "An Outline of Lectures in Systematic Theology," 3d ed. (class notes, Wheaton College, 1942), p. 9.
21. Lewis, p. 131.
22. Ibid., p. 201.
23. Lewis Sperry Chafer, *Systematic Theology,* 8 vols. (Dallas: Dallas Theological Seminary, 1948), 4:256.
24. Lewis Sperry Chafer, *Major Bible Themes* (Findlay, Ohio: Dunham, 1953), p. 265.
25. Hume, p. 145.

3

For Whom Did Christ Die?

Lewis Sperry Chafer

For many centuries the question, "For whom did Christ die?" has divided and still divides some of the most orthodox and scholarly theologians. On the one hand, those who according to theological usage are known as *limited redemptionists* contend that Christ died only for that elect company who were predetermined of God to be saved; and on the other hand, those who are known as *unlimited redemptionists* contend that Christ died for all men. The issue is well-defined, and men of sincere loyalty to the Word of God and who possess true scholarship are found on both sides of the controversy.

It is true that the doctrine of a limited redemption is one of the five points of Calvinism, but not all who are rightfully classified as Calvinists accept this one feature of that system. It is equally true that all Arminians are unlimited redemptionists, but to hold the doctrine of unlimited redemption does not necessarily make one an Arminian. There is nothing incongruous in the fact that many unlimited redemptionists believe, in harmony with all Calvinists, in the unalterable and eternal decree of God whereby all things were determined after His own will, and in the sovereign election of some to be saved (but not all), and in the divine predestination of those who are saved to the heavenly glory prepared for them. Without the

The Late Lewis Sperry Chafer
D.D., Wheaton College; Litt.D., Dallas Theological Seminary;
Th.D., Faculté Libre de Théologie Protestante
Founder and First President
Dallas Theological Seminary

slightest inconsistency the unlimited redemptionists may believe in an election according to sovereign grace, that *none* but the elect will be saved, that *all* of the elect will be saved, and that the elect are by divine enablement alone called out of the state of spiritual death from which they are impotent to take even one step in the direction of their own salvation. The text, "No man can come to me, except the Father which hath sent me draw him" (John 6:44), is as much a part of the one system of doctrine as it is of the other.

It is not easy to disagree with good and great men. However, as they appear on each side of this question, it is impossible to entertain a conviction and not oppose those who are of a contrary mind. The disagreement now under discussion is not between orthodox and heterodox men; it is within the fellowship of those who have most in common and who need the support and encouragement of each other's confidence. Few themes have drawn out more sincere and scholarly investigation.

THREE DOCTRINAL WORDS

Though common to theological usage, the terms *limited redemption* and *unlimited redemption* are inadequate to express the whole of the problem which is under consideration. There are three major aspects of truth set forth in New Testament doctrine relative to the unmeasured benefits provided for the *unsaved* through the death of Christ, and redemption is but one of the three. Each of these aspects of truth is in turn expressed by one word, surrounded as each word is by a group of derivatives or synonyms of that word. These three words are: ἀπολύτρωσις, translated "redemption," καταλλαγή, translated "reconciliation," and ἱλασμός, translated "propitiation." The riches of divine grace which these three words represent transcend all human thought or language; but these truths must be declared in human terms if declared at all. As it is necessary to have four gospels, since it is impossible for one, two, or even three to present the full truth concerning the Lord Jesus Christ, so the Scriptures approach the great benefit of Christ's death for the unsaved from three angles, to the end that what may be lacking in one may be supplied in the others. There are at least four other great words—*forgiveness, regeneration, justification*, and *sanctification*—which represent spiritual blessings secured by the death of Christ; but these are to be distinguished from the three already mentioned, in that these four words refer to aspects of truth which belong only to those who are *saved*.

Over against these, the three words *redemption, reconciliation*, and *propitiation*, though incorporating in the scope of their meaning vital truths belonging to the state of the saved, refer in particular to that which Christ wrought for the unsaved in His death on the cross. What is termed *the finished work of Christ* may be defined as the sum total of all that these three words connote when restricted to those aspects of their meaning which apply alone to the unsaved.

Redemption is within the sphere of relationship which exists between the sinner and his sins. This word, with its related terms, contemplates sin as a slavery, with the sinner as the slave. Freedom is secured only through the redemption, or ransom, which is found in Christ Jesus (John 8:32-36; Rom. 6:17-20; 8:21; Gal. 5:1; 2 Pet. 2:19).

Reconciliation is within the sphere of relationship which exists between the sinner and God, and contemplates the sinner as at enmity with God, and Christ as the maker of peace between God and man (Rom. 5:10; 8:7; 2 Cor. 5:19; James 4:4).

Propitiation is also within the sphere of relationship that exists between God and the sinner, but propitiation contemplates the larger necessity of God being just when He justifies the sinner. It views Christ as an offering, a sacrifice, a lamb slain, who, by meeting every demand of God's holiness against the offender, renders God righteously propitious toward that offender (Rom. 3:25; 1 John 2:2; 4:10). Thus it may be seen that redemption is the sinward aspect of the cross, reconciliation is the manward aspect of the cross, and propitiation is the Godward aspect of the cross. These three great doctrines combine to declare one divine undertaking.

The question at issue between the limited redemptionists and the unlimited redemptionists is as much a question of limited or unlimited reconciliation, and limited or unlimited propitiation, as it is one of limited or unlimited redemption. Having made a careful study of these three words and the group of words which must be included with each, one can hardly deny that there is a twofold application of the truth represented by each.

REDEMPTION

There is the aspect of redemption that is represented by the word ἀγοράζω ("to buy, redeem"), which means "to purchase in the market"; and although it is used to express the general theme of redemption, its technical meaning implies only the purchase of the slave, but does not necessarily convey the thought of his release from slavery. The word ἐξαγοράζω ("to redeem") implies much more, in that ἐξ, meaning "out of," or "out from," is combined with ἀγοράζω and thus indicates that the slave is purchased out of the market. (The even stronger terms λυτρόω and ἀπολύτρωσις connote "to loose" and "to set free.") There is, then, a redemption that pays the price, but does not of necessity release the slave, and there is a redemption that is unto abiding freedom.

RECONCILIATION

According to 2 Corinthians 5:19 there is a *reconciliation* declared to be worldwide and wholly wrought of God; yet the following verse indicates that the individual sinner has the responsibility to be himself reconciled to God. What God has accomplished has so changed the world in its relation to Himself that He, agreeable to the demands of infinite righteousness, is satisfied with Christ's death as the solution to the sin question for each and every one. The *desideratum* is not reached, however, until the individual, already included in the world's reconciliation, is himself satisfied with that same work of Christ (which has satisfied God) as the solution to his own sin question. Thus there is a reconciliation that of itself saves no one, but that is a basis for the reconciliation of any and all who will believe. When they believe, they are reconciled *experientially* and *eternally*. At that moment they become the children of God through the riches of His grace.

PROPITIATION

In one brief verse, 1 John 2:2, God declares that there is a "propitiation for our [the Christian's] sins: and not for ours only, but also for the sins of the whole world." While due recognition will be given later on to the interpretation of this and similar passages as offered by the limited redemptionists, it is obvious that the same twofold aspect of truth—that applicable to the unsaved and that applicable to the saved—is indicated regarding propitiation as is indicated in the case of both redemption and reconciliation.

From this brief consideration of these three great doctrinal words it may be seen that the unlimited redemptionist believes as much in unlimited reconciliation and unlimited propitiation as he does in unlimited redemption. On the other hand, the limited redemptionist seldom includes the doctrines of reconciliation and propitiation specifically in his discussion of the extent of Christ's death.

THE CROSS IS NOT THE ONLY SAVING INSTRUMENTALITY

It is one of the points most depended on by the limited redemptionists to claim that redemption, if wrought at all, necessitates the salvation of those thus favored. According to this view, if the redemption price is paid by Christ it must be the thought of ἐξαγοράζω or ἀπολύτρωσις, rather than ἀγοράζω, in every instance. It is confidently held by all Calvinists that the elect will, in God's time and way, each and every one, be saved, and that the unregenerate believe only as they are enabled by the Spirit of God. But the question here is whether the sacrifice of Christ is the only divine instrumentality whereby God *actually* saves the elect, or whether that sacrifice is a divine work (finished, indeed, as to its scope and purpose) that renders all men *savable*, but is applied in sovereign grace by the Word of God and the Holy Spirit only when the individual *believes*.

Certainly Christ's death of itself forgives no sinner, nor does it render unnecessary the regenerating work of the Holy Spirit. Anyone of the elect whose salvation is predetermined, and for whom Christ died, may live the major portion of his life in open rebellion against God and during that time manifest every feature of depravity and spiritual death. That alone should prove that men are not severally saved by the act of Christ in dying, but rather that they are saved by the divine *application* of that value when they *believe*. The blood of the Passover lamb became efficacious only when applied to the doorpost.

The fact that an elect person does live some portion of his life in enmity toward God, and in a state in which he is as much lost as any unregenerate person, indicates conclusively that Christ must not only die to provide a righteous basis for the salvation of that soul, but that that value must be applied to him at such a time in his life as God has decreed, which time, in the present generation, is almost two thousand years subsequent to the death of Christ. By so much it is proved that the priceless value in Christ's death does not save the elect, nor hinder them from rejecting the mercies of God in that period of their life which precedes their salvation.

The unlimited redemptionist claims that the value of Christ's death is extended to all men, nevertheless that the elect alone come by divine grace (wrought out by an effectual call) into its fruition, while the nonelect are not called but are those passed by. They hold that God indicates who are the elect, not at the cross, but by the effectual call and at the time of regeneration. It is also believed by the unlimited redemptionists that it pleased God to place the whole world in a position of infinite obligation to Himself through the sacrifice of Christ. Though the mystery of personal condemnation for the sin of unbelief when one has not been moved to faith by the Spirit cannot be solved in this world, the unregenerate, both elect and nonelect, are definitely condemned for their unbelief so long as they abide in that condition (John 3:18). There is nothing more clarifying in connection with this age-long discussion than the recognition of the fact that while they are in their unregenerate state no vital distinction between the elect and the nonelect is recognized in the Scriptures (1 Cor. 1:24 and Heb. 1:14 might suggest this distinction along lines comparatively unimportant to this discussion). Certainly that form of doctrine that would make redemption equivalent to salvation is not traceable when men are contemplated in their unregenerate state, and a salvation, which is delayed for many years in the case of an elect person, might be delayed forever in the case of a nonelect person whose heart God never moves. Was the objective in Christ's death one of making the salvation of all men *possible*, or was it the making of the salvation of the elect *certain?* Some light is gained on this question when it is thus remembered that the consummating divine acts in the salvation of an individual are wrought when he believes on Christ, and not before he believes.

UNIVERSAL GOSPEL PREACHING

A very difficult situation arises for the limited redemptionist when he confronts the Great Commission which enjoins the preaching of the gospel to *every* creature. How, it may be urged, can a universal gospel be preached if there is no universal provision? To say on the one hand that Christ died only for the elect and on the other hand that His death is the ground on which salvation is offered to all men is perilously near contradiction. It would be mentally and spiritually impossible for a limited redemptionist, if true to his convictions, to urge with sincerity those who are known to be nonelect to accept Christ. Fortunately, God has disclosed nothing whereby the elect can be distinguished from the nonelect while both classes are in the unregenerate state. However, the gospel preacher who doubts the basis for his message in the case of even one to whom he is appealing, if sincere, does face a real problem in the discharge of his commission to preach the gospel to every creature. To believe that some are elect and some nonelect creates no problem for the soulwinner, provided he is free in his convictions to declare that Christ died for each one to whom he speaks. He knows that the nonelect will not accept the message. He knows also that even an elect person may resist it to near the day of his death. But if the preacher believes that any portion of his audience is destitute of any basis of salvation, having no share in the values of Christ's death, it is no longer a question in his mind of whether they will accept or reject; it becomes rather a question of truthfulness in the declaration of the message. As Alexander points out:

> On this supposition [that of a limited atonement] the general invitations and promises of the gospel are without an adequate basis, and seem like a mere mockery, an offer, in short, of what has not been provided. It will not do to say, in reply to this, that as these invitations are actually given we are entitled, on the authority of God's Word, to urge them and justified in accepting them; for this is mere evasion.[1]

On the question of the beliefs of sincere gospel preachers, it would repay the reader to investigate how universally all great evangelists and missionaries have embraced the doctrine of unlimited redemption, and made it the very underlying structure of their convincing appeal.

Is God Defeated If Men Are Lost for Whom Christ Died?

One objection often raised by limited redemptionists is that if Christ died for those who are never saved, then He has experienced defeat. Of course it must be conceded that if the finished work is a *guarantee* of salvation then God is defeated if even one fails to be saved. But does Christ's redemptive work automatically guarantee salvation for all, or does Christ become the surety of salvation only when one *believes*? Christ's death is a finished transaction, the value of which God has never applied to any soul until that soul passes from death unto life. It is *actual* as to its *availability,* but *potential* as to its *application.*

To state that the value of Christ's death is suspended until the hour of regeneration is not to intimate that its value is any less than it would be were it applied at any other time. There are reasons that are based on the Scriptures why God might provide a redemption for *all* when He merely purposed to save *some.* He is justified in placing the whole world in a particular relation to Himself so that the gospel might be preached with all sincerity to all men, and so that on the human side men might be without excuse, being judged, as they are, for their rejection of that which is offered to them. Men of this dispensation are condemned for their unbelief. This is expressly declared in John 3:18 and implied in John 16:7-11, in which latter context the Spirit is seen in His work of convincing the world of but one sin, namely, that "they believe not on me."* But to reject Christ and His redemption, as every unbeliever does, is to demand that the great transaction of Calvary be reversed and that his sin, which was laid on Christ, be retained by himself with all its condemning power. It is not asserted here that sin is thus ever retained by the sinner. It is stated, however, that since God does not apply the value of Christ's death to the sinner until that sinner is saved, God would be morally free to hold the sinner who rejects Christ accountable for his sins; and to this unmeasured burden would be added all the condemnation which justly follows the sin of unbelief. In this connection, reference is made by the limited redemptionists to three passages which, it is argued, indicate that impenitent men die with their sins on them, and therefore, it is asserted, Christ could not have borne their sins.

---

*All Scripture quotations in this article are from the King James Version.

JOHN 8:24

"If ye believe not that I am he, ye shall die in your sins." This is a clear statement that calls for little exposition. It is a case of believing on Christ or dying in the condemnation of sin. It is not alone the one sin of unbelief, but "your sins" to which Christ refers. There is occasion for some recognition of the fact that Christ spoke these words *before* His death, and also that He here requires them to believe that He is the "I am," that is, Jehovah. These facts are of importance in any specific consideration of this text; but enough may be said if it be pointed out that the issue is as much a problem for one side of this discussion as for the other. Suppose the limited redemptionist were to claim that the reason these people to whom Christ spoke would die in their sins is that they were nonelect and therefore their sins were not borne by Christ. Two replies may be given to this argument: (a) The condition on which they may avoid dying in their sins is not based on the extent of His death but rather on the necessity of belief ("*If ye believe not . . .* ye shall die in your sins"). (b) If it were true that these people would die in their sins solely because of their position as nonelect for whom Christ did not die, then it would be equally true that those among them who were of the elect (cf. v. 30) and whose sins were laid on Christ, would have no need to be saved from a lost estate since their sins were already removed. Yet the context clearly stresses the necessity of belief for the removal of sin ("If you believe not . . . ye shall die in your sins. . . . *As he spake* these words, *many believed on him*"). What this important passage actually teaches is that the value of Christ's death, as marvelous and complete as it is, is not applied to the unregenerate until they *believe*. It is the effectual calling of the Spirit that indicates God's elect and not some partial, unidentified, and supposed discrimination wrought out in the death of Christ.

EPHESIANS 5:6

"Because of these things cometh the wrath of God upon the children of disobedience." The designation "children of disobedience" does not refer to the personal disobedience of any individual in this class, but rather to the fact that all unregenerate people are disobedient in the federal headship of Adam. This includes the elect and nonelect in their unsaved state; besides it should be noted that those elect saved people to whom the apostle is writing were, until saved, not only children of disobedience, but under the energizing power of Satan they were also in a state of spiritual death (Eph. 2:1-2). Thus the value of Christ's death is applied to the elect, not at the cross, but when they believe.

REVELATION 20:12

"And the dead were judged out of those things which were written in the books, according to their works." This scene is related to the great white throne judgment of the unregenerate of all ages. The sum total of sin in the present age is *unbelief* (John 16:9), as the sum total of human responsibility toward God in securing a right relation to God is *belief* (John 6:29). It is very possible that those of this vast company who were of this dispensation may be judged for the one inclusive sin of unbelief, while those of other ages may be judged for many and specific sins; but from the foregoing proofs it is evident that it is in no way unscriptural to recognize that the impenitent of this age are judged according to their own specific sins, since the value of Christ's death is not applied to or accepted for them until they believe, and these, it is evident, have never believed.

It is appropriate to consider the challenge that the limited redemptionists universally advance, namely, that if Christ bore the sins of the nonelect, they could not be lost, for it is claimed even the condemning sin of unbelief would thus be borne and therefore would have lost its condemning power. By this challenge the important question is raised whether Christ bore all the individual sins except *unbelief*.

To this it may be replied that the sin of unbelief assumes a specific quality in that it is man's answer to that which Christ wrought and finished for him when bearing his sins on the cross. There is, doubtless, divine freedom secured by Christ's death whereby God may pardon the sin of unbelief since He freely forgives *all* trespasses (Col. 2:13). "There is therefore now no condemnation to them which are in Christ Jesus" (Rom. 8:1). The sin of unbelief, being particular in character, is evidently treated as such in the Scriptures. Again, if Christ bore the sin of unbelief along with the other sins of the elect, then no elect sinner in his unregenerate state is subject to any condemnation, nor is he required to be forgiven or justified in the sight of God.

At this point some might question whether the general call of God (John 12:32) could be sincere in every instance, since He does not intend to save the nonelect. In response it may be asserted that, since the inability of the nonelect to receive the gospel is due to human sin, from His own standpoint God is justified in extending the invitation to them. In this connection there is an important distinction to be observed between God's sovereign purpose and His desires. For specific and worthy reasons, God, as any other being, may purpose to do more or less than He desires. His desire is evidently toward the whole world (John 3:16; 1 Tim. 2:4), but His purpose is clearly revealed to be toward the elect.

The Nature of Substitution

The limited redemptionists sincerely believe that Christ's substitution for a lost soul *necessitates* the salvation of that soul. This is a fair issue and there is some light available through the careful consideration of the precise nature of substitution itself.

Man did not first discover the necessity of a substitute to die in his place; this necessity was in the heart of God from all eternity. Who can declare what sin actually is in the sight of infinite rectitude? Who will assume to measure the ransom price God must require for the sinner? Who can state what the just judgments of outraged holiness were that were required by the Father and rendered by the Son? Or who can declare the cost tó God of the disposition of sin itself from His presence forever?

Two Greek prepositions are involved in the doctrine of substitution. 'Υπέρ (translated "for") is broad in its scope and may mean no more than that a thing accomplished becomes a benefit to others. In this respect it would be declared by this word that Christ's death benefited those for whom He died. However, this word is invested at times with the most absolute substitutionary meaning (cf. Titus 2:14; Heb. 2:9; 1 Pet. 2:21; 3:18). 'Αντί (also translated "for") conveys the thought of complete substitution of one thing or person in the place of another. Orthodox men, whether of one school or the other, will contend alike that Christ's death was *for* men in the most definite sense. However, substitution may be either absolute or conditional, and in the case of Christ's death for the sinner it was both absolute and conditional. Randles states this twofold aspect of truth.

> Substitution may be absolute in some respects, and conditional in others, e.g., a philanthropist may pay the ransom price of an enslaved family so that the children shall be unconditionally freed, and the parents only on condition of their suitable acknowledging the kindness. Similarly, the substitution of Christ was partly absolute, partly conditional in proportion to man's capacity of choice and responsibility. His death availed for the rescue of infants from race guilt; their justification, like their condemnation, being independent of their knowledge and will, and irrespective of any condition which might render the benefit contingent. But for the further benefit of saving men who have personally and voluntarily sinned, the death of Christ avails potentially, taking effect in their complete salvation if they accept Him with true faith.[2]

The debate between limited and unlimited redemption is not a question of the perfect character of Christ's substitution; His substitution is complete whether applied at one time or another, or if it is never applied. Likewise, it is not a question of the ability or the inability of the sinner to believe apart from divine enablement. Rather it is a question of whether the full value of Christ's death might be *potentially* provided for the nonelect, even though they never benefit from it, but are only judged because of it. The elect are saved because it is *necessary* for them to be saved in view of the fact that Christ died for them. The unlimited redemptionists believe that the substitutionary death of Christ accomplished to infinite perfection all that divine holiness could ever require for each and every lost soul, that the elect are saved on the ground of Christ's death for them through the effective call and divine enablement of the Spirit, that the value of Christ's death is rejected even by the elect until the hour that they believe, and that that value is rejected by the nonelect forever, and for that rejection they are judged.

It has been objected at this point that the belief of the unlimited redemptionist results in the end in man being his own savior; that is, he is saved or lost according to his works. One passage of Scripture will suffice to clear this matter. In Romans 4:5 it is written, "But to him that worketh not, but believeth on him that justifieth the ungodly, his faith is counted for righteousness." Here the thought is not that the candidate for salvation performs no works *except* belief, but rather that by believing he turns from all works of his own, on which he might depend, and confides in Another to do that which no human works could ever do. By so much the determination rests with man, though it is recognized that no man possesses saving faith apart from a divine enablement to that end. The peculiar manner in which God enlightens the mind and moves the heart of the unsaved to the end that they gladly accept Christ as Savior is in no way a coercion of the will; rather the human volition is strengthened and its determination is the more emphatic. It is futile to attempt to dismiss the element of human responsibility from the great gospel texts of the New Testament.

It is both reasonable and scriptural to conclude that a perfect substitution avails for those who are saved, that in the case of the elect it is delayed in its application until they believe, and that in the case of the nonelect it is never applied at all.

The Testimony of the Scriptures

In the progress of the discussion between the limited redemptionists and the unlimited redemptionists, much Scripture is noted on each side, and naturally, some effort is made by each group to harmonize that which might seem to be conflicting between these lines of proof. Some of the passages cited by the limited redemptionists are the following.

JOHN 10:15

"I lay down my life for the sheep." This statement is clear. Christ gave His life for His elect people; however, it is to be observed that both Israel's election and that of the church are referred to in this text (v. 16).

JOHN 15:13

Christ laid down His life for His friends.

JOHN 17:2, 6, 9, 20, 24

In these important verses, Christ declares that He gives eternal life to as many as are given to Him, that an elect company has been given to Him, that He prays now only for this elect company, and that He desires that this elect company may be with Him in glory.

ROMANS 4:25

Christ is here said to have been delivered for the sins of the elect and raised again for the justification of the elect. This, too, is specific.

EPHESIANS 1:3-7

In this extended text, the fact that Christ is the Redeemer of His elect people is declared with absolute certainty.

EPHESIANS 5:25-27

In this passage, Christ is revealed as both loving the church and giving Himself for it so that He might bring it with infinite purity and glory into His own possession and habitation.

In contemplating the Scriptures cited above and others of the same specific character, the unlimited redemptionists assert that it *is* the primary purpose of Christ to bring many sons into glory. He never lost sight of this purpose (that it actuated Him in all His sufferings and death is beyond question), and His heart is centered on those who are thus given to Him of the Father. However, not once do these passages *exclude* the truth, equally emphasized in the Scriptures, that He died for the whole world. There is a difference to be noted between the fact of His death and the motive of His death. He may easily have died for all men with a view to securing His elect. In such a case, Christ would have been motivated by two great purposes: to pay the forensic ransom price for the world, and to secure His elect Body and Bride. The former seems to be implied in such texts as Luke 19:10, "For the Son of man is come to seek and to save that which was lost," and John 3:17, "For God sent not his Son into the world to condemn the world; but that the world through him might be saved." The other purpose seems to be implied in such passages as John 10:15, "As the Father knoweth me, even so know I the Father: and I lay down my life for the sheep." The Scriptures do not always include all aspects of a truth in any one passage. If these texts are used in isolation to "prove" that Christ died only for the elect, then it could be argued with equal logic from other isolated passages that Christ died only for Israel (see John 11:51; Isa. 53:8) or that He died only for the apostle Paul (for Paul declares of Christ, "Who loved me, and gave himself for me," Gal. 2:20). As well might one contend that Christ restricted His prayers to Peter because of the fact that He said to Peter, "But I have prayed for thee" (Luke 22:32).

The problem that both groups face is the need to harmonize passages that refer to limited redemption with passages that refer to unlimited redemption. To the unlimited redemptionist the limited redemption passages present no real difficulty. He believes that they merely emphasize one aspect of a larger truth. Christ did die for the elect, but He also died for the sins of the whole world. However, the limited redemptionist is not able to deal with the unlimited redemption passages as easily. These passages may be grouped together in the following way:

1. Passages that declare Christ's death to be for the whole world (John 1:29; 3:16; 2 Cor. 5:19; Heb. 2:9; 1 John 2:2).

The limited redemptionist states that the use of the word *world* in these and similar passages is restricted to mean the world of the elect, basing the argument on the fact that the word *world* may at times be restricted in the extent of its scope and meaning. They claim that these universal passages, to be in harmony with the revelation that Christ died for an elect company, must be restricted to the elect. According to this interpretation, John 1:29 would read, "Behold the Lamb of God, which taketh away the sin of the elect." John 3:16 would read, "For God so loved the elect that He gave His only begotten Son that whosoever of the elect believeth on Him should not perish, but have everlasting life." Second Corinthians 5:19 would read, "God was in Christ, reconciling the elect unto Himself." Hebrews 2:9 would read, "He tasted death for every man comprising the company of the elect." First John 2:2 would read: "He is the propitiation for our [elect] sins: and not for ours only, but also for the sins of those who comprise the world of elect people."

A study of the word *cosmos* has been presented elsewhere.[3] There it was seen that usually this word refers to a satanic system which is anti-God in character, though in a few instances it refers to the unregenerate people who are in the *cosmos*. Three passages serve to emphasize the antipathy which exists between the saved who are "chosen out of the world" and the world itself: "If the world hate you, ye know that it hated me before it hated you. If ye were of the world, the world would love his own: but because ye are not of the world, but I have chosen you out of the world, therefore the world hateth you" (John 15:18-19); "They are not of the world, even as I am not of the world" (John 17:16); "And we know that we are of God, and the whole world lieth in wickedness" (I John 5:19). The limited redemptionist, then, is forced to claim that the elect, which the world hates and from which it has been saved, is the world. Shedd points to certain specific passages in an attempt to show that the word *cosmos* can at times refer to the "world" of believers.

> Sometimes it is the world of believers, the church. Examples of this use are: John 6:33, 51, "The bread of God is he which . . . giveth life unto the world" [of believers]. Rom. 4:13, Abraham is "the heir of the world" [the redeemed]. Rom. 11:12, "If the fall of them be the riches of the world." Rom. 11:15, "If the casting away of them be the reconciling of the world." In these texts, "church" could be substituted for "world."[4]

In spite of Shedd's assertion, not one of the passages quoted requires that it be interpreted in any light other than that usually accorded to the satanic system.

2. Passages that are all-inclusive in their scope (Rom. 5:6; 2 Cor. 5:14; 1 Tim. 2:6; 4:10; Titus 2:11).

Again the limited redemptionist points out that in these passages the word *all* is restricted to the elect. Indeed, such passages must be restricted if the cause of the limited redemptionist is to stand—but are these properly so restricted? By the limited redemptionist's interpretation, Romans 5:6 would read, "In due time Christ died for the elect, in their ungodly state." Second Corinthians 5:14 would read, "If one died for the elect, then were the elect dead." First Timothy 2:6 would read, "Who gave himself a ransom for the elect, to be testified in due time." First Timothy 4:10 would read, "Who is the Saviour of the elect, especially of those that believe." Titus 2:11 would read, "The grace of God that bringeth salvation hath appeared to the elect."

3. Passages that offer a universal gospel to men (John 3:16; Acts 10:43; Rev. 22:17; etc.). The word *whosoever* is used at least 110 times in the New Testament and always has an unrestricted meaning.

4. A special passage, 2 Peter 2:1, wherein the ungodly

false teachers of the last days who bring swift destruction on themselves are said to be "denying the Lord that bought them." Men are thus said themselves to be ransomed who deny the very ground of salvation and who are destined to destruction.

Two statements may be in order in concluding this section:

a. The limited redemptionist's interpretation of John 3:16 tends to restrict the love of God to those among the unregenerate who are the elect. This interpretation is supported by quoting passages that declare God's peculiar love for His saved people. There is no question but what there is a "much more" expression of the love of God for men after they are saved than before (Rom. 5:8-10), though His love for unsaved men is beyond measure; but to assert that God loves the elect in their unregenerate state more than the nonelect is an assumption without scriptural proof. Some limited redemptionists have been bold enough to say that God does not love the nonelect at all.

b. What if God did give His Son to die for all men in an equal sense to the end that all might be legitimately invited to gospel privileges? Could He, if actuated by such a purpose, use any more explicit language than He has used to express such an intent?

CONCLUSION

Again, let it be said that to disagree with good and worthy teachers is undesirable, to say the least; but when these teachers appear on both sides of a question, as in the present discussion, there seems to be no alternative. By an inner bent of mind some men tend naturally to accentuate the measureless value of Christ's death, while others tend to accentuate the glorious results of the application of His death to the immediate salvation of the lost.

The gospel must be understood by those to whom it is preached, and it is wholly impossible for the limited redemptionist, when presenting the gospel, to hide with any completeness his conviction that the death of Christ is only for the elect. And nothing could be more confusing to an unsaved person than to be drawn away from considering the saving grace of God in Christ to contemplating whether or not he is one of the elect. Who can prove that he is of the election? If the preacher believes that some to whom he addresses his message could not be saved under any circumstances, those addressed have a right to know what the preacher believes and in time they will know. Likewise, it is not wholly sincere to avoid the issue by saying the preacher does not know whether any nonelect are present. Are they absent from every service? Is it not reasonable to suppose that they are usually present when such a vast majority of humanity will probably never be saved at all? In the preaching of salvation through Christ to lost men, no greater wrong could be imposed than to reduce truths that are throbbing with glory, light, and blessing to mere philosophical contemplation. May the God who loved a lost world to the extent that He gave His own Son to die for that world ever impart that passion of soul to those who undertake to convey the message of that measureless love to men!

NOTES

1. W. Lindsey Alexander, *A System of Biblical Theology*, 2 vols. (Edinburgh: T. & T. Clark, 1888), 2:111.
2. Marshall Randles, *Substitution* (London: J. Grose Thomas, n.d.), p. 10.
3. Lewis Sperry Chafer, *Systematic Theology*, 8 vols. (Dallas: Dallas Theological Seminary, 1948), 2:76-90.
4. W. G. T. Shedd, *Dogmatic Theology*, 3 vols. (Edinburgh: T. & T. Clark, 1889), 2:479.

4

Does the Church Fulfill Israel's Program?

John F. Walvoord

THE ARGUMENT FROM GALATIANS 6:15-16

Although amillenarians often use the argument that it is not necessary for Israel to be explicitly identified with the church—just as it is not necessary for the doctrine of the Trinity to be supported by the word *Trinity* in the Bible—many of them point to Galatians 6:15-16 as the one explicit reference. Accordingly, it bears careful scrutiny.

Paul in Galatians is attempting to deal with the question of grace versus law, both as a way of salvation and as a way of sanctification. He concludes in Galatians 6:15, "For neither is circumcision anything, nor uncircumcision, but a new creation."* He then says in verse 16, "And those who will walk by this rule, peace and mercy be upon them, and upon the Israel of God." The question raised by this passage is whether the expression "the Israel of God" is identical to the "new cre-

John F. Walvoord
A.B., Wheaton College; M.A., Texas Christian University; Th.B., Th.M., Evangelical Theological College; Th.D., Dallas Theological Seminary; D.D., Wheaton College
President and Professor of Systematic Theology
Editor, *Bibliotheca Sacra*
Dallas Theological Seminary

*All Scripture quotations in this article are from the *New American Standard Bible.*

ation" described earlier in the verse, applying to the entire church.

Appeal is made to the fact that the Greek preposition καί is sometimes used in an explicative sense[1] and is equivalent to *namely*. Or it could be used in an ascensive sense and translated *even*. But the normal meaning of καί is that of a simple connective as indicated by the translation "and." Burton has a complete discussion on this matter.

> Though Rom. 9[6] 1 Cor. 10[18] show that Paul distinguished between Israel according to the flesh and the Israel according to election or promise, and Rom. 2[29] Phil. 3[3] suggest that he might use τὸν Ἰσραήλ τοῦ θεοῦ of all believers in Christ, regardless of nationality, there is, in fact, no instance of his using Ἰσραήλ except of the Jewish nation or a part thereof. These facts favour the interpretation of the expression as applying not to the Christian community, but to Jews; yet, in view of τοῦ θεοῦ, not to the whole Jewish nation, but to the pious Israel, the remnant according to the election of grace (Rom. 11[5]), including even those who had not seen the truth as Paul saw it. . . . In view of the apostle's previous strong anti-judaistic expressions, he feels impelled, by the insertion of καί, to emphasise this expression of his true attitude towards his people. It can scarcely be translated into English without overtranslating.[2]

The burden of proof is on the expositor to show that the word is used in the sense of "namely" or "even." Such proof is completely lacking. It is significant that Arndt and Gingrich avoid listing Galatians 6:16 in their study of unusual uses of καί.[3] Robertson has no reference to it in either his *Grammar* or his *Word Pictures*. It is also interesting that commentators who do not have a particular burden to prove that Israel is the church usually do not comment on the problem.

Under the circumstances, the simplest explanation is the best, that is, that what Paul is saying is that those who walk by the rule of grace as a new creation in Christ are worthy recipients of His benediction of peace and mercy, but that from his standpoint this is especially true of the Israel of God, by which Paul means Israelites who in the church age trust Jesus Christ. This is a natural and biblical explanation. In any case this verse is not an explicit statement that the Israel of God equals the church composed of both Jews and Gentiles. If those who contend for this point of view had a better verse, they obviously would not use this text. Allis, for instance, merely cites it as a proof text without discussion.[4]

THE ARGUMENT FROM ROMANS 9-11

As previously pointed out, leading amillenarians and post-millenarians are included with those who deny that New Testament references to Israel are always equivalent to the church.[5] However, both premillenarians and amillenarians who want to find fulfillment of Israel's prophecy in the church appeal to Romans 9-11.

Ladd, for instance, devotes a whole chapter to the subject "What about Israel?" in his attempt to identify Israel as the church.[6] His argument centers on the treatment by Paul of the relationship of Israel to the church in Romans 9-11. After stating the special character of Israel's relationship to God in Romans 9:4-5. Paul proceeds in verses 6-8 to distinguish between the physical seed and the spiritual seed. "But it is not as though the word of God has failed. For they are not all Israel who are descended from Israel; neither are they all children because they are Abraham's descendants, but: 'THROUGH ISAAC YOUR DESCENDANTS WILL BE NAMED.' That is, it is not the children of the flesh who are children of God, but the children of the promise are regarded as descendants."

Everyone agrees that those who are physical descendants of Abraham are not assured individual salvation or spiritual blessing. Not all of Abraham's physical descendants inherit the promises given to Jacob. Likewise, neither can all the descendants of Jacob presume on their natural lineage.

What Paul is distinguishing here is spiritual Israel or true Israel from Israelites who have only a physical connection. On this point all can agree. But there is no reference in this verse to Gentiles. While it is true according to Galatians 3:6-9 that Gentile Christians are spiritually descendants of Abraham, they are never called descendants of Jacob, and this is the point at issue.

Both the Old Testament and the New Testament agree that all the descendants of Abraham do not participate in the particular promises given to Israel. It is also true that all physical Israel will not inherit the promises, but only spiritual Israel. To expand this, however, to the statement that spiritual Israel includes Gentiles is to assume what is never taught in Scripture. The fact is that all through Romans 9-11 the thought depends on a careful distinction between Gentiles and Israel. In the past, Israel had many advantages over the

Gentiles. In the present age they have the opportunity to receive Christ on an equal basis with Gentiles. In the future, they will be restored to a privileged position, as is brought out in chapter 11.

Ladd, however, argues from Romans 9:23-26 that the quotation from Hosea applies to the Gentiles, a prophecy originally given to Israel. The passage is as follows, "And He did so in order that He might make known the riches of His glory upon vessels of mercy, which He prepared beforehand for glory, even us, whom He also called, not from among Jews only, but also from among Gentiles. As He says also in Hosea, 'I WILL CALL THOSE WHO WERE NOT MY PEOPLE, "MY PEOPLE," AND HER WHO WAS NOT BELOVED, "BELOVED." AND IT SHALL BE THAT IN THE PLACE WHERE IT WAS SAID TO THEM, "YOU ARE NOT MY PEOPLE," THERE THEY SHALL BE CALLED SONS OF THE LIVING GOD.' " Ladd states, "Then Paul does an amazing thing. He quotes two passages from Hosea which in their Old Testament context refer to Israel and applies them to the Christian church which consists largely of Gentiles, and he does this to prove that the Old Testament foresees the Gentile church."[7]

Ladd here is guilty of reading into the passage what it does not say. It is clear all the way through Romans 9 that the vessels of mercy mentioned in verse 23 include both Jews and Gentiles, and in verse 24 he specifically mentions both classes. However, in verses 25-29 the apostle reverts back to the marvelous fact that Jews can be saved in this present age, and in his quotation from Hosea he claims that there is partial fulfillment in the present age because the people of Israel can be restored and become sons of the living God. The fact that Paul is talking about Israel and not Gentiles is demonstrated in verses 27-29 where he quotes from Isaiah beginning with, "And Isaiah cries out concerning Israel. . . ." It is not until verse 30 that he returns to consider the Gentiles and this is introduced by the question, "What shall we say then?" In other words, Ladd's assertion that Hosea is referring to Gentiles is not supported by the context. In this entire chapter Paul is talking about Israel in contrast to the Gentiles.

It could be argued that there is a partial application of the Hosea prophecy to Gentiles because they were not the people of God but now in the present age can become sons of the living God. However, the entire Old Testament, including the book of Hosea, points out that Israel in covenant relationship with God forsook that covenant and has to be restored—and this was never true of the Gentiles. Accordingly, Ladd's decision to adopt a spiritualizing hermeneutic because he *"finds the New Testament applying to the spiritual church promises which in the Old Testament refer to literal Israel"*[8] is not really justified by the quotation from Hosea. Ladd is reading into it what he wants it to say rather than what it actually says. Even Ladd agrees that in chapter 11 Paul returns to literal Israel. The fact, however, is that Paul is dealing with literal Israel all the way through these chapters.

The metaphor of the olive tree in Romans 11 has occasioned a great deal of exegesis, usually influenced heavily by what the interpreter wants the passage to say. The olive tree has its natural branches cut off in order that branches from the wild olive tree could be grafted in. Paul then predicts that the day will come when the wild olive branches will be cut off and the natural branches grafted back in. The question is, What does the olive tree represent?

The most natural interpretation is that it represents the place of blessing as defined in the Abrahamic covenant in Genesis 12:3, which predicted that in Abraham all nations will be blessed. Israel was blessed by its relationship to Abraham as illustrated in the Old Testament where the Israelites were a favored people. Their rejection of Christ, however, has brought about a judicial blinding or hardening as mentioned in Romans 11:25, which states that "a partial hardening has happened to Israel until the fulness of the Gentiles has come in." This refers to the difficulty in the present age for Jews to see the truth concerning Christ. In the present age Gentiles are especially blessed, but Israel is largely in unbelief.

The passage indicates that Israel's blindness originated when Christ was on earth and will end when the time of Gentile blessing concludes with the rapture of the church. After the period of the Gentile blessing, Israel will have a further period of special blessing when "all Israel will be saved" (Rom. 11:26).

In this passage, as in earlier passages in Romans, there is no need to confuse Israel with the church. In fact, the contrast between Israel and Gentiles continues to be observed. While Paul makes clear that Israelites can be saved in the present age, it is also clear that it is a period of unusual blessing for the Gentiles, in contrast to what precedes and what follows.

That Israelites and Gentiles share blessing in the church in the present age all will affirm. However, the passage does not teach that Gentiles become Israelites. In fact Paul's entire argument is based on the *contrast* between Israel and the Gentiles in the period preceding the present age and in the period following the present age.

Much has been written on the phrase "all Israel will be saved." Here Hodge, although a postmillenarian, makes the text clear.

> Israel, here, from the context, must mean the Jewish people, and *all Israel*, the whole nation. The Jews, as a people, are now rejected; as a people they are to be restored. As their rejection, although national, did not include the rejection of every individual; so their restoration, although in like manner national, need not be assumed to include the salvation of every individual Jew. Πᾶς ʼΙσραήλ is not therefore to be here understood to mean, all the true people of God, as Augustin[e], Calvin, and many others explain; nor all the elect Jews, i.e., all that part of the nation which constitute "the remnant according to election of grace," but the whole nation as a nation.[9]

As in previous references to Israel and the Gentiles in Romans 9-11, Israel remains Israel and Gentiles remain Gentiles, and neither term is in itself equivalent to the church.

THE ARGUMENT FROM PHILIPPIANS 3:1-3

In the Old Testament the sign of the Abrahamic covenant was circumcision; anyone not circumcised was considered cut off from the covenant. "The circumcised" referred therefore to those Jews who claimed their right to the promises given to Abraham and the Jewish nation by observing this rite of circumcision. By contrast, Gentiles are called uncircumcised. Those who want to make Israel and the church identical have very often referred to Philippians 3:1-3 as contradictory evidence. The passage states, "Finally, my brethren, rejoice in the Lord. To write the same things again is no trouble to me, and it is a safeguard for you. Beware of the dogs, beware of the evil workers, beware of the false circumcision; for we are the true circumcision, who worship in the Spirit of God and glory in Christ Jesus and put no confidence in the flesh."

When Paul says "we are the true circumcision," he is, of course, referring to himself and fellow Jews. The word "true" is not in the Greek text but is added by way of explanation by the translators. Although Jews were to be physically circumcised, Paul teaches that Gentiles can fulfill the same idea by being set apart to God without the physical act. Here those ambitious to prove that Israel is the church arbitrarily state that verse 3 is referring to Gentiles, something the passage does not indicate. Although it may be conceded that Gentile Christians who are separated to God fulfill the concept of circumcision, even this concept distinguishes Gentile Christians from Christians who are of the nation Israel. Paul further points out that physical circumcision even for a Jew is not enough, and in Romans 2:28-29 he states, "For he is not a Jew who is one outwardly; neither is circumcision that which is outward in the flesh. But he is a Jew who is one inwardly; and circumcision is that which is of the heart, by the Spirit, not by the letter; and his praise is not from men, but from God." Accordingly, while Gentiles may achieve spiritually what a spiritual Jew achieves, it is not by the physical act of circumcision. Instead of making Jew and Gentile one, Philippians 3:3 continues the distinction even though they are one in Christ.

Other passages are often cited but are just as arbitrary in their interpretation as those previously examined. In James 1:1 reference is made to the twelve tribes scattered abroad, and 1 Peter 1:1 refers to the aliens, or sojourners. It is perfectly natural to take both passages as referring to Jewish Christians, not Gentiles, and to read in them anything more is imposing on the texts what they do not say. More important, however, is the argument related to Hebrews 8.

The Argument Concerning the New Covenant in Hebrews 8

From the very fact that the Bible is divided into the Old Testament and the New Testament, or the Old Covenant and the New Covenant, it is clear that Christianity fundamentally is based on a New Covenant brought in by Jesus Christ. Although the history of Christianity has revealed many attempts to return to the law as illustrated in Paul's dealing with the Galatians, and although other groups like the Seventh-day Adventists go back to the law for some of their basic theology, the whole point of the New Testament is to present the grace and truth that came by Jesus Christ. John states it very simply, "For the Law was given through Moses; grace and truth were realized through Jesus Christ" (John 1:17).

It was exceedingly difficult for many Hebrew Christians to accept the fact that the law was actually finished and that a new covenant had been introduced. Accordingly, the author of the epistle to the Hebrews offered several contrasts between the New Covenant and the Old Covenant in relation to salvation, the priesthood, and God's promises. One such contrast is developed in Hebrews 8:7-13 where the author presents an extended quotation from Jeremiah 31:31-34. Exponents of the idea that the church fulfills Israel's promises put heavy emphasis on this passage as proving their contention.

It is true that the entire passage from Jeremiah is quoted. The interpretation of the passage in Hebrews 8:13 is limited, however, to one phrase, "a new covenant," and the interpretation given is that "He has made the first obsolete. But whatever is becoming obsolete and growing old is ready to disappear." Exponents of the idea that Israel is the church are quick to point to this passage as proof of their contention. Allis, for instance, states:

> The passage speaks of the new covenant. It declares that this new covenant has been already introduced and that by virtue of the fact that it is called "new" it has made the one which it is replacing "old" and the old is about to vanish away. It would be hard to find a clearer reference to the gospel age in the Old Testament than in these verses in Jeremiah: and the writer of Hebrews obviously appeals to it as such.[10]

But is Jeremiah's New Covenant actually being fulfilled today?

Scholars in all classifications have struggled to understand completely the concept of the New Covenant. Even among premillenarians, several different views have been advanced: (a) the New Covenant belongs only to Israel but the blood of the covenant is applied to the church; (b) the New Covenant is expressly Israel's covenant but is applied in general to the church; or (c) there are two New Covenants—one for Israel and one for the church. Those who affirm that Israel and the church are one interpret the covenant as expressly made to the church, including both Old Testament and New Testament saints.

Some of the problems are semantic, and the various views

are not necessarily mutually exclusive. The problem with claiming explicit fulfillment of the promises in the New Covenant for the present age is the simple fact that all the promises of the New Covenant are not being currently fulfilled. While the church has experienced many spiritual blessings, it is not true (as is clear from Heb. 8:11) that evangelism and missionary activity are no longer necessary because everyone knows the Lord. The world has not yet reached the stage where God has declared, "I will remember their sins no more." A literal fulfillment of this passage requires the millennial kingdom with Christ reigning and bringing in the spiritual blessings that attend His reign.

A further problem for those who use this passage to support the concept that Israel and the church are one is that the explanation or exegesis limits itself to the one word "new." The writer of Hebrews does not claim that the New Covenant is now being fulfilled. All he claims is that a New Covenant has been established. What is the true explanation?

The fact that all conservative expositors accept is that Christ, through His death on the cross, has established a covenant of Grace under which those who are sinners can be justified, forgiven, and made new creatures in Christ. This is new because it provides something the law did not provide. A solution to the thorny problem of the interpretation of the New Covenant is relatively simple.

Christ in His death on the cross made it possible for God to extend grace to anyone who believes, whether Jew or Gentile. This attitude of grace, based on the death of Christ, is stated in Romans 3:23-26. It is also the basis of grace to the church in the present age and is the legal background for salvation, justification, and all the blessings that belong to the church. The grace accomplished by Christ is also the basis for millennial blessing and the fulfillment of the many promises of an age in which there will be righteousness and peace and universal knowledge of the Lord. A solution to the problem, then, is that there is one covenant with application to Israel and to the church and to anyone saved by the death of Christ. In Scripture the application of the New Covenant is explicitly to the church in the present age and to Israel as a nation in the future as far as millennial blessings are concerned. The New Covenant is also the basis for a new rule of life according to the dispensational setting of those involved.

Accordingly, the writer of Hebrews is proving that the law is dead because even the Old Testament predicted that a New Covenant would replace the law, and a faithful Jew should recognize that the Mosaic law was temporary and would be supplanted by a New Covenant of grace. Such a New Covenant has already been brought in by the death and resurrection of Christ. That the application to Israel is full and complete as anticipated in Jeremiah 31 and other similar passages, however, is not stated in the text nor is it actually true. Accordingly, the proof that Israel and the church are identical is not supported by this passage. What is taught is that both Israel and the church derive their salvation and spiritual blessing from the same covenant, that is, the covenant of grace made possible by the death of Christ.

CONCLUSION

Dispensational interpretion holds that the term *Israel* is never inclusive of Gentile Christians and that while both enjoy the same privileges in the church in the present age, the fulfillment of the special promise given to Israel of a golden age of grace and and blessing is yet to be fulfilled in the future millennial kingdom. This is based on a literal interpretation of prophecy.

In taking all references to Israel literally, dispensationalists have the support of such a postmillenarian as Hodge. Accordingly, it is not simply dispensational theology that dictates that Israel always means Israel. Correct exegesis also supports the same concept. The fact that so many scholars have spiritualized the Scriptures, including those relating to Israel, is, of course, evident. Amillennialism, which often takes this view, has been predominant since the days of Augustine. But the concept that the term *Israel* includes Gentile believers is read into the text of Scripture. It is determined by theological presuppositions rather than proper exegesis.

The implication that Israel always means Israel is important because it supports not only premillennialism, but the whole concept of the literal interpretation of prophecy in general. It leads to the conclusion that God has a special program for the nation of Israel as a nation. In the present age, Jew and Gentile can become one in Christ without losing their racial or national characteristics. In the future the distinction between

Jew and Gentile will again become more distinct as Israel receives special blessings promised to her in the millennial kingdom, whereas the Gentiles receive other blessings during the same time period. Even in the new heavens and the new earth the ethnic distinctions continue, though all believers share the same blessings. The new Jerusalem will have the names of the twelve tribes of Israel on its gates; and the names of the twelve apostles, representing the church, will be on the foundation. Individual and corporate identity will be preserved throughout eternity, even though the blessings of grace may be shared equally in the eternal state. The answer to the question, "Is Israel's prophetic program fulfilled by the New Testament church?" is no. Israel still has a glorious future that will be fulfilled literally. Wilkinson has expressed this clearly.

> Nevertheless, facts are stubborn things. It is a fact that God has declared that Israel is not to cease from being a nation before Him for ever. It is a fact that the Jewish nation, still in unbelief, survivor of all others, alone retains its national identity. . . . It is a fact that the promise of a land (the territorial limits of which were defined) to the posterity of Abraham, as also the promise of a son of David's own line to occupy David's throne for ever, were *unconditional* promises, ratified by covenant and oath. It is a fact that the posterity of Abraham has never yet fully possessed and enjoyed the whole land so granted and that no son of David occupies David's throne. . . . The O.T. promises are all as certain of fulfillment in their O.T. sense and meaning and purpose to Israel, as are the N.T. promises certain of fulfillment to the Church.[11]

NOTES

1. Henry Alford, *The Greek Testament*, 3d ed., 3 vols. (London: Revingtons, 1862), 3:66.
2. Ernest De Witt Burton, *A Critical and Exegetical Commentary on the Epistle to the Galatians*, International Critical Commentary (Edinburgh: T. & T. Clark, 1921), p. 358.
3. William F. Arndt and F. Wilbur Gingrich, *A Greek-English Lexicon of the New Testament and Other Early Christian Literature*, 4th rev. ed. (Chicago: U. of Chicago, 1957), pp. 392-94.
4. Oswald Allis, *Prophecy and the Church* (Philadelphia: Presbyterian & Reformed, 1945), pp. 109, 152.
5. John F. Walvoord, "Does the Church Fulfill Israel's Program? Part 2," *Bibliotheca Sacra* 137(April-June 1980):118-24.
6. George E. Ladd, *The Last Things* (Grand Rapids: Eerdmans, 1978), pp. 19-28.
7. Ibid., p. 21.

8.   Ibid., p. 24 (italics his).
9.   Charles Hodge, *Commentary on the Epistle to the Romans* (Philadelphia: H. B. Garner, 1883), p. 589.
10.   Allis, p. 154.
11.   Samuel Hinds Wilkinson, *The Israel Promises and Their Fulfillment* (London: John Bale, Sons, & Danielsson, 1936), pp. 56-57.

5

Premillennialism in Revelation 20:4-6

Jack S. Deere

INTRODUCTION

Many will concede that a prima facie reading of Revelation 20:4-6 and its context yields the doctrine of an intermediate Messianic kingdom, that is, a kingdom inaugurated by Christ at His second advent and terminating or merging with the eternal state. In fact, such a doctrine was held by the majority of the early church Fathers.[1] In the third century the formidable Alexandrians, Dionysius, Clement, and Origen, declared war on premillennialism.[2] The doctrine was attacked with ad hominem arguments, accused of being Judaistic, and chided for using a literal hermeneutic.[3] With the coming of Augustine and his development of the amillennial interpretation, the doctrine of premillennialism was all but obliterated, and only rarely did anyone venture to put forward a premillennial interpretation of Revelation 20:4-6.

However, the present day has witnessed a reversal in the interpretation of John's millennial vision. Hanns Lilje, T. F. Glassen, Albrecht Oepke, Austin Farrer, C. B. Caird, R. H. Charles, and Mathias Rissi, without necessarily embracing

Jack S. Deere
A.B., Texas Christian University; Th.M., Dallas Theological Seminary; graduate study toward Th.D., Dallas Theological Seminary
Assistant Professor of Semitics and Old Testament Studies
Dallas Theological Seminary

premillennialism, all understand John to be describing an intermediate messianic kingdom in Revelation 20:4-6.[4] Yet not all the commentators just mentioned think John was correct in his view of the millennium or consistent with other New Testament writers. For instance, Farrer says:

> But why did St. John believe in a millennial standstill, if St. Paul did not? It seems that the doctrine established itself in rabbinic theology towards the end of the first century A.D.; St. Paul would not have learnt it at the feet of Gamaliel, the Seer of Revelation might well learn [sic] it at whose ever feet it was he sat.[5]

According to John, however, the confirming authority for his doctrine of the intermediate kingdom was not found in rabbinic theology, but in a vision (cf. Rev. 20:4, καὶ εἶδον) which was given to him by the Master of that kingdom (Rev. 1:1). This does not mean that rabbinic theology or intertestamental literature is not important for a correct understanding of John's view of the millennial kingdom. Quite the contrary! One only has to consider how firmly entrenched the doctrine of an intermediate messianic kingdom had become before John's writing. The doctrine of an intermediate kingdom was put forth in the second century B.C. in the books of 1 Enoch and Jubilees, in the first century B.C. in the Psalms of Solomon and the Sibylline Oracles, in the early first century A.D. in the Assumption of Moses and in 2 Enoch, and in the late first century A.D. in 2 Baruch and 4 Ezra.[6] The rabbinic authorities who held the doctrine of an intermediate kingdom are conveniently cataloged by Billerbeck.[7] At least twice before the writing of Revelation the length of the messianic kingdom was held to be one thousand years! The book of 2 Enoch, which may be dated between A.D. 1 and 50, maintained that the messianic kingdom would extend for one thousand years. The well-known Rabbi Eleazar b. Hyracanus (ca. A.D. 90) also held to a one-thousand-year reign of the Messiah. One may conclude that the revelation of an intermediate messianic kingdom would not have been foreign to John or to his readers.

CONTEXT

The exegesis of Revelation 20:4-6 is determined largely by the interpreter's view of the immediate context of 19:11—

20:15. Does this section indicate a chronological progression from beginning to end, or does 20:1-6 recapitulate details in the book given before 19:11? I believe that the whole passage moves in a chronological progression.

It seems quite reasonable that 19:11-21 describes the second advent of Christ and the corresponding cataclysmic judgment on His enemies.[8] Daniel 7 offers an instructive parallel to this event. The little horn of Daniel 7 parallels the beast of Revelation 13:1-8. Both the little horn of Daniel and the beast of Revelation are said to have a worldwide empire (Dan. 7:7, 23; Rev. 13:8). Both have victory over the saints for "a time, times, and half a time" (Dan. 7:25*; Rev. 12:14).[9] Both are destroyed by the Messiah at His second advent (Dan. 7:11, 26; Rev. 19:20). Both affirm that immediately following the destruction of the world ruler the kingdom is given to the saints (Dan. 7:22, 27; Rev. 20:4-6). Thus it is apparent that at least up to the reign of the saints Revelation 19:11-20:6 is following the same pattern as Daniel 7. Since the world ruler is yet future, the millennial reign must also be future, for the saints do not reign or receive their kingdom until after his destruction.[10] Thus on the basis of Daniel 7 it is more natural to read Revelation 20:4-6 as part of a chronological progression in its larger context (19:11-20:15) than as a recapitulation.

The literary connection between 19:11-21 and 20:4-6 also indicates that 20:4-6 is yet future. Revelation 19:11-21 presents a graphic picture of the Lord coming in glory and power,[11] while 20:4-6 presents a similar picture of the saints in glory and power. Since it is taught elsewhere in the Scriptures that the saints will be revealed in glory and power at the coming of the Lord, it is only natural to view 20:4-6 as following the second advent and as, therefore, yet future.[12]

It is also evident that Revelation 20:1-3 must be future. It is customary to refer to this passage as the "binding" of Satan, yet the passage is much stronger. Satan is not only bound, but is also completely imprisoned and cut off from the earth. Those who do not believe that the millennial reign is future normally try to prove that Satan is presently bound. Rushdoony and Lenski introduce several passages in an

---

New American Standard Bible.

attempt to prove that Revelation 20:1-3 is presently being ful-filled.[13] However, on closer inspection these passages either speak about the binding of Satan in reference to individuals or they record his judgment but not its execution. None of the passages speaks about the complete imprisonment of Satan described in Revelation 20:1-3.

On the other hand, several passages in the New Testa-ment seem to indicate that Satan is not yet imprisoned, and still has a great deal of influence in the world. First John 5:19 reveals that "the whole world lies in the evil one." First Peter 5:8 also speaks of the freedom of Satan: "Your adversary, the devil, prowls about like a roaring lion, seek-ing someone to devour." In 2 Corinthians 4:3-4 Paul speaks of the power of the satanic veil that keeps men from perceiv-ing the gospel. Neither does the witness of history indicate that Satan has been unable to deceive the nations. One has only to observe Nazi Germany or present-day China or Rus-sia or even his own culture to convince him of Satan's deceptive work among the nations. Of course, one may assign all this evil to the flesh in unregenerate people. But in the kingdom, when unregenerate persons will be born, the identity of the unregenerate is not known until the release of Satan (Rev. 20:7-10). So man's sinful nature alone seems inadequate to explain the corporate evil in the world. Therefore, it may be concluded that the imprison-ment of Satan is yet future. In addition, the remainder of the twentieth chapter (20:7-15) is certainly future.

In review, Revelation 19:11-21 (the first division in this passage) must be future for it describes the second advent. The second division, the imprisonment of Satan (20:1-3), is likely future, too. The last battle and the final judgment (20:7-15) are also future. Thus between these verses (19:11—20:3 and 20:7-15), which exhibit a clear chronological progression yet future, the millennial reign is found. And the millennial reign is introduced in 20:4 with the same phrase (καὶ εἶδον, "and I saw") that introduces the visions of 19:11-21; 20:1-3; and 20:11-15. The only exception is 20:7-10, which is intro-duced with the temporal particle ὅταν ("when")! Therefore, not only do the parallels with Daniel 7 and the exegetical connec-tions with 19:11-21 argue for a futuristic interpretation of Revelation 20:4-6, but also its setting in a context that is com-pletely futuristic before and after argue for a yet-future fulfillment. Unless there are compelling exegetical reasons to the contrary, Revelation 20:4-6 must be viewed as chronologically following the second advent and as therefore future.

EXEGESIS

John begins in verse 4 by describing the saints who reign in the millennial kingdom. Charles thinks that the first line, καὶ εἶδῖον θρόνους, καὶ ἐκάθισαν ἐπ᾽ αὐτούς ("and I saw thrones, and they sat upon them") is so ungrammatical and unintelligible that it is either a marginal gloss from Daniel 7:22 or else it has been misplaced in the text.[14] However, the use of the third person plural indefinite verb is not unknown to John (cf. 12:6, τρέφωσιν; and 13:16, δῶσιν). Furthermore, John has given his readers a similar construction in 4:2-3. First, he mentions a throne, followed by the indefinite καθήμενος, and then in verse 3b he gives a more elaborate description.[15] So the present text is authentic and one must now determine who sits on these thrones.

Some have suggested that the occupants of the thrones are the twenty-four elders.[16] However, those who put forward this interpretation also view the twenty-four elders as representative of the church, or perhaps the church and Israel. Two observations preclude such a view. First, the twenty-four elders are individual beings rather than a representative group (5:5; 7:13-14). Second, Ladd points out the following concerning the vision in 7:9-11:

> First we have a great multitude of the saved which no man can number; then the various concentric ranks of heavenly beings round about the throne; first the angels, then the elders, and finally the four living creatures. See also a similar order of the heavenly beings in 19:1-4. The elders are grouped with other angelic beings in distinction to the redeemed.[17]

Since the twenty-four elders are more likely an order of angels, they cannot be the occupants of the thrones, for the saints will judge the angels (1 Cor. 6:3).

Beckwith suggests that the martyrs must be in view here.[18] However, this is not likely since the martyrs are not raised until after John has already seen the thrones and their occupants. Bullinger suggests that the occupants are Christ, God, the seven angelic assessors, and the apostles.[19] Although Christ and God have thrones and reign, it is doubtful that κρίμα ἐδόθη αὐτοῖς ("judgment was given to them") could be predicated of them. The angels are precluded by 1 Corinthians 6:3 and by Hebrews 2:5. The apostles may be likely candidates (Matt. 19:28), but why should the occupancy of the thrones be limited to them? It is more likely that all the saints are in view. In several places John records the promise of a share in Christ's throne and reign (2:26-27; 3:21; 5:10). Paul also maintains that the saints will judge the world (1 Cor. 6:2). Therefore, in 20:4 John saw the saints of all ages on the thrones.[20]

The fact that John saw them seated on thrones suggests that the phrase κρίμα ἐδόθη αὐτοῖς ("judgment was given to them") refers to their authority to judge rather than judgment passed in their favor. Regarding the nature of this judicial activity, McClain remarks:

> Since this kingdom will begin on earth with the actual situation existing here as the coming of Christ finds it, there will be many crucial matters needing to be settled by such action without delay. . . . Since throughout the millennial kingdom human life will continue with the possibilities of sin and error, though greatly restrained and controlled, it should be obvious that there will be need for such judicial activity then as well as now.[21]

After viewing the reigning saints, John saw a second group, the martyrs of the great tribulation. The participle τῶν πεπελεκισμένων ("those who had been beheaded") is more graphic than the τῶν ἐσφαγμένων ("those who had been slain") of 6:9. It stresses the fact they were put to death by the state rather than merely recording that they were slain.[22] Their "crime" is recorded in the following clauses.

First, their obedience is stated positively by the two διὰ ("because of") constructions. Ἰησοῦ ("Jesus") is probably an objective genitive, thus indicating that the martyrs were faithful in proclaiming Jesus. The second διὰ clause could be taken as a hendiadys, but since it is broader than the previous clause it probably points to the martyrs' obedience to the commandments of God. Therefore, they were put to death because they proclaimed Jesus and because they were obedient to God's Word.

Next, their obedience is stated negatively. There is some debate whether the καὶ οἵτινες ("and they") introduces a new group or further qualifies the martyrs. Lenski thinks a new group is in view because the οἵτινες is preceded by a καὶ.[23] But the καί may be ascensive in force or merely conjunctive because John is describing a new aspect of their obedience. Bullinger also thinks a new group is introduced because the οἵτινες does not agree in gender with ψυχάς.[24] Yet this phenomenon, *constructio ad sensum*, is not at all uncommon in Revelation.[25]

Two observations indicate that a new group is not in view. First, the same phrase, καὶ οἵτινες, is used in Revelation 1:7 where it includes members of the previous clause. Second, if a new group is in view, nothing is said about their death, and therefore it is difficult to see how the following ἔζησαν ("they came to life") can refer to them. Thus a new group is not in view, and instead καὶ οἵτινες gives a further qualification of the obedience of the martyrs.

The martyrs identified themselves with Jesus by proclaiming Him and obeying Him. They separated themselves from the state by refusing to worship the beast or his image and by refusing to receive his mark.[26] In doing so they paid the penalty of death (13:15). So from the state they received death, but what would they receive from God?

The answer to this question comes quickly and dramatically. These godly martyrs will receive "life" and a kingly rule from God! But what does John mean by "life"? Is John describing (1) the regeneration of the soul, (2) a symbolic resurrection, (3) the soul's entrance into heaven, or (4) a literal physical resurrection? The answer hinges on the meaning of "they came to life" (ἔζησαν) in verses 4 and 5 as well as the phrase "the first resurrection" (ἡ ἀνάστασις ἡ πρώτη) in verse 5.

Augustine argued that the resurrection in view was the regeneration of the soul.[27] Swete thinks that a symbolic resurrection is meant. The fact symbolized is the triumph of the martyrs' principles in society.[28] Both of these views may be dismissed from consideration, for they use an allegorical technique that produces interpretations that are diverse and limited only by one's fantasy. Also both views go against the usage of ἀνάστασις (which will be discussed shortly).

On the exegetical side of the question Hughes produces three arguments in favor of understanding ἔζησαν of verse 4 as a constative aorist. Therefore, he would translate ἔζησαν as "they lived" (rather than "they came to life"). That would allow him to take the ἡ ἀνάστασις ἡ πρώτη as a reference to the soul's rising into heaven at the time of death.[29] He first argues that if ἔζησαν is ingressive (i.e., "they came to life") then the following ἐβασίλευσαν must also be ingressive (i.e., "they *began* to reign"). Of course, ἐβασίλευσαν must be constative, for the martyrs did not "begin to reign for a thousand years." Yet what rule of logic or grammar dictates that ἔζησαν cannot be ingressive while ἐβασίλευσαν is constative? Recognized grammarians have not felt this tension. Nigel Turner takes ἔζησαν as ingressive.[30] A. T. Robertson also understands ἔζησαν to be ingressive while taking ἐβασίλευσαν as constative.[31] So Hughes's first argument cannot stand.

His second argument for understanding that ἔζησαν is a constative rather than an ingressive aorist is that ζάω has an ingressive force in only two places in the New Testament (Rev. 2:8 and Rom. 14:9, both of which refer to the resurrection of Christ). This is not quite correct, however, for Luke 15:32 and Revelation 13:14 are clear examples of the ingressive use of ἔζησαν, according to Turner.[32] Thus Hughes's second argument also loses some of its force.

Finally, Hughes understands the ψυχὰς of verse 4 to refer to disembodied souls, and maintains that it would be impossible for the soul to "come to life" since the soul never dies. Berkouwer, himself an amillennialist, replies, "Such a critique, however, is not decisive, for there seems to be no soul-body dichotomy in view here. John sees simply that those who had been beheaded come to life again and sit on thrones."[33] Similarly, Edvard Schweizer sees no distinction between the noncorporeal and corporeal state intended by John's use of ψυχὰς in 6:9 or in 20:4.[34] The use of ψυχή to refer to the whole person is well known (Acts 2:41, 43; 3:23). Furthermore, John has previously used ψυχή with a qualifying genitive to refer to the whole person (ψυχὰς ἀνθρώπων 18:13).[35] Also, the masculine οἵτινες, the nearest antecedent of ἔζησαν, supports the contention that John is thinking in terms of persons rather than disembodied souls. Thus it does not seem that Hughes's arguments are strong enough to preclude the natural ingressive understanding of ἔζησαν.

On the other hand, several weighty reasons can be adduced for the ingressive use of ἔζησαν. One might add to the previous four uses of ζάω as ingressive[36] the ἔζησαν of Ezekiel 37:10 in the Septuagint, which refers to dry bones coming to life. Ezekiel 37-39 has a structure similar to that of Revelation 20, and Rissi thinks John is intentionally alluding to Ezekiel

37.[37] Finally, one more thing should be noted about the ingressive use of ζάω. In both Ezekiel 37 and Luke 15 it is clear that the aorist use of ζάω is equivalent to ἀναζάω ("to come to life again"; cf. Ezek. 37:5, 10 and Luke 15:24, 32). Of course, this usage of ζάω is to be expected since, as Moulton observes, "The ingressive especially belongs to verbs of state or condition."[38] Thus both grammar and usage indicate that ἔζησαν has an ingressive force and refers to a literal physical resurrection.

Another cogent reason may be given for understanding the ἔζησαν of verse 4 to refer to a physical resurrection. Alford pointed out long ago that the ἔζησαν of verse 4 and also of verse 5 must be understood in the same sense.[39] If one is spiritual, then the other must be spiritual, and vice versa. Now the resurrection of verse 4 must refer to believers, whereas the ἔζησαν of verse 5 must refer to unbelievers.[40] If ἔζησαν in both verses refers to a physical resurrection, there is no problem. But if ἔζησαν refers to a spiritual resurrection in both verses, then the exegete is confronted with an insurmountable problem. For that would imply that the unbelieving dead of verse 5 live spiritually in heaven like the martyrs of verse 4 after the thousand years is completed. Hughes tries to escape this dilemma in the following way:

> This verse does not say that after the thousand years were finished the rest of the dead lived. In fact, the expression "the rest of the dead did not live until the thousand years were finished" is equivalent to saying that "the second death had power on the rest of the dead during the thousand years." And those on whom the second death has power are never released from its power. So the "rest of the dead" did not live until the thousand years were finished, nor did they live after the thousand years were finished. And they will never live, i.e., they will never be released from the power that the second death has on them. That the word ἄχρι (until) does not of itself imply that a change occurs after the point to which it refers is reached is shown, for example, by citing Romans 5:13a: "For until (ἄχρι) the law sin was in the world." Sin was in the world up to the point of the coming of the Mosaic expression of the law. Does this imply that sin was no longer in the world after the coming of the Mosaic expression of the law? Absolutely not! For of course sin is still in the world.[41]

This argument is invalidated by Hughes's failure to notice that ἄχρι has two basic uses. It may be used as an improper preposition with the genitive, in which case it has several forces. This is its use in Romans 5:13, where it has the mean-ing of "before." However, ἄχρι may be used as a conjunction as it is here in Revelation 20:5. When ἄχρι is used as a con-junction with the aorist subjunctive, it always has the force of a future perfect, "until, to the time that."[42] Now ἄχρι occurs three other times in Revelation with the aorist subjunctive (7:3, ἄχρι σφραγίσωμεν; 15:8, ἄχρι τελεσθῶσιν; and 20:3, ἄχρι τελεσθῇ τὰ χίλια ἔτη). In each of these uses the ἄχρι more than implies a change that "occurs after the point to which it refers is reached." Furthermore, exactly the same expressions are used in 20:3 and 20:5, ἄχρι τελεσθῇ τὰ χίλια ἔτη; and 20:3 clearly contemplates a change after the thousand years are completed. So the rule that states that the two uses of ἔζησαν must have identical meanings must also apply to the two uses of the same phrase in 20:3 and 20:5. By seeking to avoid a glaring inconsistency in regard to the two uses of ἔζησαν, Hughes has overlooked the distinctive usages of ἄχρι and fallen into an even greater inconsistency regarding the use of the ἄχρι constructions in 20:3, 5. Therefore, the only interpre-tation of ἔζησαν that is consistent with grammar, usage, and the context is that it refers to a physical resurrection.

In the context of Revelation 20:4-6 the time of the saints' reigning was shown to be future, beginning with the second advent of the Lord. Since no compelling exegetical reasons against such a view have been encountered, the place of the saints' reign may now be considered. At least four arguments favor the earth as the location of the saints' reign. First, Christ is "regarded as personally present on the earth following His return (19:11-16)"[43] and the saints are said to reign with Him (20:4). Second, at the conclusion of the thousand years the saints are still on the earth for this is where Satan comes to attack them (20:9).[44] Third, Revelation 5:10 claims that the saints will reign on the earth. Fourth, the Old Testament mes-sianic prophecies also looked forward to an earthly kingdom.[45]

If the reign is to be on earth, over whom shall the saints reign? The subjects of the reign must be the believing Gentiles and Jews who passed safely through the tribulation and were alive at the second advent. Three lines of evidence support this conclusion. First, it seems likely that they must reign over someone, for "it would be a singularly empty recognition of their services if they were to reign over a world of which they were the sole inhabitants."[46] Second, there are no unbelievers left alive for all the unbelievers followed the beast (13:8) into the battle of Armageddon, and were made to drink of the "wine of the wrath of God" (14:10; 19:15), which brought about their death (19:21). Since the reign cannot be over unbelievers it must be over believers. Third, the saints were promised a reign over the entire world, over both Jew and Gentile (Matt. 19:28; 1 Cor. 6:2; Rev. 2:26-27).

The length of the reign, τὰ χίλια ἔτη, is mentioned six times in 20:2-7. The repetition underscores the importance of this age in the divine plan. It is regarded as a great period for it begins the consummation of all history. Paul points out in Romans 8:22 that all creation longs for this epoch, all the saints long for it, and God Himself longs for it. Are the thousand years to be taken literally or symbolically? Augustine was not dogmatic about its meaning when he wrote *The City of God*, but he suggested that if it were symbolic then it was used to mark the perfection or fullness of time. "For one thousand is the cube of ten."[47] Lenski enthusiastically echoes this idea when he speaks of ten "raised to the third degree, that of highest completeness."[48] Yet one is driven to ask why ten to the third degree refers to "highest completeness." Why not ten to the fourth or fifth degree, or better still, ten to the tenth degree? What could be more complete than that, unless perhaps ten to the hundredth degree?

No one has yet demonstrated from ancient literature why the number one thousand should have any symbolic significance. In fact, there is no discernible symbolic significance of אֶלֶף in the Old Testament or of χίλιοι in the New Testament. Furthermore, a concordance study will reveal that both שָׁנָה ("year") when used with a number and ἔτος ("year") when used with a numeral are always literal years. It is futile to argue for a symbolic meaning of τὰ χίλια ἔτη in Revelation 20:4-6 on the basis of Psalm 90:4 or 2 Peter 3:8, for the latter are not saying that a thousand years *are* a day. Rather they point to God's transcendence in respect to time. Nor can one secure a symbolic sense for τὰ χίλια ἔτη merely by repeating the shibboleth that Revelation is a symbolic book, for not everything is symbolic in the book, and one must give reasons why a certain passage is symbolic. Also, it is not likely that John used τὰ χίλια ἔτη in a nontemporal way merely to indicate "the sign of the Messianic time." This interpretation is based on the view that τὰ χίλια ἔτη had become a standard expression in rabbinic theology to indicate the messianic age.[49] However, there are only two possible occurrences in earlier literature where the duration of one thousand years is assigned to the messianic kingdom.[50] Thus the only safe course to follow is Davis's dictum that all numbers "should always be taken at face value and understood as conveying a mathematical quantity unless there is either textual or contextual evidence to the contrary."[51] Therefore, the duration of the saints' reign is a literal thousand years.

The quality of the reign is described by the phrase "with Christ" (μετὰ τοῦ Χριστοῦ). Since the saints will reign by virtue of Christ's power and guidance they will fulfill their roles perfectly. For the first time in history human government will be perfectly righteous, and there will be universal peace. Some have objected to an earthly reign of glorified saints among nonglorified saints.[52] Ladd points out that a precedent was set by the Lord who "in His resurrection body enjoyed forty days of intercourse with His disciples (Acts 1:3)."[53]

In verse 5 John sees that the unbelieving dead have no part in the millennial kingdom. Since the interpretation of the phrase "the rest of the dead ..." (οἱ λοιποὶ τῶν νεκρῶν) has already been discussed, the meaning of "the first resurrection" (ἡ ἀνάστασις ἡ πρώτη) may now be considered. Although some try to view this resurrection as a regeneration of the soul or as the soul's entrance to heaven at death, the usage of ἀνάστασις precludes such an interpretation. In over forty occurrences the word always refers to the resurrection of the body. The only exception to this usage is Luke 2:34 where the word is used in its etymological sense of "rising."So the resurrection in view in Revelation 20:5 is a literal resurrection that, according to verse 6, is reserved for believers.

Aldrich points out, "The resurrection event for believers has various titles in Scripture. It is called 'the first resurrection' in Revelation 20:5, 'the resurrection of life' in John 5:29, 'the resurrection of the just' in Luke 14:14, and 'a better resurrection' in Hebrews 11:35."[54] Since not all who have a part in the "first resurrection" are raised at the same time, the term ἡ ἀνάστασις ἡ πρώτη refers not to a single event but to the kind of resurrection.[55] The participants of the "first resurrection" are all the saints who enter the millennium. The "first resurrection," therefore, precedes the "resurrection of judgment" (John 5:29) by one thousand years. Some have objected that since there seems to be no temporal distinction in John 5:29 between the two resurrections they must occur at the same time. However, just as later revelation demonstrated that there must be a temporal gap between Isaiah 61:2*a* and 2*b* (cf. Luke 4:16-21), Revelation 20:4-6 has demonstrated that there must be a temporal gap between the "resurrection of life" and the "resurrection of judgment" in John 5:29.

The stark contrast, afforded by the juxtaposition of the resurrected and reigning saints over against the "rest of the dead" calls forth the fifth of seven beatitudes in the book (20:6). The blessedness and holiness of the saints rarely seems brighter than when it is seen against the dark background of the final fate of the unbelieving. Swete points out that the ground of their blessing is threefold. First, the second death has no authority over them, and this is a great blessing, for the second death is identified in 20:14 as entrance into the lake of fire. And Revelation 14:11 vividly underscores the eternality of this death by pointing out that "the smoke of their torment goes up forever." Second, they are priests of God and of Christ. The genitives θεοῦ and Χριστοῦ are either objective (i.e., they serve God and Christ) or possessive (i.e., they belong to God and Christ). The linking together of Christ and God in the phrase "of God and Christ" is in keeping "with the general tendency of the Book to regard Christ as the Equivalent of God."[56] And the third ground of their blessing is that they reign with Christ for a thousand years. The future βασιλεύσουσιν ("they will reign") confirms the fact that this beatitude is also an interpretation of the vision of verses 4 and 5. In the vision of verse 4 the reign of the saints is seen as though it had already taken place and so is described with the aorist ἐβασίλευσαν, but the interpretation given by verse 6 places the reign in the future. This fact constitutes one of the strongest arguments for viewing Revelation 20:4-6 as future, and, therefore, as yet unfulfilled.

CONCLUSION

Both the general context and the exegetical details of Revelation 20:4-6 demonstrate that John predicted an earthly kingdom of Messiah that He will inaugurate at His second advent, and that will continue in its earthly form for one thousand literal years.

NOTES

1. Papias (c. 60-130 A.D.), Barnabas (70-132), Irenaeus (fl. c. 175-195), Justin Martyr (c. 100-165), and Tertullian (c. 160/170-215/220) were some of the more prominent early premillennialists. See Hans Bietenhard, "The Millennial Hope in the Early Church," *Scottish Journal of Theology* 6(1953):12-30.
2. Ibid., p. 20.
3. Ibid., p. 22.
4. Hanns Lilje, *The Last Book of the Bible*, trans. Olive Wyon (Philadelphia: Muhlenberg, 1957); T. R. F. Glassen, *The Revelation of John* (Cambridge: Cambridge U., 1965); Albrecht Oepke, *Theological Dictionary of the New Testament*, s.v. "αναστασις," 1:371; Austin Farrer, *The Revelation of St. John the Divine* (London: Adam and Charles Black, 1966); R. H. Charles, *Revelation*, The International Critical Commentary, 2 vols. (Edinburgh: T. & T. Clark, 1920); Mathias Rissi, *The Future of the World: An Exegetical Study of Revelation 19:11—22:5* (Naperville, Ill.: Alec R. Allenson, 1971).
5. Austin Marsden Farrer, *The Revelation of St. John the Divine* (Oxford: Clarendon Press, 1964), p. 203. According to Farrer, the Jewish doctrine had three basic causes. First, rabbinic theology developed the idea of a cosmic week, based on Psalm 90:4 and Genesis 2:2. Second, some supposed that Ezekiel 35-48 "offered a continuous prediction of the last things." Third, it seemed impossible to refer some of the messianic prophecies to the eternal state. Therefore, the doctrine of an intermediate kingdom was developed, in order to harmonize messianic prophecies with the eternal state (p. 209). Direct Old Testament support for a future messianic kingdom is found in Isaiah 24:21-37.
6. The exact dates and specific citations are conveniently catalogued in Robert Henry Charles, *Eschatology: The Doctrine of a Future Life in Israel, Judaism, and Christianity* (New York: Schocken, 1963), pp. 219-20, 239-40, 270-71, 273, 301-2, 315, 324-37.
7. Paul Billerbeck and Herman L. Strack, *Die Brief des Neuen Testaments und die Offenbarung Johannis*, 5th ed., Kommentar Zum Neuen Testament, vol. 4 (Munchen: C. H. Beckische Verlagsbuchhandlung, 1926), pp. 823-27.
8. B. B. Warfield understands 19:11-21 to be describing the conquest of the gospel during this age, but he offers no conclusive exegetical support for his view. See "The Millennium and the Apocalypse," in *Biblical Doctrines* (New York: Oxford U., 1929), p. 647.
9. In reference to the overcoming of the saints, Daniel 7:21 in the LXX (Theodotion) has ἐποιει πολεμεν μετὰ τῶν ἀγίων καὶ ἰσχοσεν πρὸς αυτούς. Revelation 13:7 has a similar description: ποῆσαι πόλεμον μετὰ τῶν γἁζίων καὶ νικῆσαι αὐτούς.
10. Paul also views the world ruler as future. He describes him as the "man of lawlessness" who will be destroyed at the Lord's coming (2 Thess. 2:1-12).
11. The effect is heightened by the interweaving of several great messianic predictions: Isaiah 49:2; 63:1-3; Psalm 2:9; and Ezekiel 39:17-20.
12. Cf. Colossians 3:4; 1 Peter 5:4; and Revelation 2:26-28.
13. E.g., Genesis 3:15; Isaiah 53:12; Luke 10:18; 11:21-22; John 12:31;

16:11; Colossians 2:15; Hebrews 2:14; and 1 John 3:8. Rousas John Rushdoony, *Thy Kingdom Come* (Philadelphia: Presbyterian & Reformed, 1971), p. 212; and R. C. H. Lenski, *The Interpretation of St. John's Revelation* (Columbus, Ohio: Lutheran Book Concern, 1935), p. 579.

14. Robert Henry Charles, *A Critical and Exegetical Commentary on the Revelation of St. John*, 2 vols., The International Critical Commentary (New York: Scribners, 1920), 2:182.

15. Rissi points out that Charles has no trouble accepting 4:2-3 as authentic (p. 96, n. 60).

16. John F. Walvoord, *The Revelation of Jesus Christ* (Chicago: Moody, 1966), p. 296.

17. George Eldon Ladd, *A Commentary on the Revelation of John* (Grand Rapids: Eerdmans, 1972), p. 75.

18. Isbon T. Beckwith, *The Apocalypse of John* (New York: Macmillan, 1919), p. 739.

19. E. W. Bullinger, *The Apocalypse* (London: Eyer & Spottiswoode, 1902), p. 613.

20. It may be likely, however, that John does not see the *totality* of the saints of all ages reigning, but rather, only those who have been faithful and who have "overcome" (see Rev. 20:26; 3:21). The same idea may be behind the promise of various "crowns" elsewhere in the New Testament (1 Cor. 9:27; 2 Tim. 4:8; James 1:12). One might also compare such passages as Matthew 25:26; 1 Corinthians 3:10-15; and 2 Timothy 2:11-13.

21. Alva J. McClain, *The Greatness of the Kingdom* (Chicago: Moody, 1959), pp. 484-85.

22. The axe was "the traditional instrument of capital punishment in republican Rome, which, though under the Empire superceded by the sword (Acts 12:2), still lingered in the memory of the provincials." See Henry Barclay Swete, *The Apocalypse of St. John* (Grand Rapids: Eerdmans, 1968), p. 262.

23. Lenski, p. 584.

24. Bullinger, p. 615.

25. Cf. Revelation 1:15, 19-20; 5:6; 11:4, 9, 15; 14:7; 17:3; 19:1.

26. The χάραγμα ("the mark"), which was the technical term for the imperial stamp, may indicate nothing more than submission to the state. (See Swete, p. 173.) Or possibly, as Charles suggests, it may travesty the Jewish custom of wearing the tephillin on the left hand and over the brow (Charles, *Revelation*, 1:362-63).

27. Augustine, *The City of God*, 20.6.

28. Swete, pp. 263, 266.

29. James A. Hughes, "Revelation 20:4-6 and the Question of the Millennium," *Westminster Theological Journal* 35(1973):290-92.

30. Nigel Turner, *A Grammar of the New Testament Greek*, 4 vols. (Edinburgh: T. & T. Clark, 1963), 3:71.

31. A. T. Robertson, *A Grammar of the Greek New Testament in the Light of Historical Research* (Nashville: Broadman, 1943), p. 833.

32. Turner, 3:71.

33. G. C. Berkouwer, *The Return of Christ* (Grand Rapids: Eerdmans, 1972), p. 304.

34. Edvard Schweizer, in *Theological Dictionary of the New Testament*, ed. Gerhard Kittel and Gerhard Friedrich, 10 vols. (Grand Rapids: Eerdmans, 1964-1976), s. v., "ψυχή," 6(1969):654.

35. Cf. ψυχὴν ἀνθρώπου in Romans 2:9.

36. Luke 15:32; Romans 4:9; Revelation 2:8; 13:4.

37. Rissi, p. 97, n. 72.
38. James Hope Moulton, *A Grammar of New Testament Greek* (Edinburgh: T. & T. Clark, 1980), p. 130.
39. Henry Alford, *The Greek Testament*, 4 vols. (Chicago: Moody, 1958), 4:732.
40. Even if one does not believe that *all* the dead of verse 5 are unbelievers, he must concede that some are, and that is enough of a concession for the present argument.
41. Hughes, pp. 301-2
42. See William F. Arndt and F. Wilbur Gingrich, *A Greek-English Lexicon of the New Testament and Other Early Christian Literature*, 4th rev. ed. (Chicago: U. of Chicago, 1957), s.v., "ἄχρι," p. 128. See also J. H. Thayer, *Greek-English Lexicon of the New Testament* (Grand Rapids: Baker, 1977), s.v., "ἄχρι," p. 91.
43. Glassen, p. 111.
44. However, this may refer not to the resurrected saints but to the believers living in the kingdom who are yet to be glorified.
45. Psalm 2:8, for example, predicts an earthly kingdom for Messiah. The connections with Daniel 7 have already been pointed out.
46. G. B. Caird, *The Revelation of St. John the Divine* (New York: Harper & Row, 1966), p. 251.
47. Augustine, 20.7.
48. Lenski, p. 577.
49. Rissi, p. 34.
50. See fns. 6 and 7.
51. John J. Davis, *Biblical Numerology* (Grand Rapids: Baker, 1968), p. 155.
52. See L. Berkhof, *Systematic Theology*, 4th ed. (Grand Rapids: Eerdmans, 1941), pp. 715-16.
53. Ladd, p. 268.
54. Roy L. Aldrich, "Divisions of the First Resurrection," *Bibliotheca Sacra* 128(1971):117.
55. Meredith G. Kline has argued that "the first resurrection" refers to the death of the Christian and presumably therefore to his entrance into heaven rather than a bodily resurrection ("The First Resurrection," *Westminster Theological Journal* 37 [Spring 1975]: 366-75). The primary support for this view is based on the usage of πρῶτος ("first") in Revelation 21; Hebrews 8-10; 1 Corinthians 15; and Romans 5. From these passages Kline concludes that πρῶτος must refer to the present world order. This argument, however, begs the question. The decisive term is not the adjective "first" but the noun "resurrection" which it modifies. It is noteworthy that Kline emphatically avoids any discussion of the New Testament usage of "resurrection," which, as mentioned above, refers to bodily resurrection. Philip Edgcumbe Hughes, himself an amillennialist, says at the outset of his discussion of the first resurrection, "In Scripture, resurrection has no proper meaning if it is not understood as *bodily* resurrection" ("The First Resurrection: Another Interpretation," *Westminster Theological Journal* 39 [Spring 1977]: 315). For a more detailed criticism of Kline's view, see J. Ramsey Michael, "The First Resurrection: A Response," *Westminster Theological Journal* 39 [Fall 1976]: 100-109, and Kline's response ("The First Resurrection: A Reaffirmation," *Westminster Theological Journal* 39 [Fall 1976]: 110-19.
56. Swete, p. 264.

6

Johannine Apologetics

Norman L. Geisler

Johannine apologetics, like Johannine theology, does not differ substantially from Pauline or Petrine apologetics. That is what one would expect in view of the central unity of Scripture resulting from the inspiration by one and the same Spirit of God. In the apostle John's writings, however, there is a unique apologetic emphasis.

THE NATURE OF JOHANNINE APOLOGETICS

John used several key words that carry much of his apologetic emphasis. The most important words are "sign" (σημεῖαν)[1] and "witness" (μαρτυρία, μαρτυρέω).

Like the rest of the New Testament, the dominant apologetic model in John is legal rather than military. That is, the background motif is a courtroom where evidence is presented for the purpose of persuading the reader. The apologetic task is not performed on a battlefield where an enemy is to be fought and defeated. In this sense John's apologetic motif fits well the *locus classicus* of 1 Peter 3:15, which urges the believer to present an ἀπολογία or defense such as one would give in court.

Norman L. Geisler
Th.B., William Tyndale College; A.B., Wheaton College; M.A., Wheaton College Graduate School; Ph.D., Loyola University of Chicago
Professor of Systematic Theology
Dallas Theological Seminary

APOLOGETICS INVOLVES A TESTIMONY OR WITNESS

The most fundamental characteristic of apologetics in John is that it is a "testimony" or a "witness." It is what a lawyer would provide in setting forth his case in court. John used four Greek words for "testimony," each from the same root: μάρτυς, μάρτυρ, μαρτυρέω, and μαρτυρία. Μαρτυρία ("witness") is the word used in the Jewish legal system: "that by the mouth of two or three *witnesses* every fact may be confirmed" (Matt. 18:16, citing Deut. 19:15). At Jesus' trial before the high priest, the latter cried, "What further need do we have of witnesses?" (Matt. 26:65).

In John's gospel, "witness" (or "testimony") is used some thirty-three times as a verb ("bear witness") and fourteen times as a noun ("a witness"). From the very first chapter it is clear that the testimony is about the Lord Jesus Christ. John the Baptist "came for a *witness*, that he might *bear witness* of the light [Christ]" (1:7,* italics added). John the apostle wrote, "I have seen, and have *borne witness* that this is the Son of God" (1:34, italics added). Apologetics, then, is first of all a witness to the truth about Christ.

APOLOGETICS INVOLVES AN EYEWITNESS TESTIMONY

It is important in a court of law that one have firsthand or eyewitness testimony. John repeatedly said "I saw" or "I heard."[2] John bore witness saying, "I have *beheld* the Spirit descending as a dove out of heaven, and He remained upon [Christ]" (1:32). Jesus Himself bore witness of the Father by "what He has *seen* and *heard*" (3:32). John also stated that when "the people *saw* the sign which [Jesus] had performed, they said, 'This is of a truth the Prophet who is to come into the world' " (6:14). The same is said later of the "multitude" when "they *heard* these words [of Jesus]" (7:40, all italics added).

After the resurrection the emphasis is the same. "Mary Magdalene came announcing to the disciples, 'I have *seen* the Lord' " (20:18, italics added); and "the other disciples therefore were saying to [Thomas], 'We have seen the Lord!' " Even

---

*All Scripture quotations in this article are from the *New American Standard Bible.*

Thomas's desire to "*see* in His hands the imprint of the nails" (20:25, italics added) was granted by the Lord.

Literally dozens of times throughout John's gospel, he was careful to point out that his apologetic for Christ was not hearsay or secondhand. It was an eyewitness—an "I saw" and "I heard" kind of testimony that would count as evidence in court.

APOLOGETICS INVOLVES A TESTIMONY TO THE SUPERNATURAL

John's testimony is about the supernatural, not the ordinary. It is a testimony about seven "signs" (miracles) or supernatural confirmations. These "signs" were for the confirmation of revelation. As Hebrews clearly states, the message of Christ "was confirmed to us by those [apostles] who heard [Christ], God also bearing witness with them, both by signs and wonders and by various miracles and by gifts of the Holy Spirit according to His own will" (Heb. 2:3-4). This means that the "sign" is the substantiation of the revelation given by Christ. The sign is the miracle to support the message God gave through His Son (Heb. 1:1-2).

John's witness is to the empirical and the historical. He wrote in his first epistle, "What we have *heard*, what we have *seen* with our eyes, what we *beheld* and our hands handled, . . . we proclaim to you" (1:1-3, italics added). But what John gave witness to was also *more* than empirical;[3] he testified to what was divine. It is for this reason that a "sign" is needed, since it points beyond the merely empirical to the spiritual, from the natural to the supernatural realm. Hence apologetics for John is an eyewitness testimony of the supernatural confirmation of the revelational truth claims of Christ. When asked what "sign" He gave of His claims, Christ pointed to the supernatural sign of His resurrection (John 2:18-19; cf. Matt. 12:40-41). Only the supernatural is sufficient to confirm His supernatural claims.

APOLOGETICS INVOLVES A CONFIRMED TESTIMONY

Another important aspect of courtroom testimony is confirmation. It is essential to place an issue "beyond reasonable doubt." The same fact must be witnessed by more than one person. As the law put it, "by the mouth of *two or three* witnesses every fact may be confirmed" (Matt. 18:16, citing Deut. 19:15, italics added).

John's gospel presents in two ways a confirmed testimony of who Jesus is. First, the "signs" indicating who Jesus is were multiple. Indeed, seven (the number of completeness) "signs" are given in John. In addition John noted, "Many other signs therefore Jesus also performed in the presence of the disciples, which are not written in this book" (20:30). Second, there were many human witnesses to the signs and to whom Jesus was. Sometimes multitudes saw the signs (see John 6). Even the resurrection in John was witnessed by the eleven disciples plus the women and on repeated occasions (John 20-21).

Chapter 5 of John lists a fourfold testimony about Jesus. (a) *John* the Baptist testified about Jesus (5:32-33). (b) Also "the very *works* that I do, bear witness of Me," Jesus said (5:36). (c) "And the *Father* who sent Me, He has borne witness of Me" (5:37). By this Jesus meant the voice that spoke three times from heaven (two of which were recorded by John in 1:32-34 and 12:28). (d) Jesus said, "You search the *Scriptures*, . . . it is these that bear witness of Me" (5:39).

According to Jewish law, two or three witnesses were sufficient. Yet John presented seven miracles in four major areas by eleven disciples, and at times with even thousands of people as eyewitnesses (cf. John 6). This is an overwhelming ἀπολογία ("defense").

APOLOGETICS INVOLVES A SWORN TESTIMONY

After the words *sign, witness,* and *I saw,* perhaps the most apologetically significant phrase in John is *verily, verily* or *truly, truly.* It occurs twenty-five times, and in the context of John's apologetic testimony it becomes the rough equivalent of the courtroom phrase "I swear to tell the truth, the whole truth, and nothing but the truth." This is its meaning because (a) it is unique to John, (b) it is used numerous times (twenty-five), (c) its repetitive form ("truly, truly") has the flavor of an oath, and (d) it is used in direct connection with the truth and trustworthiness of the eyewitness testimony about God. Jesus said, "Truly, truly, I say to you, we speak that which we know, and bear witness of that which we have seen" (3:11; cf. 8:58). Jesus said to Nathaniel, "Truly, truly, I say to you, you shall see the heavens opened, and the angels of God ascending and descending on the Son of Man" (1:51).

To sum up thus far, apologetics in John's gospel involves

an eyewitness, confirmed, sworn testimony about the super-natural confirmation of the truth of Christ's claims.

APOLOGETICS INVOLVES A "SEALED" TESTIMONY

Another word that fits John's legal apologetic motif is *sealed*. One of the earmarks of an official document in ancient times—and even today—is a seal that is placed on it. What was sealed by the king was considered to be a binding (and by some, an unbreakable) authority (e.g., Dan. 6:12).

Twice John spoke of a "seal" on the testimony about Christ. "He who has received His witness has set his *seal* to this, that God is true" (3:33, italics added). This is the seal of approval to God's truth by believers. But even more significant is God's seal on Christ. For "on Him the Father, even God, has set His seal" (6:27).

So the testimony about Christ is not only a confirmed, sworn, eyewitness testimony, but it is sealed by man and also by God who cannot lie (John 8:26; cf. Heb. 6:18).

APOLOGETICS INVOLVES A LAST-WILL-AND-TESTAMENT TESTIMONY

It is almost universally conceded that a sane, sober, deathbed testimony is eminently trustworthy. Few men deliberately deceive when standing at death's door. Men have sometimes died for what they believe to be true but is false, but few, if any, die swearing to what they know to be false. It is most interesting in this regard that the very word for *witness* is the word μάρτυρ or "martyr." In point of fact, to extend Johannine apologetics to the Apocalypse, John referred several times to those who died for their "testimony" for Christ. They literally became martyrs for their μαρτυρία ("testimony"). In Revelation 2:13, God speaks about "Antipas My *witness* [μάρτυρ], My faithful one, who was killed among you (italics added)." Likewise, Revelation 6:9 speaks of "those who had been slain because of the . . . *testimony* [μαρτυρία] which they had maintained (italics added)." Those who are "beheaded [during the Tribulation] because of the testimony [μαρτυρία] of Jesus . . . came to life and reigned with Christ for a thousand years" (Rev. 20:4).

In short, John extended the concept of witness to include those who would witness unto death for the truth about Christ, as indeed did many of the first-century eyewitnesses of Christ. This kind of deathbed or last-will-and-testament testimony carries with it the highest degree of integrity and thereby has the greatest apologetic value.

APOLOGETICS INVOLVES AN APOSTOLIC TESTIMONY

One very important fact of Christian apologetics is tucked away in a phrase in John 15:27. Jesus said to the eleven disciples, "You will bear witness also, *because you have been with Me from the beginning* (italics added)." This is precisely the same condition set forth as a qualification to be one of the twelve in Acts 1. "It is therefore necessary that of the men who have accompanied us all the time that the Lord Jesus went in and out among us—*beginning with the baptism of John, until the day that He was taken up from us*—one of these should become a witness with us of His resurrection" (Acts 1:21-22, italics added). In brief, to become one of the twelve, one had to be with Jesus "from the beginning" (cf. Luke 1:2). One who has known an issue from the very beginning is in a more credible position as a witness. Further, anyone who is a special part of the "in group" from the beginning has access to information not available to others.

Jesus gave special authority to the apostles. It was in "the apostles' teaching" (Acts 2:42) that the early church continued. It was only through "the laying on of the apostles' hands" (Acts 8:18; 19:6) that the Holy Spirit was given to the early Samaritan and Gentile believers. Paul said that the church is "built upon the foundation of the apostles and prophets" (Eph. 2:20). Even the writer of Hebrews said that the message was "confirmed to us by those [apostles] who heard [the Lord Jesus]" (2:3). An important apologetic conclusion can be drawn from these facts: The only apologetic Christian evidence that exists is *apostolic and first-century evidence*. Once the eyewitness, first-century, inner circle, to whom Jesus gave special authority and miracles (Heb. 2:4), died, there was no more apologetic evidence. The evidence ended with the apostles. Of course the evidence is available for today, but only through the historically authentic apostolic documents. Nothing else would stand up in court, since any other kind of evidence would be indirect, hearsay, or second-hand.[4] For this reason, both the apostolic testimony and the miracles are of supreme apologetic value. Neither "experiences," "visions," or alleged "miracles" since that time provide the least substantiation for any revelatory truth about

Christ. Jesus said to the apostles, the Holy Spirit "will teach you all things, and bring to your remembrance all that I said to you" (John 14:26; cf. 16:13). It should also be noted that Jesus promised the apostles "*all* truth." The canon of revelation ends with the apostolic age.

APOLOGETICS IS VERDICT-DEMANDING EVIDENCE

Johannine apologetics takes place in a courtroom. The eyewitness, confirmed, sealed, sworn, last-will-and-testament evidence is offered to the unbelieving jury; but by the very nature of the case, it is evidence that demands a verdict![5] The jury may not be dismissed from the momentous claims of Christ until it has reached a verdict. All must vote. Some may vote that He is mad (cf. John 8:48). Others may come to the verdict that He is bad (cf. John 9:16). However, those who are truly open to the evidence will conclude with Thomas that He is God (John 20:28). But a verdict *must* be reached.

THE PURPOSE OF APOLOGETICS IN JOHN

The purpose of apologetics is threefold. John wished (a) to give evidence of the truth (b) in order to bring glory to God and (c) in order to bring the willing to salvation.

APOLOGETICS GIVES EVIDENCE OF THE TRUTH

God never calls on a person to make a blind leap of faith. The wise man "looks before he leaps." He looks at the evidence and, if the evidence warrants belief, takes the step of faith based on the sufficiency of the evidence.[6]

The gospel of John provides evidence of truth about God (3:33; 10:38; 18:37), evidence of truth about Scripture (2:17; 19:24), and evidence of truth about Christ (2:18; 5:36). John set forth his "case" (Isa. 41:21), and God bids, as it were, "Come now, and let us reason together" (Isa. 1:18). One purpose of John's apologetic, then, is to give evidence of the truth. In John's words, "He who has received His witness has set his seal to this, that God is true" (John 3:33). Again, "believe the works; that you may know and understand that the Father is in Me, and I in the Father" (10:38). Jesus said very clearly to Pilate, "for this I have come into the world, to bear witness to the truth" (18:37).

Likewise, by fulfilling prophecy Jesus gave evidence to the disciples that the Scriptures are true (cf. John 2:17; 19:24). Repeatedly the gospel states that Jesus gave evidence to those who asked proof of who He is. Once it was the evidence of His resurrection (2:18-22), and at other times it was the evidence of the "works" that He did (5:36).

APOLOGETICS BRINGS GLORY TO GOD

There is a doxological aspect of Johannine apologetics. Providing evidence for men to believe—even if they do not believe it—brings glory to God. God does *not* place any premium on blind faith; on the contrary He is glorified when evidence and "arguments" (see Acts 17:2) are presented for His truth. When the incarnation occurred, which is perhaps the best evidence of the truth and nature of God, John wrote, "We beheld His *glory,* glory as of the only begotten from the Father, full of grace and truth" (John 1:14, italics added). As a matter of fact, even the "signs" (miracles) of Christ, which give the greatest evidence of His claims, declared His glory. "This beginning of His signs Jesus did in Cana of Galilee, and manifested His *glory* ..." (2:11, italics added). Hence, presenting this apostolic and miraculous evidence for Christ is a doxological duty of the believer. Those who give the ἀπολογίας, no less than those who preach the κήρυγμα or the εὐαγγέλιον, bring glory to God.

APOLOGETICS IS TO BRING PERSONS TO CHRIST

One purpose of apologetics—an important one—is to bring to salvation those who are willing. Those who are not willing will *not* be positively influenced by apologetics, and in fact apologetics will actually harden them in their unbelief. (This will be discussed further in the next point.) God's purpose, however, is that the evidence will convince men to believe. John made this abundantly clear in his conclusion when he wrote, "These have been written *that* you may believe that Jesus is the Christ, the Son of God" (20:31, italics added). The direct purpose of giving the eyewitness testimony of the unusual evidence about Christ was to elicit faith. So not only does God desire faith to rest on evidence,[7] but the producing of faith is the very purpose of presenting the evidence. This same point is hinted at in other Johannine passages (e.g., 10:25; 16:27).

THE RESULTS OF APOLOGETICS

Some have wrongly suggested that no one is ever brought to Christ by means of apologetics. If true, this would mean that the God who created human reason and provides evidence never uses good reasons or evidence to bring a man to Christ. But why would the Holy Spirit short-circuit the very evidential procedure He calls on believers to use in *testing* spirits (1 John 4:1) and in knowing "false prophets" from true ones (Deut. 18)? Some fideists overstep the bounds of Scripture by chastising Paul for his "rationalistic" Mars Hill escapade, insisting that Paul had no success when he tried evidence and argument instead of trusting the Holy Spirit![8] If they would read further in Acts 17 they would see that Paul did have good results in his apologetic effort on Mars Hill. Many were saved, including a philosopher named Dionysius (v. 34).

When Paul presented evidence for Christ, the results were not unlike those in John where the Jews were presented with the evidence of His diety: some believed and some were more confirmed in their unbelief, and thus their guilt was more manifest.

APOLOGETICS HELPS BRING SOME TO FAITH

It is clear that John made a direct connection between the "sign" evidence and the consequent faith of the disciples and the crowd.[9] For "many believed in His name, beholding His signs which He was doing" (2:23). Nicodemus concluded that Jesus must "have come from God as a teacher; for no one can do these signs that You do unless God is with him" (3:2). The nobleman and his household believed after seeing Jesus raise his son (4:53). The same is true of the blind man who was healed (9:31), and of the friends of Lazarus after his resurrection (12:11, 18).

The key to those who were influenced to believe, however, seemed to be their "willingness." Even miracles do not produce faith in the obstinate (see Luke 16:31). As Jesus said, "If any man is *willing* to do His will, he shall know of the teaching, whether it is of God" (7:17, italics added). Apologetics, then, is only effective in eliciting faith in those who are "open" to the evidence and "willing" to believe it.

APOLOGETICS CONFIRMS SOME IN UNBELIEF

One of the shocking realities of a fallen world is that even the best apologetic arguments will not convince some people. As the old proverb says, "A person convinced against his will is of the same opinion still." In fact, when it comes to the evidence for the deity of Christ, it would seem that the greater the evidence, the more obstinate is the unbelief of the unwilling. By extrapolation, persistent unbelief in the face of Christ's miracles became at its apex the "unpardonable sin" (see Mark 3:29-30).

Jesus, in a complaint to the Jews, hinted of the truth that miracles do not help those who are unwilling to believe: "Unless you people see signs and wonders, you simply will not believe" (John 4:48). The same seems to be implied elsewhere (cf. 10:25-26). This point becomes most evident in John 12:37. "But though He had performed so many signs before them, *yet* they were not believing in Him" (italics added). In fact, those miraculous signs had "blinded their eyes" (12:40). The Jews of Jesus' day were like Pharaoh, who "hardened his heart" (Exod. 8:15; cf. 7:14) as more signs and wonders were performed by God. Indeed, the very miracles intended to bring men to faith became, by willful rejection, a contributing cause of their unbelief. Perhaps this is the sense in which the phrase "the LORD hardened Pharaoh's heart" should be understood (Exod. 9:12; 11:10). Hardened unbelief is a *result,* but not a real *purpose,* of miracles. John made this same point when he noted that all the judgmental miracles by the two witnesses during the Tribulation, which were designed to lead men to repentance, simply made them more recalcitrant against God's desires. In spite of all God's supernatural efforts to reach them, John wrote of these people that "they did not repent, so as to give Him glory" (Rev. 16:9).

The point is a simple one: *With greater evidence comes greater responsibility to believe.* In the face of overwhelming apologetic evidence, unbelief becomes perverse and the guilt of the unbeliever becomes more manifest. But even here apologetics has performed an important function. For by presenting evidence for the truth of Christ's claims, the unbeliever is left "without excuse" (Rom. 1:19-20).

THE SCOPE OF APOLOGETICS

John presented primarily an apologetic about Christ. It is, properly speaking, *Christian* apologetics. Since Jesus was speaking to people who were already theists, John did not concentrate on theistic apologetics (i.e., arguments for God's existence). John did give, however, some hints in the direction of theistic apologetics, as will be considered below. But Johannine apologetics is primarily focused on the testimony about Jesus.

THE TESTIMONY ABOUT JESUS

John bore witness to many truths about Jesus. Primarily John's gospel is a testimony about Jesus' deity (1:1; 5:18; 8:58; 10:30; 20:28, 30-31) and His saviorhood (1:29; 4:42) and messiahship (1:21-49, esp. vv. 31, 45, 49). There are, nevertheless, some important indications of Christ's humanity found in John (see 4:6; 11:35).

THE TESTIMONY ABOUT GOD

In John's gospel much of Jesus' personal testimony was centered on the Father. Jesus claimed that His *words* were received from the Father and that He spoke for the Father (3:11, 32-34; 8:26, 38, 40). Likewise, Jesus claimed that His *life* manifested the Father: "He who has seen Me has seen the Father," He said to Philip (14:9; cf. 1:14). Also, Jesus insisted that His *works* gave evidence of the Father: "The very works that I do, bear witness of Me, that the Father has sent Me" (5:36).

There remains one interesting question: Did John, like Paul (Acts 14; 17; Rom. 1-2), give any reasons for the existence of God? In other words, did he have any *theistic* apologetics along with his Christian apologetics? Since John's main audience, and that of Jesus', already believed in God, one should not expect John to develop any argument for God. He did, however, give some possible hints about the need for theistic apologetics. One of the things indicated by the "voice from heaven" incident in John 12 is that even the most direct empirical "evidence" will not convince a complete naturalist that God exists. For the naturalists, exposed to the same phenomenon from the sky which believers recognized as the voice of God, believed it to be mere thunder (12:29). The reason for this is that they had another world view. Within a naturalistic world view, nature is the "whole show." Hence any alleged miracle will automatically be given a *natural* interpretation. Perhaps Jesus' words elsewhere could be applied to them: "Neither will they be persuaded if someone rises from the dead" (Luke 16:31). The reason is obvious enough: If someone does not even believe in God, then surely he will not consider the resurrection an *act of God*.[10] How can God act if He does not exist? The gospel of John is not geared to deal with the problem of such a person. What he needs is some indication that God exists.

For the theistic apologetic task John gives only hints. The world does have order; it is a cosmos, not a chaos, because of God's creative activity. Indeed, John does refer to the works of creation—of things that "came into being" (1:3). From this it may be reasoned that since "nothing comes from nothing— nothing ever could," then there must be some eternal and necessary Being who created everything that "came into being." John, however, did not develop this. It was not his purpose. But for those who already believe in God, John did present a sworn, sealed, confirmed testimony of an eyewitness that Jesus is indeed "the Christ, the Son of God" (John 11:27).

NOTES

1. Merrill C. Tenney noted the apologetic value of the word *sign* in John in his excellent article, "Topics from the Gospel of John: Part II: The Meaning of the Signs," *Bibliotheca Sacra* 146(April-June 1975):229.

2. The early date now being assigned to John by liberals, like John A. T. Robinson who dates it around A.D. 40-65 (*Redating the New Testament* [Philadelphia: Westminster, 1976]), and evangelicals, like John Wenham who dates it in the early 60s ("Gospel Origins," *Trinity Journal* 8 [Fall 1978]:112-34), certainly fits well with the vividness and freshness of John's eyewitness record.

3. Two extremes are to be avoided in defining miracles. One is the Bultmannian attempt to make them purely suprahistorical or *Heilsgeschichte*. In this case they are no longer events of history; nor are they verifiable. The other extreme is to make miracles purely historical and empirical. In this case they lose their supernatural character. A miracle is an event *in* the natural world but not *of* it; it is *of* God. Hence a miracle is only empirically verifiable in part, since a miracle has a dimension that is "more than" the purely historical, natural, or empirical world.

4. As F. F. Bruce correctly observes, evidences outside the New Testament are not really independent and sufficient evidences but are at best only supplementary and confirmatory of the New Testament witness (*Jesus and Christian Origins Outside the New Testament* [Grand Rapids: Eerdmans, 1974]). Courts do accept ancient documents as evidence

under "the ancient document rule" (*McCormick's Handbook of the Law of Evidence*, 2d ed. [St. Paul: West, 1972], section 223).

5. In this sense there could not be a more Johannine title for an evidential apologetic text than that chosen by Josh McDowell in his popular and helpful *Evidence That Demands a Verdict* (Arrowhead Springs, Calif.: Campus Crusade for Christ, 1972).

6. In this sense John Carnell was right when he defined faith as "a whole-soul trust in God's word as true" and added that "proper faith . . . rests in the sufficiency of the evidence" (*An Introduction to Christian Apologetics* [Grand Rapids: Eerdmans, 1950], pp. 66, 69).

7. The failure to distinguish "belief *that*" and "belief *in*" seems to be at the root of much confusion in apologetics. The fideists are right that belief *in* God needs no evidence; it is an act of the will based in the revelation of God. However, evidentialists are right in pointing to the fact that rational men ought not believe in something for which they have no evidence *that* it is there. No one should step into an elevator shaft without evidence *that* there is an elevator there. Likewise, one should have evidence *that* Christ is the Son of God before he believes *in* Him. See the author's *Christian Apologetics* (Grand Rapids: Baker, 1976), chapters 3 and 5.

8. For an excellent statement on the relationship of evidence, faith, and the Holy Spirit, see Gordon T. Lewis, *Testing Christianity's Truth Claims* (Chicago: Moody, 1976), pp. 21-34.

9. That effective, persuasive reasoning can be used by the Holy Spirit to bring men to Christ is evident from the ministry of Paul who "reasoned with them from the Scriptures" (Acts 17:2) and spoke so effectively that a great number of Jews and Gentiles believed (Acts 14:1).

10. A contemporary example of this unbelief is G. D. Chryssides, "Miracles and Agents," *Religious Studies* 11(September 1975):319-27. He insists that, even if Jesus willed and accomplished it, His walking on water would not be a miracle (p. 326).

7

The Chief Characteristic of Early English Puritanism

Edwin C. Deibler

From the days of the apostles until now a certain tension may be traced in the history of the Christian church, a tension that stems from the fact that "from the beginning Christians felt themselves to be in opposition to what they called 'the world.' "[1] Christians understood themselves to be those who possessed a spiritual power or treasure, yet a treasure that was contained in earthen vessels (2 Cor. 4:7). How that treasure and the earthen vessels and the world interacted with each other becomes an interesting and important chapter in the story of Christian history. In succeeding ages the church was influenced in differing degrees and manners by the world, and conversely, the world was influenced by the church. Moreover, Christians did not always agree among themselves to what degree the world should be permitted to infiltrate the church, and how pure the church should seek to remain from such infiltration. Such disagreements sometimes led to serious controversy between contending schools of thought. Matters of doctrine were sometimes involved as well as practice and ritual.

In some instances the whole cause of Christianity was weakened by such controversy. Before North Africa was lost

Edwin C. Deibler
A.B., University of Pennsylvania; Th.M., Dallas Theological
Seminary; Ph.D., Temple University
Professor of Historical Theology
Dallas Theological Seminary

to the Christian church as the result of Moslem advance, "the seeds of permanent religious division had been sown"[2] by the Donatist controversy, a disagreement between groups of Christians growing out of differing views of how the church and the world should be interrelated.

In other places and times the cause of Christianity seems to have been strengthened as a result of recurring concern among Christians that purer standards of life and thought be maintained. The story of Christian monasticism is punctuated by pulsations of recurring piety. When established monasteries tended to become less concerned that they retain "otherworldly" standards, new leaders arose to rekindle the spark of purity. "The old established monasteries were no longer strict enough to satisfy some of the converts; new orders were founded which made greater demands on their members."[3] So a modern scholar traces the beginnings of a movement that begat the Cluny reforms, the Carthusians, and the Cistercians, and that mightily strengthened the church in her conflict with the political rulers of Europe. "Fervor and piety gave the new orders great prestige; the most influential men in the West during the late eleventh and early twelfth centuries were the abbots of the great reformed monasteries."[4]

These are but examples of a conviction persisting among Christians that although they were *in* the world, they should not be, in some respects, *of* the world. In its larger connotation the term *puritan* might be applied to them and to those other individuals, groups, and movements that in the course of the church's history sought to bring the doctrine and practice of the church of their times into closer proximity to what they felt should be the proper relationship with the world surrounding them.

WHAT IS PURITANISM?

A contemporary author, writing from the point of view that describes English Puritanism as political utopianism, touches on this theme of recurring waves of piety in the development of the church when he defines English Puritanism as a "periodic revival of devotion whose coincidence with secular upheavals led it to seize and dominate a revolution till its holy zeal for power was discredited."[5] This article is not concerned with the latter portion of that definition, nor does it agree with it. Even so, the phrase "periodic revival of devotion" expresses a helpful insight into the true nature of the Puritan spirit.

In this narrower context, the term *Puritan* is employed to delineate a movement, or the adherents thereof, that powerfully affected the Church of England in the sixteenth century, and that in later ages exerted a worldwide influence, as English culture became increasingly prominent in the expansion of Europe around the globe. English Puritanism was also involved with the tensions generated by the setting of the "in the world, but not of the world" in its own place and time. That situation, the Elizabethan settlement, the church of the middle way, became the matrix in which was developed the early English Puritanism that is the concern of this study.

It is interesting that some of the leaders in the Church of England who were imbued with this spirit were not particularly happy with the term *Puritan*, which was attached to them by unsympathetic onlookers. William Perkins, for example, complained that "the pure heart is so little regarded, that the seeking after it is turned to a byword: those that most endeavor to get and keep the purity of heart . . . are so branded with vile terms of Puritans and Precisians."[6] This phrase "keep the purity of heart" is of considerable import here, because it serves to indicate a leading characteristic of Puritanism, namely, an emphasis on inner experience.

The present purpose is not to trace the development of the Puritan movement in detail; others have treated that subject in varying degrees of exhaustiveness. The chief concern here is to note the leading characteristics of the movement—those features, developments, and convictions existing in the minds and lives of a growing number of Elizabeth's subjects that caused them to object to and oppose important elements of the Church of England.

THE UNIQUENESS OF ENGLISH PURITANISM

It is recognized that various emphases are represented among early English Puritans. Some were more concerned with effecting changes in the presentation of Christianity by the Establishment, by doing away with such remnants of the medieval church as vestments and liturgy. Thus, a recurrence of controversy about the use of vestments, which figured prominently in the career of Bishop John Hooper in the early 1550s, broke out again under the leadership of men such as William Whittingham, Thomas Sampson, Lawrence Humphrey, and others between 1559 and 1567.[7] Others, like Thomas Cartwright, were more concerned about the form of church government.[8] As the movement grew numerically and in its influence on English life, yet other leaders emphasized more subjective aspects of pietistic Puritanism. William Perkins, a man of immense influence in his generation, developed the notion that theology is the science of living blessedly forever.[9]

In his introductory chapter, Patrick Collinson sounds a proper note of caution in regard to the temptation to overgeneralize in describing the early Puritan movement. "The wise observer of Elizabethan religion will resist the temptation to impose on a confused scene the clear-cut pattern of denominations not yet born. He will be equally on his guard against the tendency to treat early puritanism as a monolith."[10]

J. C. Brauer, in a helpful investigation into the nature of English Puritanism, agrees with M. M. Knappen[11] that English Puritanism must be viewed as a distinct historical entity, not to be confused with other entities of its own or any other time. He also is aware of the complexity of the movement—that it "embraces men and ideas so diverse one wonders if all can be called Puritan."[12]

BASIC CHARACTERISTICS OF EARLY ENGLISH PURITANISM

Whatever their individual peculiarities, however, all early Puritans concurred in the notion that religion was, at root, a matter of personal experience. Not the outward connection to an ecclesiastical society, but the inward relation to God was the sine qua non of true religion for them. In his definitive work on the early development of Evangelical Pietism, a contemporary American scholar holds that all Pietists are marked by four characteristics or emphases; they are experiential, perfectionistic, biblical, and oppositive in nature.[13] In my judgment, F. Ernest Stoeffler wisely places the emphasis on the experiential note in first place.

Brauer feels that, in spite of the differences among early Puritans, there are qualities common to all of them. He lists four: (1) There is a deep dissatisfaction with the Anglican idea of Reformation and the Roman Catholic faith. (2) The root of that dissatisfaction lies in a deep religious experience. (3) This dissatisfaction results in a rising zeal for reform in the use of ecclesiastical vestments to every facet of daily life. (4) Covenant theology is employed as the vehicle for structuring an understanding of the Christian faith. Although Brauer lists a deep religious experience in second place, he terms it the heart of the matter.[14]

Why the dissatisfaction? It was because of the Puritans' religious experience. "Every Puritan had it and could not doubt the certainty of it."[15] To these men, regeneration and conversion were not theological terms but were realities. The Anglican did not feel he had to go through the pangs of the new birth and engage in a strenuous pilgrimage. But "every Puritan had to."[16] Christ had to be formed in him.

The collected works of John Flavel (1628-1691) have already been reprinted. One of the most popular Puritan writers of the seventeenth century (his works were issued five times in the eighteenth century and at least three times in the nineteenth), his work carried on and illustrated this primary characteristic of the earlier English Puritans. Concerning the present reprint, Martyn Lloyd-Jones has commented, "I am glad to hear of the reprinting of the six volumes of John Flavel. Having read his work for many years, I have always regarded him as one of the warmest and *most experimental* of the Puritan writers."[17] In these words, Lloyd-Jones conveys his own understanding of Puritan piety; it dealt in the main with experience.

The advertisement assures one that Flavel possessed all the characteristics of the Puritan pietistic tradition to which he belonged—"a tradition which believed that preaching should be 'hissing hot,' searching and expository." It describes Flavel as preeminent in his ability to combine instruction with an appeal to the heart. Such appeal to the heart must be given high prominence in any attempt to describe early pietistic Puritanism.

It was this experiential side of religion that made other Puritan characteristics necessary: the preaching of the Word of God, a strict personal discipline (almost at times to the point of asceticism), a strong doctrine of the Holy Spirit, and the confident activisim of the Puritans. Brauer is correct in his conviction that "the source of Puritan activism and reforming zeal does not arise out of the doctrine of predestination. . . . The Puritan did not engage in his vigorous action to prove his own election. It arose from his conversion experience. Once converted—he could not rest."[18]

Alan Simpson also notes that although Puritanism occurred in many stages, a Puritan could always be identified as anyone who had the root of the matter in him. He is correct in asserting that "a movement which began by exhorting men to prepare themselves for a miracle of grace and ended by asserting the presence of the Holy Spirit in every believer is one movement."[19] The movement was one that had at its root the necessity of an inner experience of grace.

EARLY PURITAN PREACHING

In a recent, excellent work on the godly preachers of the Elizabethan church, the author describes the preaching of those early Puritans as spiritual, romantic, expository, and evangelical.[20] He also gives first place to the spiritual nature of that preaching. These men objected to much of the ceremonialism carried over into the Elizabethan church from the medieval church; they objected to the vestments worn by the clergy. They had little use for any religion that was mainly ceremonial. Early Puritans spent much time in their meetings discussing how much or how little support should be given to the ceremonial side of worship. "To them religion was a spirited movement and not capable of being confined in a ceremonial worship, for the Kingdom of God was not meat and drink and apparel, but righteousness, peace and joy in the Holy Ghost."[21]

In time these early Puritan preachers became characterized by this emphasis on the spiritual rather than the ceremonial and came to be known as "spiritual preachers," in contrast to the "witty" preaching of their opponents.[22] Their hearers considered preaching to be the "ordinary means of faith," and their preaching begat "lively, rather than formal faith."[23]

Collinson quotes the prayer of an Elizabethan preacher of the 1570s:

I beseech God bless my good Uncle Brant and make him to know

[that] which in his tender years he could not see. . . .And the Lord
open His gracious countenance . . . unto my aunt, that she may
also make a blessed change.[24]

One heartily concurs with Collinson's judgment that no
account of this period of the English Reformation can suffice
that is so confined by statutes and prayer books that it fails to
take into account this "blessed change."

THE ROOT OF THE MATTER: INNER SPIRITUAL REALITY

One concludes, then, with others, that the characteristic
of experientialism—innerness, the necessity of inner change—
is the notion that the outer life—the daily practice of Christianity—must be nothing other than a reflection, or an overflow,
of an inner reality. Puritans might have disagreed among
themselves on the degree of ceremonialism they might have
been content to retain in their public worship, but they concurred in the conviction that the outward ritual was a secondary matter; religion was for them primarily an affair of the
heart. "This deep concern with the . . . potential holiness of
the human heart prevailed in all of Puritanism. No other facet
of Puritan spirituality so dominated the written expression of
the interior life."[25]

It was this inner experience that prompted Puritans to the
practice of "godliness," which was their chief concern. In a
prefatory note to *Two Elizabethan Puritan Diaries*,[26] Knappen
allows that, because of the variations in temperament from
individual to individual, it is difficult to find a single mold of
character to which all the adherents of a movement conform.
Nevertheless, he is persuaded that Richard Rogers and
Samuel Ward are typical of the Puritans of their day. I agree
with this view.

The Puritan concern for godliness is well illustrated by an
entry in the diary of Rogers, dated November 29, 1587:

> The lord also this month hath granted me the libertie of the
> morneinges to my study, and to enter the same with prayer and
> med[itation] and to the better keeping of mine hart and lif all the
> day after. And espec[ially] this I may say that idle wanderings
> after the world, frowardness, or such other boisterous corrup-
> tions have been much abated, though I see them riseing at times,
> since I entred into this cours more faithfully. *And this is mine
> harty desire, that I may make godliness, I mean one parte or
> another of it, to be my delight through my whole lif,* as this

> month hath been a good beginninge thereof, which in this time
> hath been no hard yoke to me . . . (italics added).[27]

That Rogers was not alone in this pursuit of godliness is
evident in his account of a meeting with fellow ministers
about a month later. The date of the entry is December 22,
1587.

> The 6 of this month we fasted betwixt our selves, min[isters]
> to *the stirringe up of our selves to greater godliness.* Very good
> thinges we gathered to this purpose, ef[esians] 1:2, and then we
> determined to bring into writinge a direction for our lives, which
> might be both for our selves and others (italics added).[28]

The diary of Samuel Ward is replete with lamentations
about his frequent failures to manifest in the smallest details
of daily life those outward evidences of godliness that might
be expected from a man in whom the grace of God had
wrought an inward experience. He complains of his longing
after damson plums, after he had made a vow not to eat in
the orchard, of his anger, of his negligence and sleepiness in
reading the Bible, of his long sleeping in the morning that
prevented his making an analysis of a chapter in the Bible, of
his bragging, of his going to the tavern with lewd fellows, of
his impatience, of his negligence in prayer, of his slack attention at the sermon.[29] The prayer he wrote in January, 1598 is
most instructive as to the longing of the Puritan heart for
godliness.

> O Lord, give us grace to consider how that all our night
> watching and all ought to tend to this end, to the winning of
> Christ. Grant that by thy manifold benefites, both spirituall and
> temporall, we may be brought to repentance to the dying to our
> sinnes and living to thee in newnes of lif, and that not only for a
> tyme but so long as we live in this world.[30]

The Puritan felt it to be dangerous in meditating on the
Word of God to "feed only on the outward letter without any
desire of the spirit."[31] He exhorted every man to use such hearing, reading, and meditating on the Word of God as would
lead him to see and confess sin and wretchedness in himself,
and would prompt him to prayer for God's mercy and grace.
His prayer was, "Grant me true and living faith . . . that of
practice and not of naked speculation.[32] His thrust was toward
experiential religion, a *living* faith.

A Puritan catechism, dated 1585, stresses this need of

inner experience. Holding that faith is the badge of a Christian, it confesses that faith is difficult to describe. It raises the question, "What does faith work in us?" and answers with the Puritan insistence on experience: "The knowledge of God. The assurance of our redemption and the consolation of conscience through the Holy Ghost." It proceeds to describe faith as an "assurance sent from God to us and nothing else."[33]

Still another helpful glimpse into this basic characteristic of early Puritan thought and practice is afforded by the introductory sentence of the classic work by William Ames, the well-known *Medulla*. Ames opens his theological system with the words, "Theologia est doctrina Deo vivendi." (Theology is the teaching of living unto God.) This speaks of experience. Ames writes of faith, but a faith in God as a person, the Person who meets humans as persons. Douglas Horton feels that this is the fundamental characteristic of Ames's thought, a "characteristic which he drew from Puritanism, refined, and bequeathed to the modern church."[34] One would agree with Horton in his conviction that it was this idea that produced Pietism in Europe, and that Pietism is one of the most important movements in Europe in recent centuries, producing "Bible study, better liturgical practices, hymnology, religious poetry, philanthropic institutions of all kinds, and foreign missions."[35]

In an older study of Puritanism from the literary point of view, a work recently reprinted, one finds another confirmation of this note of experience at the heart of the matter. The author states that one of the first effects of Puritanism was a quickening of self-consciousness in matters of religion. He points out that external rites, ordinances, and ceremonies seemed to lose much of their virtue for many devout people, deemed by some simply to be matters of indifference, while for others they become actually stumblingblocks to the true life of the soul.

> To discover the dominant idea of Puritanism we must look beyond dogma to something common to every phase of the great contention. And undoubtedly the unvarying central element was this—Puritanism maintained, as far as was possible, that the relation between the invisible spirit of man and the invisible God was immediate rather than mediate. It set little store by tradition, because God had spoken directly to man in the words of Revelation. It distrusted human ceremonies because these stood between the creature and his Creator; the glory of the Christian

temple is the holiness of the living temple which rises in the heart of the child of God.[36]

Thus reality for the Puritan was an immediate experience, not an indiscriminate mysticism, for the Bible was consulted and doctrine was not neglected. Yet there was little use for mediating devices of whatever sort, and a system heavily weighted with ritual, however beautiful, became irrelevant.

THE BASIC CHARACTERISTIC OF EARLY ENGLISH PURITANISM

On March 8, 1951, the annual lecture of the Evangelical Library was delivered in London by J. I. Packer on the subject, *Practical Writings of the English Puritans*. In his lecture, Packer considers five characterizing marks of early English pietistic Puritanism. He notes first that the men who gave direction to the Puritan spirit (Greenham, Chaderton, Perkins, Baynes, Cotton, Preston, Sibbes, Goodwin, Baxter) were pastors who wrote with the practical aim of edifying the church of Christ and who, therefore, felt that theological controversy was a waste of time. Second, he points out that they were expositors whose works deal with doctrine, reproof, correction, and instruction in righteousness; works in which doctrine is first stated but then always applied to the practical life. Third, Packer goes on to say, these Puritan pastors were nearly all university men who were systematic and thorough in their treatment of texts and doctrines, aiming to be so exhaustive in the treatment of their texts that no sinner might be able to find a loophole through which to escape the claims of the gospel. Fourth, he states that these Puritans sought to be popular preachers always seeking to reach the common people, therefore disdaining tricks of rhetoric and the ornaments of flourishing style. They determined to present their message in the idiom of the people.

Packer reserves until last the mark that has been put first, that of spiritual experience. But he leaves no doubt that he also considers it to be the one of primary importance.

> The fifth and most significant mark of the great Puritans, without which no other distinction could give them more than historical interest for us, is that they were above all *spiritual* men; and their writings bear witness to the quality and depth of their Christian living.[37]

The men believed themselves to be sinners before they were preachers; therefore they needed a deep experience of grace in their own souls. The Word of God, they felt, must dwell with power in them before it could go forth with power from them. Their preaching could produce little effect unless it reflected a life of practical, experiential holiness in the preacher. Scripture in experience was the heart of pietistic Puritanism.

This "root of the matter," as it was worked out in the practicalities of daily life by millions of followers of these pioneer Puritans, wrought mightily for God and for good in America and England in succeeding generations. Dare one pray that a widespread return to it in the present generation might effect a significant revival of godliness and spiritual power.

NOTES

1. Kenneth Scott Latourette, *A History of Christianity* (New York: Harper, 1953), p. 241.
2. Wh. H. C. Frend, *The Donatist Church* (Oxford: Clarendon, 1952), p. 2.
3. J. R. Strayer, *Western Europe in the Middle Ages* (New York: Appleton, 1955), p. 80.
4. Ibid.
5. Alan Simpson, "Saints in Arms," *Church History Magazine*, June 1954, p. 119.
6. William Perkins, *Works*, vol. 3 (on microfilm, Southern Methodist University Library, Dallas, Texas), p. 15 (italics added).
7. W. H. Frere and C. E. Douglas, *Puritan Manifestoes* (London: 1954), pp. xiff.; Roberts Crowley, *A Brief Discourse Against the Outward Apparel and Ministering Garments of the Popish Church*, McAlpin Collection of British History and Theology, Union Theological Seminary Library, New York, 1566, pages unnumbered; J. H. Primus, *The Vestments Controversy* (Kampen, Holland: J. H. Kole, 1960), pp. 79-83.
8. Patrick Collinson, *The Elizabethan Puritan Movement* (London: Cape, 1967), p. 131.
9. William Perkins, *The Golden Chain* (on microfilm, Southern Methodist University Library, Dallas, Texas), p. 9
10. Collinson, p. 28.
11. M. M. Knappen, *Tudor Puritanism* (Chicago: U. of Chicago, 1939), pp. vff.
12. J. C. Brauer, "The Nature of English Puritanism," *Church History Magazine*, June 1954, p. 100.
13. F. Ernest Stoeffler, *The Rise of Evangelical Pietism* (Leiden: E. J. Brill, 1965), pp. 13, 23.
14. Brauer, p. 100.
15. Ibid.
16. Ibid., p. 101.
17. D. Martyn Lloyd-Jones, brochure (London: Banner of Truth).
18. Brauer, p. 101.

19. Simpson, p. 119.
20. Irvonwy Morgan, *The Godly Preachers of the Elizabethan Church* (London: Epworth, 1965), pp. 13-32.
21. Ibid., p. 13.
22. Ibid., p. 16.
23. Collinson, p. 23.
24. Ibid.
25. Norman Pettit, *The Heart Prepared: Grace and Conversion in Puritan Spiritual Life* (New Haven, Conn.: Yale U., 1966), p. 1.
26. Richard Rogers and Samuel Ward, *Two Elizabethan Puritan Diaries*, ed. Marshall M. Knappen (Gloucester, Mass.: P. Smith, 1966), p. 31.
27. Rogers and Ward, p. 65 (italics added).
28. Ibid., p. 69 (italics added).
29. Ibid., pp. 110-18.
30. Ibid., p. 118.
31. John Bradford, *Godly Meditations upon the Ten Commandments* (London: 1567), copy of original edition in the McAlpin Collection, Union Theological Seminary Library, New York, n.p.
32. Ibid., "On a Treatise Against the Fear of Death."
33. William Chub, *A Christian Exercise for Private Householders* (London, 1585), in the McAlpin Collection, Union Theological Seminary Library, New York, n.p.
34. Douglas Horton, "Let Us Not Forget the Mighty William Ames," *Religion in Life* 29(Summer 1960):440.
35. Ibid., p. 442.
36. Edward Dowden, *Puritan and Anglican: Studies in Literature* (Freeport, N.Y.: Books for Libraries, 1967), p. 11 (italics added).
37. J. I. Packer, *Practical Writings of the English Puritans* (typed and bound copy of the lecture published by the Evangelical Library, London, 1951), p. 27.

8

Chalcedon and Christology: A 1530th Anniversary

Craig A. Blaising

Anniversaries are times of remembering a special event or occasion in the past. The kind of anniversary dear to most people is the one that looks back to the forming of a relationship. For example, when the word "anniversary" is heard, who does not think of a wedding anniversary? Furthermore, the older the relationship, the more special its anniversary becomes. How very special is a silver or golden wedding anniversary!

Thirty years ago many articles and some books were written commemorating the fifteen-hundredth anniversary of the Council of Chalcedon.[1] Chalcedon was both an event to remember and the forming of a relationship. The event was the coming together of over five hundred bishops and other representatives from all the various portions of the church under the order of the Emperor Marcian in A.D. 451. The purpose was to establish ecclesiastical unity throughout the church by resolving the tension in Christology stemming from the differences of expression in Alexandrian and Antiochian traditions. That tension was resolved to an extent by a definition of faith agreed on finally in the fifth session of the council (on Oct. 22).[2] The definition of faith not only excluded the

Craig A. Blaising
B.S., University of Texas at Austin; Th.M., Th.D., Dallas Theological Seminary; Ph.D. cand., University of Aberdeen
Assistant Professor of Systematic Theology
Dallas Theological Seminary

extremes of Nestorianism and Eutychianism from orthodoxy, but also provided some positive considerations on the person of Christ. The most important section of the definition is as follows:

> Following therefore the holy Fathers, we confess one and the same our Lord Jesus Christ, and we all teach harmoniously [that he is] the same perfect in Godhead, the same perfect in manhood, truly God and truly man, the same of a reasonable soul and body; consubstantial with the Father in Godhead, and the same consubstantial with us in manhood, like us in all things except sin; begotten before ages of the Father in Godhead, the same in the last days for us; and for our salvation [born] of Mary the virgin *theotokos* in manhood, one and the same Christ, Son, Lord, unique; acknowledged in two natures without confusion, without change, without division, without separation—the difference of the natures being by no means taken away because of the union, but rather the distinctive character of each nature being preserved, and [each] combining in one Person and *hypostasis*— not divided or separated into two Persons, but one and the same Son and only-begotten God, Word, Lord Jesus Christ; as the prophets of old and the Lord Jesus Christ himself taught us about him, and the symbol of the Fathers has handed down to us.[3]

With the development of this definition of faith, Chalcedon became more than just an event. It marked the beginning of a relationship, a relationship between Chalcedon and Christology that has continued in the history of theology down to the present day. However, the relationship has not always been peaceful. Chalcedon has always had its detractors, but the advent of higher criticism in the nineteenth century brought the greatest challenge of all. New Christologies were formed that declared their independence from Chalcedon.

In the last half decade, the attack on Chalcedon has been renewed. The purpose of this article on the 1530th anniversary is to review these most recent attacks with a view toward answering the question, What is the relationship between Chalcedon and Christology? This question will be considered from two perspectives: the significance of that relationship at its formation, and its significance today.

"THE MYTH OF GOD INCARNATE"

In 1977 a group of seven Anglican theologians, later labeled "the seven against Christ," launched a full scale

attack on traditional Chalcedonian Christology. Their mani-
festo was entitled *The Myth of God Incarnate* and was edited
by John Hick.[4] Since its appearance, several other books have
been written on both sides of the issue.[5]

An important point to note about the myth-of-God-Incarnate debate is that there is nothing new among the views and
presuppositions of the participants. Many of these can be
traced directly to early nineteenth-century liberalism. Most of
their views reflect the more radical side of the historical-criti-
cal tradition. What is new is perhaps the way in which many
theological and philosophical opinions together with results
from the critical tradition have been brought to focus on one
doctrine, the hypostatic union as expressed in the *definitio
fidei* of Chalcedon. As a result, the myth-of-God-Incarnate
theologians are quite definite on how they think the relationship between Chalcedon and Christology should be
understood.

THE RELATIONSHIP BETWEEN CHALCEDON AND CHRISTOLOGY

In order to address the relationship between Chalcedon
and Christology, one must come to grips with the issue of
authority in theological expression. To their credit, the contributors to *The Myth of God Incarnate* discuss this issue
directly. In the preface Hick admits that the contributors
accept the basic presuppositions of nineteenth-century liberalism that include a dynamic view of God and the world and
the judgment that "the books of the Bible ... cannot be
accorded a verbal divine authority."[6] The reason for this rejection of Scripture is that the contributors all accept a basic
tenet (which began with Schleiermacher) that truth about God
is not discerned through rational propositions but is felt
through an experience of Him. Statements about God are simply testimonies to an otherwise inexpressible experience. They
are to be taken not literally but as myth.

Young addresses the nature of biblical and patristic writings and concludes that in both cases, "it was the dynamic
reality of their experience which they sought to preach to and
articulate for their contemporaries."[7] In her article she
attempts to show an evolutionary development between the
New Testament and the church Fathers. Both are efforts to
create statements about Jesus due to the inexpressible reality
of the experience of salvation through Him.[8] As time went on,
these formulations resorted more and more to "supernatural

and mythical categories" derived from the surrounding Hellenic culture and world view "to envisage his nature and origin."[9]

More could be said here, but this gives the foundation for understanding what the contributors to *The Myth of God Incarnate* would see as the relationship between Chalcedon and Christology. The Chalcedonian definition of faith, like Scripture, is a formula created out of the experience of the early church cast in terms and expressions drawn from and consistent with the philosophical and mythological world view of that day. The purpose of such formulation was to create a representation of Christ that would give the greatest significance to the inexpressible reality of the experience of salvation through Him. Furthermore, not only is this the method of Christology at Chalcedon (as well as the entire biblical and patristic era), but also this is the method that the myth-of-God-Incarnate theologians recommend today. Houlden, in his essay "The Creed of Experience," gives precisely this positive assessment of Chalcedon.[10]

On the other hand, the Chalcedonian declarations that Jesus Christ is truly God and truly man, are rejected by these theologians. The inexpressible reality of the experience of salvation in Christ is supposedly the same today as it was then. The method of going to one's world view to find the concepts for constructing Christological statements that seem consistent with that experience is the same. However, the world view held today differs from that of the early church. Consequently the religious and philosophical concepts from which one must choose in constructing a Christology are decisively different from those used at Chalcedon.[11]

How, then, should one perceive the relationship between Chalcedon and Christology today? The answer of *The Myth of God Incarnate* is that the method is similar, but the content of the two must definitely be different.

It should be noted that other specific objections against the Chalcedonian definition of faith are raised in *The Myth of God Incarnate*. These include charges of logical incoherence, an abstract and metaphysical approach that ignores existential significance, a distortion of the biblical faith, and a hellenizing of the gospel. These are all related to the problem of world view discussed above.

One further note should be made before criticizing this approach to Chalcedon and Christology. What if it is objected that this approach removes any real historical continuity in theology? The myth-of-God-Incarnate theologians recognize this problem and offer a solution of reinterpreting the creeds similar to the hermeneutical method of demythologization used on Scripture. Hick, for example, expressly calls the Incarnation "a mythological idea" and then explains what he means by myth and what one should do with such a myth.

> And I am using the term "myth" in the following sense: a myth is a story which is told but which is not literally true, or an idea or image which is applied to someone or something but which does not literally apply, but which invites a particular attitude in its hearers. Thus the truth of a myth is a kind of practical truth consisting in the appropriateness of the attitude to its object. *That Jesus was God the Son incarnate is not literally true*, since it has no literal meaning, but it is an application to Jesus of a mythical concept whose function is analogous to that of the notion of divine sonship ascribed in the ancient world to a king.[12]

One cannot help but be distressed at such blatant Arianism. The distress increases as Hick proceeds to "demythologize" the Incarnation to an essential belief that Jesus is (in some way) efficacious for a salvation experience (whatever that means and certainly not in an exclusive sense) with the Ultimate![13] Maurice Wiles honestly admits that there is no telling where this procedure will lead, but he insists that it is necessary, since religion is "an evolving, living tradition" and is confident that the results "can only be regarded as a gain."[14]

CRITICISM

There is certainly much for which *The Myth of God Incarnate* deserves to be criticized, and there are many avenues on which to proceed (theological, philosophical, biblical, and historical). Obviously a comprehensive criticism is impossible here. One should survey the various review articles as well as the literature of the debate. The main problem is the acceptance of the presuppositions of higher criticism including a Kantian epistemology combined with a theology of religious experience. From the perspective of this article, however, the point to be made is that the method of forming Christological doctrine that these theologians attribute to Chalcedon is historically inaccurate and misleading. The low view of Scripture on the part of these theologians combined with a theory about the evolution of religion apparently prevents them from appreciating the high view of Scripture maintained by the Fathers at Chalcedon and the central stabilizing role played by Scripture in the development of the early conciliar theology. An examination of Chalcedonian Christology will attempt to demonstrate this point.

CHRISTOLOGY AT CHALCEDON

Certainly one of the factors that came out of Chalcedon that created a continuing relationship between Chalcedon and Christology was a Christological method. Furthermore, this method was employed to produce a definition of faith that was the most detailed statement of Christology at that time. Both the method and the definition should be examined.

CHRISTOLOGICAL METHOD AND TRADITION

Christology, of course, did not begin at Chalcedon. Prior to Chalcedon the early church had already attempted to deal with various inadequate views of Christ. These attempts were recorded in the writings of various church Fathers. In addition, various church councils, both local and ecumenical, had met to deal with Christological issues. Some of these produced statements of faith, the most important of which prior to Chalcedon was the Council of Nicea in 325.

The creed of Nicea figured prominently in the Christological thinking of Chalcedon. In fact, the bishops who assembled at Chalcedon would have been happy not to have produced a statement of faith at all, but simply to reaffirm their agreement to the creed of Nicea as had been the case in the two previous councils.[15] The emperor, however, wanted a formula, and as usual, what the emperor wanted, he got. Thus Chalcedon produced a certain advance in formal Christology with a new theological formula. However, the method for this advance included a careful acceptance of and harmonization with the previous level of Christological development, specifically the Nicene creed. As Sellers put it, Chalcedon employed a method containing the two principles of Christological confession and Christological inquiry.[16]

Since the Nicene creed played a confessional or traditional role in the Christology of Chalcedon, it is important to examine its view of authority. To do so, one can simply turn to Athanasius's defense of Nicea, *De Decretis*. Here there is no picture of theologians grappling with an inexpressible experience of the Ultimate, scanning the Hellenic philosophical and religious world view for an apt description of Christ. Instead they were earnestly seeking to be faithful to Scripture. They believed "that the sayings of Scripture are divinely inspired" (εἶναι θεόπνευστα τὰ τῆς γραφῆς ῥήματα), and attempted to refute the Arians on the basis of Scripture.[17] It was not the Nicene Fathers who were attempting to hellenize Christ, but the Arians. Athanasius writes that "they proceeded to borrow from the Greeks" certain philosophical terms such as "unoriginate" (ἀγένητον) which they attempted to make the primary attribute of deity "that, under the shelter of it, they might reckon among the things originated and the creatures, that Word of God, by whom these very things came to be."[18]

In formulating the creed of Nicea, the bishops attempted to present a statement about Christ using as much as possible the titles and descriptions of Him in the Scriptures. However, as they were putting the statement together using exact scriptural terms and phrases, Athanasius stated that the Arians were observed "whispering to each other and winking with their eyes . . . that it was no difficulty to agree to these."[19] Recognizing the Arian deceit, "the Bishops . . . were again compelled on their part to collect the sense of the Scriptures, and to re-say and re-write what they had said before, more definitely still, namely, that the Son is 'one in essence' (ὁμοούσιον) with the Father."[20] This then is the origin of the doctrine of the *homoousion*. It was not the product of philosophizing about what Christ must be, but rather the attempt to be precise about the scriptural presentation of Him.

Space does not permit a more thorough examination of the Nicene creed, but this brief discussion should help illustrate the point that it was Scripture, not Greek philosophical opinion, that played the authoritative role. The same point is made continuously in Athanasius's *Orations against the Arians*. It was the Arians who were using Hellenic concepts foreign to Scripture to produce a heretical view of Christ.[21]

The same point could be made about the creed of Constantinople, which Chalcedon also affirmed. Chalcedon states its own opinion on the matter when it says that the creed of Constantinople was drawn up "not by adding anything which was left out by their predecessors but by clarifying, through scriptural testimonies, their understanding of the Holy Spirit in opposition to those who were trying to reject his rule."[22]

It is important to see the authority of Scripture at the

formative stage of that which was to play the role of tradition at Chalcedon. Many analyses of patristic theology focus on the authoritative *use* of developing tradition by the Fathers without paying enough attention to its formation. This leads many times to an uncritical acceptance of the Roman view of tradition on an equal level with Scripture. It is not being denied that such a view of tradition did develop. Already by the time of Chalcedon, there is Cyril's statement in his third letter to Nestorius that the Nicene fathers drew up their confession "as the Holy Spirit spoke in them."[23] Nevertheless, it seems more accurate to note that the Nicene Creed enjoyed wide theological authority at the time of Chalcedon because of its success in expressing the sense of Scripture against Arianism, as had been noted by Athanasius.

CHRISTOLOGICAL METHOD AND SCRIPTURE

In addition to the ecumenical creeds, Chalcedon accepted as *de fide* Cyril of Alexandria's letters to Nestorius and to John of Antioch as well as Leo of Rome's *Tome*. Much has been written by way of helpful insight on how Chalcedon drew from these sources in putting together, phrase by phrase, its definition of faith.[24] These works are examples of the development of Christology in the fifth century that included and culminated in the *definitio fidei* of Chalcedon. It has already been noted that the Christological advance proceeded with a sense of continuity and harmony with the existing traditional Christology. When this method of advance is examined carefully, one does not find the Fathers scouring the Hellenic world view to express the inexpressible. Rather, one finds the same method that was operative in the formation of the traditional Christology (the Nicene Creed). It is an attempt to make a precise statement about the person of Christ as found in the Scriptures. Of particular concern were certain passages that demonstrate what has become known as the communion of attributes, which simply means that the attributes of both humanity and deity are predicated of the same person, Jesus Christ.[25]

Cyril, for example, in his third letter to Nestorius wrote:

We do not divide the terms used in the Gospels of the Saviour as God or man between two *hypostases*, or Persons, for the one and only Christ is not twofold, though he is thought of as out of two, and as uniting different entities into indivisible unity.... All the terms used in the Gospels are to be referred to one Person,

the one incarnate hypostasis of the Word. There is one Lord
Jesus Christ, according to the Scriptures. . . .[26]

Again, in Cyril's letter to John of Antioch, also known as the
Formula of Union of 433, he wrote, "as to the evangelical and
apostolic phrases about the Lord, we know that theologians
treat some in common, as of one person, and distinguish
others, as of two natures, and interpret the God-befitting ones
in connection with the Godhead of Christ, and the humble
ones of the manhood."[27]

The *Tome* of Leo is essentially an extended exegesis of
many passages that demonstrate the communion of Christ's
attributes. When it was read, it was immediately accepted
with shouts of "so we all believe."[28] The Council of Chalcedon,
at the conclusion to the definitive portion of its declaration,
explains its source of authority for recognizing the unity of
Christ's person and the differences in His natures: "as the
prophets of old and the Lord Jesus Christ himself taught us
about him, and the symbol of the Fathers has handed down to
us."

THE DEFINITION OF FAITH

Many have stressed the negative character of this defini-
tion. Certainly, terms such as "without confusion" ($\dot{\alpha}\sigma\upsilon\gamma\chi\dot{\upsilon}\tau\omega\varsigma$),
"without change" ($\dot{\alpha}\tau\rho\dot{\epsilon}\pi\tau\omega\varsigma$), "without division" ($\dot{\alpha}\delta\iota\alpha\iota\rho\dot{\epsilon}\tau\omega\varsigma$),
and "without separation" ($\dot{\alpha}\chi\omega\rho\dot{\iota}\sigma\tau\omega\varsigma$)—all of which refer to the
union of Christ's two natures—are negative in force. Their
presence helps to define the boundaries within which proper
Christological thinking should take place.

The definition, however, is also positive. He is "one and
the same Christ, Son, Lord, unique," being "the same perfect
in Godhead, the same perfect in manhood, truly God and truly
man." This positive content is offered as a proper Christological statement within the boundaries set by the negative terminology. It is offered as a true description of the communion of
His attributes, as found in the Scriptures.

The definition of faith also makes use of terms that were
present in the Hellenic culture, such as $o\dot{\upsilon}\sigma\dot{\iota}\alpha$, $\dot{\upsilon}\pi\dot{o}\sigma\tau\alpha\sigma\iota\varsigma$, and
$\phi\dot{\upsilon}\sigma\iota\varsigma$.[29] However, the thesis of *The Myth of God Incarnate* that
herein is a hellenizing of Christianity cannot be maintained.
The Chalcedonian Fathers were not engaged in a philosophical discussion as to how the infinite *could* relate to the finite
in *an* Incarnation in such a way as would make sense to the

Greek philosophical mind. They were engaged not in a specu-
lative task but in a descriptive task. They were concerned to
make a precise as well as accurate (to the data) statement
about *the* Incarnation *recorded* in the Scriptures. Like Nicea
before them, they found it necessary to use terms not in Scripture to express the sense of Scripture. Herein is not a helleni-
zation of Christianity but its protection from such hellemiza-
tion because of the false teachings of Nestorianism and
Eutychianism.

CHALCEDON AND CHRISTOLOGY TODAY

What about the relationship between Chalcedon and
Christology today? Chalcedon demonstrates a method of
Christology which recognizes (a) the central authority of Scripture and also (b) the necessity of making theological statements which are descriptive of Christ as He is revealed in the
Scriptures in order to protect the church from misleading
presentations of Him. Protestant evangelicalism, continuing
in the tradition of *sola Scriptura*, shares this same method
and purpose. *The Myth of God Incarnate* not only stands out
of continuity with this Christological method but also is an
example of that very kind of distortion such a method is
designed to avoid.

The definition of faith at Chalcedon has now taken its
place in a tradition of Christological formulation that includes
other elements that have also taken their place during the history of theology. The basic reason Protestant evangelicalism
has continued to make use of these formulations is not
because of a doctrine of the authority of tradition, but because
those formulations are in fact descriptive of what is in
Scripture.

Seeing in traditional Christology an authority derived
from Scripture rather than one equal to it also makes it both
possible and necessary to reexamine those formulations to see
if they continue to fulfill the needs of Christological expression
today or whether new expressions might more accurately present the picture of Christ in Scripture. Thus, it is possible to
critique the definition of Chalcedon, but only from the standpoint of Scripture.[30] Such a high view of Scripture in Christology today is not only a fitting observance of the anniversary of
that relationship begun 1,530 years ago, but is also the only

way to keep it vital in years to come. In like manner Calvin wrote:

> But whenever a decree of any council is brought forward, I should like men. . .to examine by the standard of Scripture what it dealt with—and to do this in such a way that the definition of the council may have its weight and be like a provisional judgment, yet not hinder the examination which I have mentioned. . . . Thus to councils would come the majesty that is their due; yet in the meantime Scripture would stand out in the higher place, with everything subject to its standard. In this way, we willingly embrace and reverence as holy the early councils, such as. . .Chalcedon. . .which were concerned with refuting errors— in so far as they relate to the teachings of faith. For they contain nothing but the pure and genuine exposition of Scripture, which the holy fathers applied with spiritual prudence to crush the enemies of religion who had then arisen.[31]

EDITOR'S NOTE

The year 1981 marked the 1530th anniversary of the significant Council of Chalcedon of A.D. 451. Interestingly, it also marked the 1600th anniversary of the Council of Constantinople (A.D. 381) and the 1550th anniversary of the Council of Ephesus (A.D. 431).

NOTES

1. Note especially the work by R. V. Sellers, *The Council of Chalcedon* (London: SPCK, 1953).
2. Complete agreement was not achieved at Chalcedon, for a faction of the Alexandrian party rejected the definition of faith. This formed the nucleus of the Monophysites who permanently split from the rest of the church. Reconciliation of the schism was attempted at Constantinople in 553 and again in 680, where the monophysite and monothelite questions were addressed. The schism was still not reconciled and continues today in the Orthodox churches between Eastern Orthodox (Chalcedonian) and Oriental Orthodox (Monophysite). Modern-day attempts to heal the schism along with continued discussion of the events and the formulary of Chalcedon can be found in *The Greek Orthodox Theological Review* 10 (Winter 1964-65); 13 (Fall 1968); and 16 (Spring and Fall 1971).
3. This translation is given by Edward R. Hardy, ed., *Christology of the Later Fathers*, The Library of Christian Classics (Philadelphia: Westminster, 1954), p. 373.
4. John Hick, ed., *The Myth of God Incarnate* (London: SCM, 1977).
5. See, for example, Michael Green, ed., *The Truth of God Incarnate* (London: Hodder & Stoughton, 1977); M. D. Goulder, ed., *Incarnation and Myth, The Debate Continued* (London: SCM, 1979); Don Cupitt, *The Debate about Christ* (London: SCM, 1979).
6. Hick, p. ix.

7. Ibid., p. 30.
8. This follows the thesis of Harnack that beginning with Athanasius, the Fathers produced a Christology on the basis of soteriology.
9. Hick, p. 30.
10. Ibid., pp. 125-32.
11. Wiles writes: "The setting in which the process [of developing theological expression] took place was one in which the idea of supernatural divine intervention was a natural category of thought and faith, in a way that is no longer true of the main body even of convinced believers today. It was within the context of such a general belief in divine intervention that belief in the specific form of divine intervention which we know as the incarnation grew up" (Maurice Wiles, "Myth in Theology," in *The Myth of God Incarnate*, p. 4). This objection is essentially the same which Bultmann raised and stated so clearly in his essay "New Testament and Mythology," in *Kerygma and Myth*, ed. Hans Werner Bartsch (New York: Harper & Row, 1961) pp. 1-16.
12. Hick, p. 178 (italics added).
13. Ibid., pp. 178-79.
14. Ibid., pp. 6, 9. He does note, however, that "the most likely change would be towards a less exclusive insistence on Jesus as *the* way for all peoples and all cultures." Hick's article deals with this very issue.
15. On the relationship of the creed of Constantinople to the Nicene creed see J. N. D. Kelly, *Early Christian Creeds*, 3d ed. (New York: McKay, 1972), pp. 296-331.
16. Sellers, p. xiii.
17. Athanasius, *De Decretis*, trans. J. H. Newman, 15. "The Council wished to do away with the irreligious phrases of the Arians, and to use instead the acknowledged words of the Scriptures, that the Son is not from nothing but 'from God,' and is 'Word' and 'Wisdom,' and not creature or work, but a proper offspring from the Father" (ibid., 19).
18. Ibid., 28.
19. Ibid., 20.
20. Ibid.
21. Athanasius also accused the Arians of using such concepts as a hermeneutical device to distort Scripture (Athanasius *Orationes Contra Arianos* 1.12.52).
22. Richard A. Norris, Jr., ed. and trans., *The Christological Controversy*, Sources of Early Christian Thought, ed. William G. Rusch (Philadelphia: Fortress, 1980), p. 158.
23. Hardy, *Christology of the Later Fathers*, p. 349.
24. See Sellers, pp. 207-53.
25. See John F. Walvoord, *Jesus Christ Our Lord* (Chicago: Moody, 1969), pp. 117-18.
26. Hardy, p. 352.
27. Ibid., p. 356.
28. Sellers, p. 110.
29. See the examination of these terms in Sellers. Also see the discussion in G. Christopher Stead, *Divine Substance* (London: Oxford U., 1977). An excellent discussion by Stead of οὐσία and ὁμοούσιος is also found in his article, "The Significance of the Homousios," *Studia Patristica* 3(1961):397-412.
30. See G. C. Berkouwer, *The Person of Christ*, Studies in Dogmatics (Grand Rapids: Eerdmans, 1954), pp. 90-97.
31. John Calvin, *The Institutes of the Christian Religion* (trans. F. L. Battles), 4.9.8.

Biblical Studies

9

The Purpose of the Law

J. Dwight Pentecost

What is the purpose of the law? Such is the question the apostle Paul faced with his readers in the third chapter of Galatians as he taught them the doctrine of sanctification by faith in Jesus Christ. Paul is dealing with the problem as to how a person is sanctified, made perfect, or how he attains experientially the promises and blessings that are his in Christ. The Galatians had been led to believe that sanctification is by the law and that through keeping of the law believers obtain the promises that were given to them by God. In order to show the fallacy of this interpretation, the apostle has cited the experience of Abraham. Abraham was given promises by God (Gen. 12), which were repeated (Gen. 13) and ratified by a blood covenant (Gen. 15). All that Abraham obtained he obtained by faith in the promise of God. Such teaching would be incontrovertible by virtue of the fact that no law had been given in Abraham's time. Therefore, all that Abraham realized he had to realize by faith in the promise of God.

The error that had been propagated among the Galatians was that, although Abraham attained by faith alone, the giving of the law altered the basic plan by which God dealt with men, so that Abraham's children subsequent to the giving of the law must attain by keeping the law rather than by faith in

J. Dwight Pentecost
A.B., Hampden-Sydney College; Th.M., Th.D., Dallas Theological Seminary
Professor of Bible Exposition
Dallas Theological Seminary

the promise of God. In order to dispel this error, Paul shows in Galatians 3:17 that "the law, which was four hundred and thirty years after, cannot disannul, that it should make the promise of none effect."* Paul adds in verse 19 that, rather than disallowing or nullifying the law, the law was added, or better added alongside the existing promise, in order to serve a specific function. He further shows in verse 21 that there is no basic conflict between the law and the promises of God and that the two can coexist. Anticipating certain objections or questions in the minds of his readers, Paul faces the question specifically. "Wherefore, then, serveth the law?" (v. 19). It is this specific question that must be considered now.

It should be observed that many who lived under the law had the deepest reverence, respect, and love for the law. David, writing in Psalm 119, frequently reflects this attitude. In verse 97 he said, "O how love I thy law! It is my meditation all the day." Or in verse 77 he said, "Thy law is my delight." Again, in verses 103 and 104, he wrote, "How sweet are thy words unto my taste! yea, sweeter than honey to my mouth! Through thy precepts I get understanding." Or once again, in verse 159, he said, "Consider how I love thy precepts." David shows a love for and dependence on the law. In contrast with much current antinomianism, which treats the law as a worthless worn-out garment to be discarded, the apostle Paul in Romans 7:12 says, "The law is holy, and the commandment is holy and just and good." That which was loved, revered, and respected by Old and New Testament writers must have served a worthy function.

It needs to be noted that the law of Moses was given to a redeemed people. The writer to the Hebrews in Hebrews 11:28-29 says of Moses, "Through faith he kept the passover, and the sprinkling of blood, lest he who destroyed the first-born should touch them. By faith they passed through the Red Sea as by dry land." On the night of the Passover in Egypt, Israel was redeemed by blood. By faith they began a walk through the wilderness toward the land of promise. It was on the basis of that blood redemption that God could say to the nation as recorded in Isaiah 43:1, "But now thus saith the

---

*All Scripture quotations in this article are from the King James Version.

LORD that created thee, O Jacob, and He that formed thee, O Israel, Fear not: for I have redeemed thee, I have called thee by thy name; thou art mine." The nation that was redeemed by faith through blood was brought to Mount Sinai. Although that nation had been redeemed, it was a nation which was viewed as being in spiritual immaturity. They recognized a responsibility to the Redeemer which they did not know how to discharge.

The fact of Israel's infancy at the time of the giving of the law is recognized by the apostle Paul who writes in Galatians 3:23-26, "But before faith came, we were kept unto the law, shut up unto the faith which should afterwards be revealed. Wherefore the law was our schoolmaster to bring us unto Christ, that we might be justified by faith. But after that faith is come, we are no longer under a schoolmaster. For ye are all the children of God by faith in Christ Jesus." Or again in Galatians 4:1-5, "Now I say, That the heir, as long as he is a child, differeth nothing from a servant, though he be lord of all; but is under tutors and governors until the time appointed of the father. Even so we, when we were children, were in bondage under the elements of the world: but when the fullness of the time was come, God sent forth his Son, made of a woman, made under the law, to redeem them that were under the law, that we might receive the adoption of sons." Paul views those living under the law as children in a state of immaturity and he views the law as a pedagogue, a child trainer or overseer whose responsibility it was to supervise every area of the life of the child committed to its care. It is because of this fact of immaturity that Israel needed the law. Thus the law was given as a gracious provision by God to a redeemed people who were in a state of spiritual infancy to meet their needs.

As the Scriptures are studied, a number of reasons may be derived why the Mosaic law was given to the nation Israel. First, it was given to reveal the holiness of God. Peter writes in 1 Peter 1:15-16, "But as he which hath called you is holy, so be ye holy in all manner of conversation; because it is written, Be ye holy; for I am holy." The fact that God was a holy God was made very clear to Israel in the law of Moses. Perhaps the primary function of the law was to reveal to Israel the fact of the holiness of God and to make Israel aware of the character of the God who had redeemed them from Egypt. All the requirements laid on the nation Israel were in the light of the holy character of God as revealed in the Mosaic law.

Second, the Mosaic law was given to reveal or expose the sinfulness of man. It is of this that Paul writes in Galatians 3:19-22, when he says, "It [the law] was added because of transgressions, till the seed should come to whom the promise was made; and it was ordained by angels in the hands of a mediator. . . . But the scripture hath concluded all under sin, that the promise by faith of Jesus Christ might be given to them that believe." The holiness of God as revealed in the law became the test of man's thoughts, words, and actions, and anything that failed to conform to the revealed holiness of God was sin. It is this fact that Paul has in mind when he writes in Romans 3:23, "For all have sinned, and come short of the glory of God." That in which God finds His highest glory is His own holiness. Sin is not only want of conformity to the law, but want of conformity to the holiness of God, of which the law is a revelation. Consequently, the holiness of God becomes the final test of sin; rather than the law, which is the reflection of that holiness. Because all of Abraham's seed were born in sin, the law was given by which Israel might readily determine their sinfulness before a holy God. The law made very specific the requirements of divine holiness, so that even children in spiritual infancy could determine whether their conduct was acceptable to a holy God.

A third purpose of the law, related to the above, was to reveal the standard of holiness required of those in fellowship with a holy God. Israel had been redeemed as a nation—redeemed in order to enjoy fellowship with God. As these redeemed ones faced the question of what kind of life was required of those who walk in fellowship with their Redeemer, the law was given to indicate the standard God required.

The psalmist recognized this, as he wrote in Psalm 24:3-5: "Who shall ascend into the hill of the LORD or who shall stand in his holy place? He that hath clean hands, and a pure heart; who hath not lifted up his soul unto vanity, nor sworn deceitfully. He shall receive the blessing from the LORD, and righteousness from the God of his salvation." Those who were redeemed were redeemed to enjoy the Redeemer, and the law made very clear the kind of life that God required of them, if they were to walk in fellowship with Him.

A fourth purpose of the law is stated by the apostle in

Galatians 3:24: "Wherefore the law was our schoolmaster to bring us unto Christ." The word "schoolmaster" refers to the slave selected by the father whose responsibility it was to supervise the total development of the child—physically, intellectually, and spiritually. The child was under the pedagogue's constant supervision until he should move out of childhood into adulthood. Every area of the child's life was under the supervision of the pedagogue until he came to maturity.

The apostle's teaching says that the law served to supervise the physical, mental, and spiritual development of the redeemed Israelite until he had come to maturity in the Lord. The psalmist reflects this same concept in Psalm 119:71-72, when he says, "It is good for me that I have been afflicted; that I might learn thy statutes. The law of thy mouth is better unto me than thousands of gold and silver." David confesses that he learned of God's requirements through the law that had been revealed.

A fifth purpose of the law is that it was given to be the unifying principle that made possible the establishment of the nation. In Exodus 19:5-8 one reads, "Now therefore, if ye will obey my voice indeed, and keep my covenant, then ye shall be a peculiar treasure unto me above all people: for all the earth is mine: And ye shall be unto me a kingdom of priests, and an holy nation. These are the words which thou shalt speak unto the children of Israel. And Moses came and called for the elders of the people, and laid before their faces all these words which the LORD commanded him. And all the people answered together, and said, All that the LORD hath spoken we will do." One notices in the eighth verse that in response to the instruction given by Moses as to what God had revealed, the nation voluntarily submitted themselves to the authority of the law. Apart from voluntary submission to a unifying principle there could have been no nation. And the people redeemed out of Egypt by blood who had begun a walk by faith are constituted a nation when they voluntarily submit themselves to the law.

This same truth is reaffirmed in Deuteronomy 5:27-28, "Go thou near, and hear all that the LORD our God shall say: and speak thou unto us all that the LORD our God shall speak unto thee; and we will hear it, and do it. And the LORD heard the voice of your words, when ye spake unto me; and the LORD said unto me, I have heard the voice of the words of this people, which they have spoken unto thee: they have well said all that they have spoken." From the divine viewpoint Israel was constituted a nation at the time they voluntarily submitted themselves to the law.

It is significant that the prophet Jeremiah warns the people that because they have abandoned the law God will deliver them into the hands of the Gentiles. The Babylonian captivity by which Israel lost their national identity came about because of their failure to observe the law. In Deuteronomy 28 Moses had made it very clear that if the people abandoned the law, God would deliver them into the hands of the Gentiles. And it is not without significance that until Israel submits to the authority of the law of her Messiah-King she will not be recognized by God as a nation again.

Related to this, in the sixth place the law was given to Israel to separate them from the nations in order that they might become a kingdom of priests. In Exodus 31:13 one reads, "Speak thou also unto the children of Israel, saying, Verily my sabbaths ye shall keep: for it is a sign between me and you throughout your generations; that ye may know that I am the LORD that doth sanctify you." Israel was sanctified or set apart, according to Exodus 19:5-6, to become a kingdom of priests, that is, a nation that mediated the truth of God to the nations of the earth. The law became a hedge that separated Israel from the nations of the earth. The law separated and preserved the nation and kept them intact. In order that Israel might serve the function of a light to the world, they were given the law.

In the seventh place the law was given to a redeemed people to make provision for forgiveness of sins and restoration to fellowship. In Leviticus 1-7 there are the five offerings that God instituted for the nation. Whereas the nation as a nation was preserved before God because of the annual offering of the blood of atonement, individuals in the nation were restored to fellowship and received forgiveness for specific sins through the use of the offerings that God provided. The God who had redeemed the nation by faith through blood provided that the redeemed could walk in fellowship with Himself. The same law that revealed their unworthiness for fellowship also provided for restoration to the fellowship. That was one of the primary functions of the law.

In the eighth place the law was given to make provision

for a redeemed people to worship. A redeemed people will be a worshiping people, and a people who walk in fellowship with God will worship the God with whom they enjoy fellowship. In Leviticus 23 the law revealed a cycle of feasts that the nation was expected to observe annually. These feasts were the means by which the redeemed nation worshiped God. In the cycle of feasts Israel's attention was directed backward to the redemption out of Egypt and forward to the final redemption that would be provided through the Redeemer according to God's promise.

The law, in the ninth place, provided a test as to whether one was in the kingdom or the theocracy over which God ruled. In Deuteronomy 28 as Israel stood on the border of the Promised Land, Moses revealed the principle by which God would deal with the nation. The first portion of the chapter outlines the blessings that would come on the nation for obedience. A great portion of that extensive chapter deals with the curses that would come on the nation because of disobedience. Even though the nation as a whole entered into the Promised Land, because not all had believed God, not all were eligible to receive the blessings promised to those in the land. The law, then, revealed whether or not a man was rightly related to God. Those who submitted to and obeyed the law did so because of their faith in God, which produced obedience. Those who disobeyed the law did so because they were without faith in God, and lack of faith produced their disobedience. Whether a man obeyed the law or not, then, became the test as to whether he was rightly related to God and thus, in God's kingdom.

Finally, it becomes clear from the New Testament that the law was given to reveal Jesus Christ. The great truths concerning the person and the work of the Lord Jesus Christ are woven throughout the law, and the law was given in order to prepare the nation for the coming Redeemer King. It was because of that that the Lord on the Emmaus road could expound to His companions great truths concerning the Messiah that had been revealed in the law and the prophets. Israel, through the law, was being prepared for the coming Messiah through the revelation of Him which it contained.

As one looks back over these reasons for the giving of the law, he can observe that there was in the law that which was *revelatory* of the holiness of God. This aspect of the law was permanent. Holiness does not change from age to age, and that which revealed the holiness of God to Israel may still be used to reveal the holiness of God to men today. That which reveals the holiness of God reveals concomitantly the unholiness of man, and the law may still be used to reveal the unholiness of man today. It is this revelatory aspect of the law that Paul refers to as holy, just, and good.

There was also that in the law which was *regulatory.* The law regulated the life and the worship of the Israelite. It is this regulatory aspect of the law that was temporary, that has been done away. Paul in 1 Timothy 1:8 writes, "But we know that the law is good, if a man use it lawfully." How can the law be used lawfully in an age in which it is said that the law had been done away? If a law is used to reveal the holiness of God, the unholiness of man, the requirements of those who would live in fellowship with the holy God, or to learn of the person and work of Christ, it is used lawfully. One who attempts to use the regulatory portions of the law which were "only until Christ" is using the law unlawfully. Although one sings, "Free from the law, oh happy condition," he still recognizes that the law is "holy, just and good."

10

A Fresh Look at the Imprecatory Psalms

J. Carl Laney

Included in the Psalter are various psalms containing appeals for God to pour out His wrath on the psalmist's enemies. These psalms are commonly classified "imprecatory psalms" for the imprecation forms a chief element in the psalm. These psalms have been problematic for Bible students, because of the difficulty in reconciling them with Christian thought. Albert Barnes comments on this problem.

> ... perhaps there is no part of the Bible that gives more perplexity and pain to its readers than this; perhaps nothing that constitutes a more plausible objection to the belief that the psalms are the productions of inspired men than the spirit of revenge which they sometimes seem to breathe and the spirit of cherished malice and implacableness which the writers seem to manifest.[1]

The purposes of this article are to define an "imprecation," identify the imprecatory psalms, pinpoint the problem that interpreters have with such psalms, recount proposed solutions to the difficulty, and present a suggested solution to this problem.

J. Carl Laney
B.S., University of Oregon; M.Div., Th.M., Western Conservative Baptist Seminary; Th.D., Dallas Theological Seminary
Associate Professor of Biblical Literature
Western Conservative Baptist Seminary
Portland, Oregon

THE DEFINITION OF IMPRECATION

An "imprecation" is an invocation of judgment, calamity, or curse uttered against one's enemies, or the enemies of God. The morning prayer of Moses was an imprecation that the enemies of Yahweh, who were Moses' enemies as well, would be scattered and flee from His presence (Num. 10:35). The song of Deborah and Barak concludes with an imprecation that Yahweh's enemies might perish (Judg. 5:31). Jeremiah the prophet used repeated imprecations against his enemies (Jer. 11:20; 15:15; 17:18; 18:21-23; 20:12). Such imprecations are not limited to the Old Testament, but are found in the New Testament as well (Rev. 6:9-10). Other portions of the New Testament are considered by some to contain imprecations (Acts 13:10-11; 23:3; 1 Cor. 16:22; Gal. 1:8-9; 5:12; 2 Tim. 4:14), but although these verses contain a curse element, they do not have a specific prayer to the Lord that the judgment would be carried out.[2] Imprecations from the Psalms, however, are quoted in the New Testament (Acts 1:20; Ps. 69:25; 109:8). Crucial to the definition of an imprecation is that it (a) must be an invocation—a prayer or address to God, and (b) must contain a request that one's enemies or the enemies of Yahweh be judged and justly punished.

THE IDENTIFICATION OF THE IMPRECATORY PSALMS

Although many imprecations are in the book of Psalms,[3] it is evident that in some psalms the imprecations form the chief element. These "imprecatory psalms" have been said to contain "expressions calling for divine judgment to fall upon the Psalmist's enemy,"[4] which would involve not only the enemy's personal destruction but also the overthrow of his family and the crushing of all hope for his future. H. C. Leupold states that the term "imprecatory psalms" is used to designate "those psalms in which the writer prays that God may afflict the evildoer and punish him according to his just deserts."[5] Roland K. Harrison remarks that these psalms constitute "a reply to the national enemies" and a call to God "to exercise retribution."[6] In the imprecatory psalms the imprecation, instead of being a minor element, is greatly multiplied until it becomes a major element or leading feature. An imprecatory psalm, then, is one in which the imprecation is a major element or leading feature of the psalm.

Although opinion varies as to the number and identity of the imprecatory psalms, at least these nine may be included, based on the preceding definition: Psalms 7, 35, 58, 59, 69, 83, 109, 137, and 139. A reading of these psalms reveals that the imprecatory element is a leading feature of each psalm and is crucial to the psalmist's argument. All these imprecatory psalms are Davidic except for Psalm 83, which is attributed to Asaph, and Psalm 137, which is exilic.

THE PROBLEM WITH THE IMPRECATORY PSALMS

The basic problem with the imprecatory psalms is an ethical one. Johannes Vos asks, "How can it be right to wish or pray for the destruction or doom of others as is done in the Imprecatory Psalms? . . . Is it right for a Christian to use the Imprecatory Psalms in the worship of God, and if so, in what sense can he make the Psalms his own?"[7] J. W. Beardslee also calls attention to the ethical problem of these psalms.

> In our private reading we can scarcely understand why they should find a place in a book otherwise so universally fitted to stimulate devotional life. In the public service of the church they are passed in silence by the preacher as having in them nothing calculated to educate and elevate the moral character of the people.[8]

The problem with the imprecatory psalms, or more correctly, the interpreter's problem with them, is how an apparent spirit of vengeance can be reconciled with the precepts of the New Testament and Jesus' command to "love your enemies, and pray for those who persecute you" (Matt. 5:44).* Essentially three problems are confronted: (1) How can the presence of these imprecations in the Hebrew hymnal be explained? (2) Do they have application to the life and worship of Christians? (3) Can these heart cries for vengeance and retribution be as inspired as other portions of the book of Psalms, which magnify and elevate God's character? Evangelicals must answer the second and third questions in the affirmative, and then

---

*All Scripture quotations in this article are from the *New American Standard Bible.*

begin to deal with the first question—the ethical or moral problem of the psalms of imprecation.

THE UNSATISFACTORY SOLUTIONS

Many possible solutions to the problem of the imprecatory psalms have been formulated. A brief review and evaluation of some major suggestions is necessary before setting forth a fresh approach to dealing with the ethical problem.[9]

THE IMPRECATIONS BY DAVID'S ENEMIES

It has been suggested that the imprecations in Psalm 109:6-20 are not the utterance of David against his enemies, but are the fierce cursing of David's enemies against David himself.[10] To adhere to this solution one must insert the participle אָמַר ("saying") at the end of verse 5 so that the imprecation would appear to be sourced in the mouths of David's persecutors. Justification for this solution is based on the insertion of an implied participle in Psalm 2:2 in the King James Version to explain the quotation in 2:3, which obviously must be attributed to the psalmist's enemies.

However, this proposed solution is very strained. The transition from verse 5 to verse 6 in Psalm 109 does not give any intimation that the words pass from David's prayer to an imprecation by his enemies, and the alleged "quotation" (vv. 6-20) is far longer than the single verse of Psalm 2. Also this solution would certainly not work in Psalms 7, 35, 58, 59, 69, 83, 137, or 139, where the imprecation is against a plurality of the psalmist's enemies. This view must therefore be rejected as an inadequate explanation.

THE EXPRESSION OF DAVID'S OWN SENTIMENTS

A second solution offered is that in these imprecations David is uttering the sentiments of his own heart and not those of the Holy Spirit. This view is taken by Kittel, who considers the imprecatory psalms to have originated from mean-spirited individuals who thought only of conquest and revenge. The presence of these psalms in the Hebrew Psalter witnesses to the fact that at one time they were accredited to God.[11] The suggestion is made that if David had been a better man, he would not have uttered such perverse thoughts. This view, however, overlooks the biblical record of David's character as a man who did not indulge in a spirit of personal revenge (1 Sam. 24:1-7; 26:5-11). Also the New Testament reveals that David wrote the psalms under the personal and direct inspiration of the Holy Spirit ("who by the Holy Spirit, through the mouth of our father David Thy servant, didst say . . ." [Acts 4:25], and "men moved by the Holy Spirit spoke from God" [2 Pet. 1:21]). To dissect a psalm or any portion of Scripture into inspired and uninspired sections is a fundamental error, and therefore an unacceptable solution to the problem of the imprecatory psalms.

THE INFERIOR PRINCIPLE OF SPIRITUAL LIFE IN THE OLD TESTAMENT

Still another view offered is that the inspiring principle underlying the spiritual life of the Old Testament differs from that of the New.[12] It is suggested that, since David lived prior to the full light of the truth about spirituality, as developed in the New Testament, broad ethical teaching and practice should not be expected from him. However, although those in the present dispensation of grace do enjoy the benefits and spiritual life provided by the teachings of Jesus, the Mosaic covenant did provide David with adequate guidelines for ethical conduct. Hatred for one's neighbors is forbidden in the Old Testament, as is vengeance (Deut. 32:35), while love is commanded (Lev. 19:17-18). This solution to the problem of the imprecatory psalms is inadequate because it underestimates the Old Testament's provision of ethical guidelines. Christians do enjoy the benefits of progressive revelation, but that progress is not from error to truth; instead, it is a progression from incomplete revelation to a more full and complete revelation or divine disclosure.

THE IMPRECATIONS AGAINST DAVID'S SPIRITUAL FOES

It has also been suggested that the imprecatory psalms are the psalmist's *spiritual* antagonists rather than human personages. According to this view, evil spiritual influences are personified as evil men. Mowinckel suggests that the imprecations in these psalms are curses uttered in the name of God who is a sure defense against the powers of darkness and is able to defy and overthrow the hosts of evil which stir themselves up against His servants.[13] This solution introduces an unfortunate subjectivity and indefiniteness to the meaning of the biblical language. How is one to determine when to make the transition from a literal to a spiritual interpretation of a particular passage? Also, if the psalmist's enemies are evil principles and forces of darkness, it is strange that their families should be mentioned in Psalm 109. Many of the psalms were written in a time of oppression from enemies like Doeg the Edomite (Ps. 52:1; 1 Sam. 21:7) and Shimei (2 Sam. 16:5-8), and it is therefore difficult to believe that David would have had nonphysical enemies in mind.

THE IMPRECATIONS ARE PROPHETIC

Another proposed solution to the problem is that the imprecatory psalms are to be understood as prophetic. The psalmist was not only a poet, but was also a prophet declaring what would happen to the ungodly. This is one of the solutions offered by Barnes, and was held by Augustine, Calvin, and Spurgeon.[14] This view throws the responsibility for the imprecation on God, and thus relieves the psalmist from the charge of speaking out of a spirit of bitterness or revenge. It is pointed out by advocates of this view that the imprecations are quoted in the New Testament (Ps. 69:25 and 109:8 in Acts 1:20; and Ps. 69:22-23 in Rom. 11:9-10), and that therefore all the imprecations are prophetic. Against this view is the fact that the imperfect form of the verb is sometimes preceded by an imperative, in which case the imperfect form is translated as a jussive (Ps. 69:25-26).[15] The imprecation in such a case is not a simple declaration of what will happen, but is a wish or prayer that it may happen. In Psalm 137 the imprecation involves the third person in such a way as to show that the speaker is not simply uttering the divine will as a prophet, but is expressing his own feeling as a man. Psalm 137:8-9 is an expression of the personal satisfaction the psalmist will feel when judgment overtakes the wrongdoers.

THE HUMANITY OF THE PSALMIST

A recent view of Psalm 137 is that it simply expresses the full humanity of the psalmist who loved Zion but who hated his foes passionately. According to John Bright, the psalmist is "God's wholly committed man, yet a man who is estranged from God's spirit."[16] Bright asserts that the psalm must not be read and received as God's Word for today in and of itself, but that it must be read in light of the gospel. The psalmist expresses a conclusion which is "unworthy and sub-Christian," but he records the frustration of the whole man who must be confronted by Christ. The psalmist's thoughts are not approved, but are understood to be an expression of humanity's need for Christ. Although Bright deals only with Psalm 137, presumably he would also apply this principle of interpretation to the other imprecatory psalms. This view does offer an application of these psalms to Christians, but it does not adequately explain the inspiration of Psalm 137 and the reason for its inclusion in the Psalter. This view appears to deny the divine authorship of the imprecatory psalms in an arbitrary attempt to distinguish between that which is the expression of humanity and that which is the expression of the Spirit. Such a dichotomy fails to grasp the unity of the divine and human authors of Scripture (see Acts. 4:25).

STEPS TOWARD A SATISFACTORY SOLUTION

Having investigated several unsatisfactory solutions to the ethical problem of the imprecatory psalms, several factors toward a satisfactory solution may now be considered.

THE PURPOSES OF THE IMPRECATIONS

An awareness of the ethical and revelational purposes of the imprecatory judgments will enable one to understand better the imprecatory psalms. Six purposes are evident.

1. One major purpose of the judgments against evildoers is to establish the righteous. As God judges the wicked, He is also invoked to establish the righteous (Ps. 7:8-9). A concern for righteousness and the righteous is foundational to the imprecation found in Psalm 7:6-11.

2. A second purpose of the imprecatory judgments is that God may be praised when the psalmist is delivered (7:17; 35:18, 28). Closely related to this is the anticipation of rejoicing when the psalmist sees the vindication taking place (58:10).

3. A third purpose in requesting judgment against the wicked is that men will see the reward of the righteous and recognize that it is God who judges the earth (58:11). Both the righteous and the wicked will know that God is concerned with justice and that He executes judgment on the earth.

4. The imprecatory judgments are also designed to

demonstrate to everyone that God is sovereign. David prayed that his enemies would be destroyed so that men from the ends of the earth "may know that God rules in Jacob" (59:13).

5. A fifth purpose of the imprecatory judgments is to prevent the wicked from enjoying the same blessings as the righteous. David prays that those who persist in wickedness may be blotted out of the book of life (the register of the living), that is, may be judged by physical death (69:28).

6. A sixth purpose of the imprecatory judgments is to cause the wicked to seek the Lord. Asaph prays that God would judge and humiliate His enemies so that they would seek His name and acknowledge Him as the sovereign God (83:16-18).

These purposes of the imprecations give a divine perspective to the seemingly human cries for judgment. It would appear that the high ethical and revelational purposes of the imprecatory psalms clear them of the charge of being sourced in the bitter spirit of a bloodthirsty, carnal man.

THE COVENANTAL BASIS FOR A CURSE ON ISRAEL'S ENEMIES

The fundamental ground on which one may justify the imprecations in the Psalms is the covenantal basis for a curse on Israel's enemies. The Abrahamic covenant (Gen. 12:1-3) promised blessing on those who blessed Abraham's posterity, and cursing (אָרַר) on those who would curse (קָלַל) Abraham's posterity. Because of the unconditional nature of the covenant, its promises and provisions remain in force throughout Israel's existence as a nation. Balaam is an example of one who received judgment for cursing Israel (Num. 22-24; 31:16). Actually, Balaam was unable to curse Israel, and he fell under God's judgment because of his attack on Israel by undermining the spiritual life of the nation (31:8). All the Midianites except for the little ones and the virgin girls were slain because of their part in the attack against the spiritual life of Israel (31:1-18). Truly, those who had cursed were cursed!

On the basis of the unconditional Abrahamic covenant, David had a perfect right, as the representative of the nation, to pray that God would effect what He had promised—cursing on those who cursed or attacked Israel. David's enemies were a great threat to the well-being of Israel! The cries for judgment in the imprecatory psalms are appeals for Yahweh to carry out His judgment against those who would curse the nation—judgment in accordance with the provisions of the Abrahamic covenant.

THE ATTITUDE OF THE IMPRECATOR

The attitude of the psalmist is a key consideration in seeking to interpret and appreciate the imprecatory psalms. Although the psalmist might appear to be a bloodthirsty and vindictive avenger, a closer examination demonstrates that this is not the case. Four significant points must be taken into consideration.

1. It is significant that David never prayed that he may be permitted to take vengeance on his enemies, but always that *God* would become his avenger. David's prayer was always that Yahweh would rise against his adversaries (Pss. 7:6; 35:1; 58:6; 59:5) and overthrow, smite, and destroy as the psalmist's own Avenger. The power and right to avenge belonged to God (Deut. 32:35), and David, realizing that a crisis had come, simply requested that God use judgmental retribution for His own glory and for the deliverance of His servant.

2. It is also important to distinguish between "vindication" and "vindictiveness." The psalmist's passion was for justice, and the imprecatory psalms are not sourced in personal vindictiveness or bitter malice that seeks revenge. David was capable of generosity under personal attack (2 Sam. 16:11; 19:16-23), yet no ruler was more deeply stirred to anger by unscrupulous actions, even when they appeared to favor his cause. What David pleaded for in his imprecations was that justice be done and that right be vindicated. He simply asked for the judgmental intervention that any victim of injustice deserved. David's concern was for vindication—justice— a concern which also the New Testament upholds (e.g., Luke 18:1-8).

3. David's concept of kingship sheds considerable light on the attitude of the imprecator. The king of Israel was God's chosen man (Deut. 17:15), sitting on an earthly throne as God's representative. David had great respect for the anointed king and refused to stretch forth his hand against Yahweh's anointed (1 Sam. 24:10; 26:11). To have done so would have been not only treason but also utter sacrilege and disregard

for the theocratic office. When the office of king was conferred on David, he then regarded himself and everything that concerned him in light of his official relationship to God and the theocratic government. As the representative of God to the people, an attack on the king—the theocratic official—differed in no way from an attack on Yahweh! David saw attacks against him as attacks on the name of Yahweh. He thus prayed for the destruction of the wicked, not out of personal revenge, but out of his zeal for God and His kingdom.

4. It is also helpful to see that the imprecations in the book of Psalms reflect an Old Testament saint's abhorrence of sin and evil. Those against whom the imprecations were directed were not the private enemies of David, but those who opposed God and His cause. Divine judgment was called down on those who were the very incarnation of wickedness. David's heart was sensitive to sin (Pss. 51:3, 9; 139:23-24), and out of his abhorrence for sin and evil he appealed to God for justice and the execution of judgment on the wicked.

CONCLUSION

The imprecatory psalms present Bible students with the problem of reconciling the apparent spirit of vengeance with the precepts of the New Testament and the teachings of Jesus. The key to solving this ethical problem is to understand that the imprecations are grounded in the Abrahamic covenant (Gen. 12:1-3), in which God promised to curse those who cursed Abraham's descendants. The psalmist, then, merely appealed for God to fulfill His covenant promise to Israel. It is also helpful to note that the imprecations were motivated by a desire to promote righteousness (Ps. 7:6-11), to demonstrate God's sovereignty (58:11; 59:13), to cause the wicked to seek the Lord (83:16-18), and to provide an opportunity for the righteous to praise God (7:17; 35; 18, 28). Therefore, out of zeal for God and abhorrence of sin, the psalmist called on God to punish the wicked and to vindicate His righteousness.

In light of the fact that the Abrahamic covenant reflects God's promise to Abraham and his descendants, it would be inappropriate for a church-age believer to call down God's judgment on the wicked. One can appreciate the Old Testament setting of the imprecatory psalms and teach and preach from them. However, like the ceremonial dietary laws of the applied to church-age saints. This is clear from Paul's exhortation in Romans 12:14, "Bless those who persecute you; bless and curse not." Paul admonished the Romans, "Never take your own revenge, beloved, but leave room for the wrath of God, for it is written, "VENGEANCE IS MINE, I WILL REPAY", says the Lord' " (12:19). Paul's words in 2 Timothy 4:14 indicate that he practiced what he preached. Rather than calling down divine wrath on Alexander the coppersmith, Paul simply stated, "The Lord will repay him according to his deeds." And John makes it clear that God in the future will judge the wicked for their sin (Rev. 20:11-15).

NOTES

1. Albert Barnes, *Notes, Critical, Explanatory, and Practical on the Book of Psalms*, 3 vols. (London: Blackie & Son, 1868), 1:xxv-xxvi.
2. The cry of the martyred tribulation saints in Revelation 6:10 for God's vengeance, while similar to the psalmist's imprecations, is not applicable to the church age.
3. Psalms 5:10; 6:10; 9:19; 10:2, 15; 17:13a; 28:4; 31:17b-18; 40:14-15; 55:9, 15; 68:1-2; 70:2-3; 71:13; 79:6, 10, 12; 94:1; 97:7; 104:35; 129:5-6; 140:9-11; 141:10; 143:12.
4. J. W. Beardslee, "The Imprecatory Element in the Psalms," *Presbyterian and Reformed Review* 8(1897):491.
5. H. C. Leupold, *The Psalms* (Grand Rapids: Baker, 1969), p. 18.
6. Roland K. Harrison, *Introduction to the Old Testament* (Grand Rapids: Eerdmans, 1969), p. 997.
7. Johannes G. Vos, "The Ethical Problem of the Imprecatory Psalms," *Westminster Theological Journal* 4(May 1942):123.
8. Beardslee, p. 491.
9. For an overview of other solutions that have been proposed, see Roy B. Zuck, "The Problem of the Imprecatory Psalms" (Th.M. thesis, Dallas Theological Seminary, 1957), pp. 45-58.
10. Beardslee, pp. 491-92.
11. Rudolf Kittel, *The Scientific Study of the Old Testament*, trans. J. Caleb Hughes (New York: G. P. Putnam's Sons, 1910), p. 143, quoted from G. S. Gunn, *God in the Psalms* (Edinburgh: Saint Andrews Press, 1965), p. 102.
12. Beardslee, pp. 491-92.
13. Sigmund Mowinckel, *The Psalms in Israel's Worship*, trans. D. R. Ap-Thomas, 2 vols. (New York: Abingdon, 1962), 1:44-52.
14. Barnes, 1:xxx.
15. E. Kautzsch, ed., *Gesenius' Hebrew Grammar*, trans. A. E. Cowley, 2d English ed. (Oxford: At the Clarendon, 1910), p. 322.
16. John Bright, *The Authority of the Old Testament* (Nashville: Abingdon, 1967), p. 238.

11

Jeremiah's Ministry and Ours

Kenneth L. Barker

The Word of the Lord came to Jeremiah (1:4) in a period of history when conditions were strikingly similar to those of the present day.[1] Politically, it was a time of upheaval in the ancient Near Eastern world—an upheaval involving the great world powers of Assyria, Egypt, and Babylonia, and also involving such momentous events as the fall of Nineveh in 612 B.C., the battle of Carchemish in 605 (in which Babylon was victorious over Egypt), and the fall of Judah and the destruction of Jerusalem, including the first Temple, i.e., Solomon's Temple, in 586.

Religiously, there was moral and spiritual decay. Even in little Judah, society was rotten to the core. The ultimate reason for this appalling condition was given by God Himself in Jeremiah 2:13: "For my people have committed two evils: they have forsaken Me, the fountain of living waters, to hew for themselves cisterns, broken cisterns, that can hold no water."* Now this indicates that Josiah's reform was apparently only superficial, external, and temporary. No real repentance or inner change in the national character had resulted from it. Many were foolishly and erroneously reasoning that

Kenneth L. Barker
A.B., Northwestern College; Th.M., Dallas Theological Seminary; Ph.D., Dropsie University, College of Hebrew and Cognate Learning
Vice-President for Bible Translation
New York International Bible Society
East Brunswick, New Jersey

*All Scripture quotations in this article, except those noted otherwise, are from the *New American Standard Bible.*

because of these outward religious reforms, Judah would now be secure and exempt from divine judgment. The reform itself, then, seems to have actually contributed to the general attitude of complacency, along with the dangerous notion of the people that the presence of the Temple, the house of God, in Jerusalem automatically brought security with it. All of this meant that judgment was now certain, that Judah as a country or separate national entity was soon to die.

At such a time as this, God called a man who is known as both the weeping prophet and the prophet of loneliness, a weeping prophet because he was a man of pathos, feeling, and compassion. This aspect of the nature, personality, and emotion of this man of God may be ascertained from such references as 9:1 and 14:17, and the entire book of Lamentations. He was the prophet of *loneliness* because God Himself commanded him never to marry as a sign of the impending disruption of the whole social life of Judah (16:2-4). Thus, he was never to know the joys of home and family. Then, too, any man in any age who faithfully proclaims the Word of God will at times find himself standing virtually alone. This was certainly true in Jeremiah's case, so much so that he was even accused of being unpatriotic—a traitor! His life became a veritable history of persecution. But, above all else, Jeremiah was a man who, though tempted to relinquish his prophetic work, nevertheless, continued *faithfully to proclaim the Word of God*, and who, in the face of mounting pressure from all sides, refused to temper the message God had given him, refused even to water it down a bit, and refused to be silent. Using his own phraseology (20:9), the Word of God was like a fire shut up in his bones which, try as he might, he could not hold in. This brings us to our subject: "Jeremiah's Ministry and Ours." The writer here presents a very brief devotional exposition of Jeremiah 1:1-10, which records the call of this great prophet who had such a sensitive heart.

THE TITLE PAGE (1:1-3)

The passage includes, first, the preface, superscription, or title page to the whole book in verses 1-3. The meaning of Jeremiah's name is uncertain. Possibly it means "the Lord throws," in other words, "the Lord throws down," which would be appropriate to his message of judgment. Jeremiah was a priest, as verse 1 indicates: "The words of Jeremiah, the son of Hilkiah, of the priests who were in Anathoth in the land of Benjamin." Prophets came from practically all walks of life. The real stamp that marked a prophet was not what he was before his call, but the fact that he had received a supernatural call from God to his prophetic office and ministry. The word "Anathoth" is modern Anata, and it includes the name of the Phoenician or Canaanite goddess, Anat. This town is not quite three miles northeast of Jerusalem. Note also that it is in the land of Benjamin. Jeremiah, then, was from the same tribe or territory as both the Old and New Testament Sauls.

Verses 2-3a read, "To whom the word of the LORD came in the days of Josiah, the son of Amon, king of Judah, in the thirteenth year of his reign [approximately 626 B.C.]. [The Word of the Lord] came also in the days of Jehoiakim, the son of Josiah, king of Judah." Josiah was the last good and godly king of Judah. Actually, before Jehoiakim, Jehoahaz reigned for three months. Perhaps his name is omitted because his reign was so brief and not particularly significant.

Verse 3 continues, "until the end of the eleventh year of Zedekiah, the son of Josiah, king of Judah." Again, before the reign of Zedekiah, Jehoiachin reigned for the short space of three months. Verse 3 concludes, "until the exile of Jerusalem in the fifth month." Of course, this catastrophic event occurred in 586 B.C. This means that Jeremiah's public ministry covered a period of about forty years, not counting his ministry in Jerusalem and Judah *after* 586 B.C. and his ministry in Egypt. If those were included, another five to ten years should be added.

JEREMIAH'S CALL AND APPOINTMENT (1:4-5)

Jeremiah's call and appointment to the prophetic office occurred in 626 B.C.; verse 4 refers back to verse 2, the thirteenth year of Josiah's reign. Verse 5 indicates when Jeremiah was called from the divine viewpoint, and appointed to the prophetic office. "Before I formed you in the womb I knew you, and before you were born I consecrated you; I have appointed you a prophet to the nations." In the synonymous parallelism of the beautiful poetry of this verse, God informs Jeremiah that, before that historical moment in time when he was born—even before he was formed, shaped, or fashioned in the womb, God did three things: He knew; He sancitifed; and He ordained. Because of the parallelism, these three words are roughly synonymous. But, at the same time, it is possible to make certain distinctions between them. First, God declared, "I knew you". In the Old Testament and, for that matter, in all Semitic usage, "knowing" implies a personal relationship, indeed a very personal inward relation.[3] When used of God toward an individual or nation, it is tantamount to such a close personal relation or interest in the person or nation that it is virtually the same as such other words as "selection," "singling out," or "choice," and that would be a bad translation here: "I chose you." This usage is clear in several other references. In Amos 3:2, God says of the nation of Israel, "You only have I chosen of all the families of the earth." That is to say, "I entered into a very close personal covenant relationship with you," that is, "I had such a personal interest in you that I singled you out; I selected you; I chose you" (see Exod. 33:12; Ps. 144:3). God *chose* His servant Jeremiah.

Second, God said, "I consecrated you." To paraphrase, stressing the root idea of "consecrated": "I *separated* you unto Me,"[4] God said. "I *set* you *apart* for the service or ministry of the prophetic office."

Third, God told Jeremiah, "I appointed you". Actually, the word used here literally means, "to give." But the best translation would be, "I ordained you."[5] Implied in the meaning also is an appointment that carries with it the impartation of spiritual gifts, the necessary gifts for the office. "I appointed thee" in that sense. Then, "I appointed you a prophet (i.e., 'as one called to be my spokesman'[6]) to the nations." The nations are referred to, because Jeremiah's ministry was not restricted to Judah (cf. chaps. 25; 46-51). His ministry encompassed many great nations.

Verse 5 presents the doctrine of divine sovereign election. This is a puzzling and disconcerting doctrine to some, but actually it ought to be a comforting and encouraging doctrine. If a minister of God today has a similar consciousness that, before he was born or even fashioned in the womb, God in His eternal counsels sovereignly elected or chose him, set him apart for the work of the gospel ministry, and appointed him to His service—if he has that kind of conviction, assurance, or consciousness, then this will comfort him more than anything else. It will anchor him, as it did Jeremiah, through all the testings and onslaughts of Satan and will make him a faithful man of God with unshakable convictions. All servants of Christ need to keep the knowledge and awareness of this constantly before them.

JEREMIAH'S RETICENCE (1:6)

Jeremiah's reticence to accept God's call is evident: "Then I said, 'Alas, Lord GOD! Behold, I do not know how to speak, because I am a youth.' " Jeremiah does what other servants of God have done. In the face of such an awesome responsibility and task, he hesitates. He recognizes his weaknesses and lack of qualifications, so he shrinks back. He says, "I cannot speak." Actually, the Hebrew word for "know" is also present in this expression. Literally, it reads: "I do not know how to speak" (i.e., "I do not know *how* to speak"). But the word *know* also often means "to be skilled or experienced in doing something."[7] The idea here, then, is: "I am not experienced in speaking, for I am a child."

"Child" is a poor translation. The word could be better rendered, "young man" or "youth."[8] Perhaps Jeremiah was nineteen or twenty years of age at this time. In this expression he is pleading immaturity, the fact that he is a novice. In this verse, then, is a cry of weakness on the part of Jeremiah before such an awesome responsibility, but not necessarily a cry of unwillingness. He pleads his immaturity and inexperience; he needs to discover that God never calls a man to any work without imparting the necessary gifts and enablement for performing it.

An interesting question could be raised at this point. Why does God often choose the weak (or those who are cognizant of their weakness and who cry out in their hearts, "Who is sufficient for these things?")? The answer is given in 1 Corinthians 1:26-31. God often chooses the weak (in the eyes of men), so that "no man should boast before God" (v. 29). God will not share His glory with another. The reason is also stressed in 2 Corinthians 4:7: "But we have this treasure in earthen vessels, that the surpassing greatness of the power may be of God and not from ourselves." He must receive all the credit, honor, and glory for what is accomplished.

Paul was such a man. Physically, he was weak, and he felt very inadequate and insufficient. In one of those moments of weakness, when he was praying that God would deliver him from whatever physical malady or abnormality plagued him, Christ reassured him with the words of 2 Corinthians 12:9. "My grace is sufficient for you, for My power is perfected in weakness." All of us as believers need to learn to draw our strength daily from God by faith, so that we can constantly experience the truth of Ephesians 3:16, "strengthened with power through His Spirit in the inner man."

JEREMIAH'S REVELATION (1:7-10)

CONCERNING HIS MINISTRY

At this point, God, in response to Jeremiah's hesitation, was pleased to give him a revelation, first, concerning his ministry, particularly the nature of it. "But the LORD said to me, 'Do not say, "I am a youth," because everywhere I send you, you shall go, and all that I command you, you shall speak' " (v. 7). Essentially God declared, "Go where I command, and speak what I say." In other words, "Speak the Word of God." The Word of God was to be central in Jeremiah's ministry. We find too little of this kind of preaching and teaching ministry today. The typical speaker reads a few verses and then merely uses them as a takeoff for whatever *he* wants to say, instead of reading a passage from the Word of God and then sharing with the people what *God* has to say from that passage of Scripture to them and their needs.

Second Timothy 4:2 urges the man of God to "Preach the word." What does that mean? Above everything else, it ought to mean, "Here is a man who preaches and heralds the Word of God, who even in the sometimes necessary changing, adapting, or adjusting of methods and approaches to meet the needs of a changing society, nevertheless adheres to the truths of the Word of God." Just how seriously is this taken in the teaching and preaching of today's ministers? It is possible to discuss some topic, tell some interesting stories, issue an appeal or challenge, and still not preach the Word! Today's minister must never forget that it is only His *own* Word that God has promised to bless.

In this same chapter (v. 12), the Lord said, "I am watching over My word to perform it." In Isaiah 55:11, in a simile, God promised, "So shall my word be that goeth forth out of my mouth; [my word] shall not return unto me void [or "empty"], but [my word] shall accomplish that which I please, and [my word] shall prosper in the thing whereto I sent it" (KJV).＊ This is surely one of the goals or objectives of seminary profes- sors—namely, to equip called and gifted men to expound the Scriptures, and to do it accurately, effectively, and in terms that are relevant to our day. Many people are still hungry for a word from God; they want to hear someone open the Scrip- tures to them and tell them what *God* has to say. Ministers ought not to disappoint them. God's servants must be known, not just as "men of the cloth," but as men of the Book. True men of God are always men of the Book. Jeremiah was, for his was to be a ministry of the Word.

God reassures His prophet. " 'Do not be dismayed before them . . . for I am with you to deliver you,' declares the LORD" (vv. 17*b*, 19*b*). God spoke similar words to Moses, Joshua, and many others. "I am with you." (v. 8). Regardless of the nature of the problems, obstacles, or difficulties a servant of God may encounter in his ministry, these words, "I am with you," should give him backbone, put iron in his blood, and cause him to cry out triumphantly, "If God is for us, who is against us?" (Romans 8:31*b*). On several occasions, men actually sought to have Jeremiah executed, but God kept His promise and rescued His prophet.

CONCERNING HIS MESSAGE (1:9-10)

God was pleased to give Jeremiah a revelation concerning the *general* content of his message. "Then the LORD stretched out His hand and touched my mouth. And the LORD said to me, 'Behold, I have put My words in your mouth' " (v. 9). This statement, made by the Lord, is an explanation of the sym- bolic act in the first part of the verse. That is, the touching of Jeremiah's mouth by God's hand symbolized the fact that God had placed His words in the prophet's mouth. This also points back to verse 6, in which Jeremiah had said, "I do not know how to speak." God's answer is, "I have put My words in your mouth." This, then, is to be the *general* content of his message: "my words." Of course, this verse also has bearing on the doctrine of inspiration—these are inspired words.

＊King James Version.

Then God gave Jeremiah a word concerning the some-
what more *specific* content of his message. The specific content is twofold. First, it was to be a message of destruction—
that is the negative aspect. "I have appointed you this day
over the nations and over the kingdoms, to pluck up [note the
figure of planting] and to break down [note the figure of build-
ing], to destory [referring back to "pluck up" and the figure of
planting] and to overthrow [referring to "break down" and the
figure of building], to build and to plant" (v. 10). In these
verbs, the energy and power of the Word of God is evident, for
it is the ministry of the Word that is in view here. He who
utters the Word destroys and builds with it.

In this same book (Jer. 23:29), God said, "Is not My word
like fire . . . and like a hammer which shatters a rock?" Four
words are used in the negative sense, whereas only two are
employed in the positive sense, evidently because the prophecies threatening destruction and judgment in the book far out-
number those promising construction, hope, and salvation.
But the verse ends with a positive emphasis: "to build and to
plant." From Jeremiah 31:28 it is clear that these words of
construction will find their primary fulfillment and application in the New Covenant.

Preaching or teaching the Word of God is much like building and planting. Those same two figures appear in the new
Testament. In 1 Corinthians 3:11, Paul wrote that "No man
can lay a foundation other than the one which is laid, which is
Jesus Christ." Again, in verse 10, he warned, "Let each man
be careful how he builds upon it." The building is done primarily through a ministry of the Word of God. In 1 Corinthians 3:5-8 the figure is that of planting. If one faithfully sows or
plants the good seed of the Word of God, then someone else, or
perhaps even the sower again, will water it, and God will ultimately give the increase, fruit, or harvest.

God is still calling men for a mission similar to that of
Jeremiah. The question is: will God's ministers today be as
faithful to God and His Word as Jeremiah was? Just how committed are we in our adherence to the Word, both in our personal lives and in our public ministry? If we submit to the
Word, we will be planted and built up. But if we rebel and
refuse to bow to the authority of Scripture, we may be
uprooted and torn down. The writer heartily commends to
today's ministry a minister of the Word of God.

Study it diligently,
Believe it implicitly,
Obey it completely,
Expound it faithfully!

NOTES

1. For an excellent portrayal of the historical setting of the book of Jeremiah, see John Bright, *Jeremiah* (New York: Doubleday, 1965), pp. xxvii-liv.
2. See Ronald F. Youngblood, "The Prophet of Loneliness," *Bethel Seminary Quarterly* 13 (May 1965):3-19.
3. See James Muilenburg, "The Intercession of the Covenant Mediator (Exodus 33:1a, 12-17)," in Peter R. Ackroyd and Barnabas Lindars, eds., *Words and Meanings* (New York: Cambridge U., 1968), pp. 159-81; cf. also the literature cited there in notes on pp. 177-80.
4. Francis Brown, S. R. Driver, and Charles A. Briggs, *A Hebrew and English Lexicon of the Old Testament* (New York: Cambridge U., 1968), p. 873.
5. Ibid., p. 680.
6. For the etymology and meaning of "prophet," see William F. Albright, *From the Stone Age to Christianity*, 2d ed. (Baltimore: Johns Hopkins, 1967), p. 303; Hobart E. Freeman, *An Introduction to the Old Testament Prophets* (Chicago: Moody, 1969), pp. 37-40.
7. Brown, Driver, and Briggs, p. 394.
8. Ibid., p. 655.

12

A Reemphasis on the Purpose of the Sign Gifts

J. Lanier Burns

The charismatic movement continues to grow, despite the repeated warnings of sober students of Scripture. James D. G. Dunn, a leading scholar of contemporary pneumatology, has noted, "Pentecostalism has now become a movement of worldwide importance, reckoned as 'a third force in Christendom' (alongside Catholicism and Protestantism) by not a few leading churchmen."[1] Frederick Bruner, another leading scholar in the field, adds:

> The Pentecostal movement is on the growing edge of the Christian mission in the world today. And while some within the church might find that edge untidy and a few might even question if the movement propelling it may properly be called Christian at all, none can deny that the movement is growing. It is to be recognized that, whether approved by us or not, the Pentecostal movement is in the world with increasing numbers and significance.[2]

In view of the continuing need to deal with Pentecostalism this article will seek to reaffirm the true purpose of sign gifts and to introduce 1 Corinthians 1:4-9 as fresh confirmation of that purpose.

One of the primary refutations of the Pentecostal movement through the years has been the purpose of the sign gifts

J. Lanier Burns
A.B., Davidson College; Th.M., Th.D., Dallas Theological Seminary
Assistant Professor of Systematic Theology
Dallas Theological Seminary

as revealed in Scripture. The Pentecostalists believe that even the spectacular gifts were and are given for edification. The refutation has been that at least some gifts were spectacular and extraordinary, and these sign gifts authenticated new special revelation. When special revelation ceased, then the sign gifts ceased as well. In other words, one can be as certain about the cessation of sign gifts as he can about the close of the biblical canon. This was an emphasis of Warfield:

> There is, of course, a deeper principle recognizable here, of which the actual attachment of the charismata of the Apostolic Church to the mission of the Apostles is but an illustration. This deeper principle may be reached by us through the perception, more broadly, of the inseparable connection of miracles with revelation, as its mark and credential; or, more narrowly, of the summing up of all revelation, finally, in Jesus Christ. Miracles do not appear on the page of Scripture vagrantly, here, there, and elsewhere indifferently, without assignable reason. They belong to revelation periods, and appear only when God is speaking to His people through accredited messengers, declaring His gracious purposes. Their abundant display in the Apostolic Church is the mark of the richness of the Apostolic Age in revelation; and when this revelation period closed, the period of miracle-working had passed by also, as a mere matter of course.[3]

Gerlach emphasized the authenticating purpose of tongues.

> Thus glossolalia was a gift given by God, not primarily as a special language for worship; not primarily to facilitate the spread of the gospel; and certainly not as a sign that a believer has experienced a second "baptism in the Holy Spirit." It was given primarily for an evidential purpose to authenticate and substantiate some facet of God's truth. This purpose is always distorted by those who shift the emphasis from objective sign to subjective experience.[4]

The Pentecostalists, to the contrary, have contended that the purpose of all gifts is edification (which is usually the reinforcement of some facet of their spiritual lives such as prayer). The Pentecostal theologian, Ernest Swing Williams, has stated, "Those who have spoken in tongues in private worship and devotion can testify to the enriching, spiritual rest, and refreshing to the soul that results from such communion with God."[5] E. D. O'Connor, a leading Roman Catholic charismatic theologian, has written that the charismata "always seem to be spoken of as a normal function of the Christian life

. . . [in which the Holy Spirit] makes them willing and able to undertake various works for the renewal and upbuilding of the Church."[6] These men have influenced some. For example, Bernard Ramm, though critical of the movement as a whole, has written:

> Obviously some sort of unusual phenomenon took place in the Corinthian church. According to I Corinthians 12-14, and according to the witness of contemporary charismatics or neo-Pentecostals, this speaking in tongues is for worship, edification, and personal devotions. This is apparently the legitimate and proper use of tongues in the Christian fellowship.[7]

But there is ample evidence in Scripture for the view that sign gifts authenticated new revelation. Acts 2:22 reveals that the incarnation inaugurated a new period of attestation. Peter spoke of "Jesus the Nazarene, a man attested to you by God with miracles and wonders and signs which God performed through Him in your midst."[*] Mark 16:20, if genuine, associates confirmation (βεβαιοῦντος) with revelation (λόγον) through signs: "And they went and preached everywhere, while the Lord worked with them, and confirmed the word by the signs that followed." Interestingly, Stephen cited Moses' "wonders and signs" in connection with Moses' receiving the "living oracles" for Israel, which that generation and Stephen's generation were unwilling to obey (Acts 7:36-39, 51). A study of Acts shows that Jews always were present when the phenomena took place, which not only would highlight their particular need for authentication[8] but also would complement the Jewish orientation referred to in 1 Corinthians 14:20-22.[9] Furthermore, the startling effect of the phenomena on those who in difficult circumstances desperately wished otherwise (as in Acts 4:13-16; 10:28-29; 11:1-3, 15-18; and 15:1-12) supports the purpose of authentication (and not edification) for the sign gifts.

A frequently cited passage that confirms the above is Hebrews 2:2-4. This sentence was a solemn warning to its Jewish readers not to treat lightly revelation (cf. τοῖς ἀκουσθεῖσιν and λόγος) concerning salvation, which had been revealed by Christ and had been authenticated by apostolic eyewitnesses

---

[*]All Scripture quotations in this article, except those noted otherwise, are from the *New American Standard Bible*.

as well as by God Himself through the apostolic signs, wonders, miracles, and μερισμοῖς of the Holy Spirit.[10] The emphasis
of the passage is captured by James Moffatt.

> If the Sinaitic Law ἐγένετο βέβαιος, the Christian revelation was
> also confirmed or guaranteed to us . . . . It reached us, accurate
> and trustworthy. No wonder, when we realize the channel along
> which it flowed. It was authenticated by the double testimony of
> men who had actually heard Jesus, and of God who attested
> and inspired them in their mission.[11]

Thus these verses contain all essential elements of the non-
Pentecostal emphasis: subject (new revelation), scope in time
(Christ and the apostles), and purpose (authentication).

Two implications of this passage may be emphasized.
First, the recipients of the phenomena seemed to be clear to
the author and his audience. They were the first-generation
associates of Christ, and the author seems to have had no one
outside that circle to cite.[12] In support of this point the aorist
ἐβεβαιώθη would seem to indicate that from the author's perspective the phenomena were already a matter of history. This
is convincing evidence for the temporary, limited nature of the
miraculous phenomena and some of the gifts. "Thus the book
is addressed to second generation Christians," concludes
Robert Lightner, "the point being that Christians of the first
generation experienced some things even the second generation Christians did not."[13]

Second, the phenomena apparently were well known in
spite of their limited circulation. The εἰς ἡμᾶς would suggest
their personal familiarity with and possible knowledge of the
authenticating purpose as Jews. That is, the author seems to
be reminding them in exhortation rather than teaching them
about these matters. Bruce has set forth this implication well.

> The New Testament writers . . . would not have appealed to the
> evidence of these miraculous manifestations if there was any
> possibility that their readers would reply that they had never
> seen or heard of such things. They were matters of common
> knowledge and widespread Christian experience, and the refer-
> ence to them here is calculated to restore the reader's faith in the
> gospel as God's authoritative message.[14]

It would seem that the case could be closed at this point.
Have we not demonstrated that the sign gifts according to purpose authenticated revelation and according to time were temporary? Many would agree, but a surprising number would

disagree. The writers noted earlier (Williams, O'Connor, Ramm, etc.) among others would cite 1 Corinthians 12-14 as indicating most strongly that sign gifts (especially glossolalia) were for edification. Thus it is important to determine whether this letter's teaching is consistent with or distinctive from the nature and purpose of sign gifts as established elsewhere in Scripture.

Two lines of evidence indicate that it is consistent. First, 1 Corinthians 14:22-25, according to Hodges, teaches that tongues were a final gracious sign to rouse the nation to repentance.[15] Beyond Hodges's argument it may be noted that σημεῖαν here are by nature "miracles and wonders by which God authenticates the men sent by him, or by which men prove that the cause they are pleading is God's"[16] (as in 1 Cor. 1:22 and 2 Cor. 12:12). The objects of the sign in the letter were Jewish unbelievers as demonstrated by 1:22 ('Ιουδαῖοι) and 14:21 (τῷ λαῷ τούτῳ). And the purpose of the sign in 14:20-25 was to admonish[17] Jewish unbelievers (14:21-22a) by demonstrating that the new revelation (προφητεία) in the church was of God (22b-25) and by showing them their need for affiliation with it through faith in Christ (cf. 1:18-25). It seems that tongues exemplify all essential elements of the sign gifts here as to their nature, purpose, and object.

A second line of evidence has seldom been discussed. This evidence concerns Paul's introductory sentence in 1 Corinthinas 1:4-9 as a governing consideration for his later discussion of spiritual gifts. The main thought here is Paul's thankfulness for God's grace in their lives (v. 4). The flow of the following verses is that Paul's μαρτύριον was accompanied and authenticated by spiritual gifts (χαρίσματι, v. 7) with the effect that they received the grace (χάριτι, v. 4) of God by faith and were enriched by apostolic doctrine (v. 5).

Of special interest is Paul's use of χάρισμα, which is used only here in 1:7 and in 7:7 before chapter 12 (12:4, 9, 28, 30-31). One must begin by understanding Paul's nuance here. Does χάρισμα in 1:7 refer to salvation through Christ (Rom. 5:15; 6:23), divine favor in general (2 Cor. 1:11), or spiritual gifts (1 Cor. 12)? Many commentators prefer "divine favor in general" because of the emphasis on the Corinthians' state of grace in verses 4 and 8.[18] However, it seems best to view χαρίσματι as spiritual gifts (1 Cor. 12-14) in view of Paul's later preoccupation with that subject in the same letter. Μηδενὶ thus would mean that they had experienced not only the edifying gifts but also the sign gifts in confirmation of new revelation. This is supported by the specific contextual tie of ὥστε in 1:7 to ἐβεβαιώθη.[19] That is, their need for confirmation of truth resulted in the manifestation of extraordinary sign gifts in addition to normal functional gifts. It also seems that revelation was confirmed as it was progressively revealed to them (καθώς). In Paul's construction Christ's confirmation (βεβαιώσει) is analogous to the gifts' confirmation (καί), but it does not govern the preceding syntactically. Furthermore, if χαρίσματι refers to mere divine favor, as Robertson and Plummer suggest, it seems strange that they preferred the meaning, "brought home to your deepest conviction as true by the witness of the Spirit," for ἐβεβαιώθη (v. 6).[20] That meaning is more consistent with the specific nuance suggested in this article than with the meaning of "divine favor." Ironically, the view of confirmation has been summarized best by Robertson and Plummer in their paraphrase of Paul's words.

> These gifts ye received in exact proportion to the completeness with which our testimony to the Messiah was brought home to your hearts and firmly established there; so that (as we may hope from this guarantee) there is not a single gift of grace in which you find yourselves to be behind other Churches, while you are loyally and patiently waiting for the hour when our Lord Jesus Christ shall be revealed.[21]

In this case the gifts authenticated τὸ μαρτύριον τοῦ χριστοῦ (1:5). While the subjective genitive ("testimony of Christ"; cf. Heb. 2:3) is not impossible, the objective genitive ("testimony about or concerning Christ") is best here. Probably verses like 2:2 and 15:3-4 are in the near background of Paul's mind as he wrote this epistle. The revelational aspect of μαρτύριον is strengthened by the ἀποκάλυψιν which follows in 1:7. Paul's thought seems to be that this revelation about Christ has been authenticated by gifts as a normative and inviolable basis for living, so that with assurance believers can anticipate His personal ἀποκάλυψιν (15:52-58). Therefore once again all important elements of the sign gifts are present; spiritual gifts (ἐν μηδενὶ χαρίσματι) in authentication (ἐβεβαιώθη) of revelation (τὸ μαρτύριον τοῦ χριστοῦ).

The implication of this interpretation is significant. Paul gives us the clue at the beginning of his letter as to his view of the purpose and function of the χαρίσματα (or at least some of them), and chapters 10-12 could hardly be considered apart from this. In other words, there is no reason to doubt that sign gifts such as tongues were *edifying in result* (14:4-5), but there is every reason to doubt that they were *for the explicit purpose of edification*. The fact that 1:22 and 14:20-25 are in accord with this would make any alternative extremely tenuous. But if the sign gifts were for authentication of new revelation for Jewish unbelievers, then there is no possibility for their existence today unless the canon is open for new revelation for the same audience. Ryrie has concluded:

> Consequently, then, it does not follow that if one considers the gifts of miracles and healings temporary, he also is saying that God does not perform miracles or heal today. He is simply saying that the gifts are no longer given because the particular purpose for which they were originally given (i.e., to authenticate the oral message) has ceased to exist.[22]

One may conclude from this study that the enduring argument against Pentecostalism concerning the authenticating purpose of the sign gifts should be stated with fresh conviction. The argument is grounded in clear and consistent statements of Scripture from several New Testament authors. Careful exegesis indicates that 1 Corinthians is consistent with Hebrews 2:3-4 and Acts. There seems to be no basis for saying that there is a different nature and purpose of sign gifts in the respective books. First Corinthians 1:4-9 and 14:20-25 (cf. 1:22) are consistent with each other and with the rest of Scripture. Only by allowing one's experience to govern his view of the passages could a different conclusion be reached.

NOTES

1. James D. G. Dunn, *Baptism in the Spirit* (London: SCM, 1970), p. 2.
2. Frederick Dale Bruner, *A Theology of the Holy Spirit* (Grand Rapids: Eerdmans, 1970), p. 19.
3. Benjamin B. Warfield, *Counterfeit Miracles*, reprint (London: Banner of Truth Trust, 1972), pp. 25-26.
4. Joel C. Gerlach, "Glossolalia," *Wisconsin Lutheran Quarterly* 70(October 1973):251. See also John F. Walvoord, *The Holy Spirit at Work Today* (Chicago: Moody, 1973), p. 41.
5. Edwin Swing William, *Systematic Theology*, 3 vols. (Springfield, Mo.: Gospel Publishing, 1953), 3:50.
6. E. D. O'Connor, *The Pentecostal Movement in the Catholic Church* (Notre Dame: Ave Maria, 1971), pp. 280, 283. See also John Sherrill, *They Speak with Other Tongues* (Old Tappan, N.J.: Revell, 1964), pp. 79-88, for the same emphasis from a popular vantage point.

One of the most overt statements is found in the catalog of Oral Roberts University: "The baptism of the Holy Spirit is an experience which brings an enduement of Christ's power to the Christian, the ability of edifying himself in the inner man through 'devotional' tongues and which subsequently pray more effectively through his intellect . . . .This experience is available to all believers (Acts 2:38). However, the baptism of the Holy Spirit with the Spirit-given ability to pray and praise God in tongues in one's private and personal devotions IS NOT THE GIFT OF TONGUES. The Gift of Tongues is one of the nine gifts of the Spirit . . . .The nine gifts are resident in the Holy Spirit and are manifested by Him (as He wills) through the believer to meet special needs and bring help and profit to the body of Christ (1 Cor. 12:7-11)" (Tulsa, Okla.: Oral Roberts University Catalog, 1973), pp. 26-27.

7. Bernard Ramm, *Rapping About the Spirit* (Waco, Tex.: Word, 1974), p. 115.

8. A God-fearing Jew faced a dilemma, for he was faced with new truth in place of his already authenticated Scripture, which had been revered from the time of Moses.

9. Other evidence from Acts supporting the same conclusion is given by S. Lewis Johnson, Jr., "The Gift of Tongues and the Book of Acts," *Bibliotheca Sacra* 120(July-September 1963):309-11.

10. The idea is that the eyewitness testimony was sufficient confirmation (ἐβεβαιώθη) but above and beyond that God "joined them in the authentication" (συνεπιμαρτυρέω) through the miraculous phenomena. Bruce cites the usual and best interpretation of μερισμοῖς: "The reference then is to God's distribution of spiritual gifts to His people" (F. F. Bruce, *Commentary on the Epistle to the Hebrews*, The New International Commentary on the New Testament [Grand Rapids: Eerdmans, 1964], p. 30).

11. James Moffatt, *A Critical and Exegetical Commentary on the Epistle to the Hebrews*, The International Critical Commentary (Edinburgh: T. & T. Clark, 1924), p. 19.

12. Hebrews is usually placed in the mid to late sixties (cf. Bruce, pp. xlii-xliv).

13. Robert P. Lightner, *Speaking in Tongues and Divine Healing* (Des Plaines, Ill.: Regular Baptist, 1965), p. 31.

14. Bruce, pp. 30-31.

15. Zane C. Hodges, "The Purpose of Tongues," *Bibliotheca Sacra* 120(July-September 1963):226-33.

16. Joseph Henry Thayer, *Greek-English Lexicon of the New Testament Being Grimm's Wilke's Clavis Noti Testamenti*, rev. ed. (Grand Rapids: Zondervan, 1962), pp. 573-74.

17. Ibid.

18. Archibald Robertson and Alfred Plummer, *A Critical and Exegetical Commentary on the First Epistle of St. Paul to the Corinthians*, The International Critical Commentary, 2d ed. (Edinburgh: T. & T. Clark, 1914), p. 7.

19. The force of ἐβεβαιώθη with the personal ἐν ὑμῖν has been brought out by Schlier: "The σημεῖα do not prove the validity of the λόγος; they are a way in which the valid Logos is more forcefully put into effect. This gives us the clue to 1 C. 1:6; In the Corinthian community the μαρτύριον τοῦ χριστοῦ has been given legal force by the apostles, even to the institution of rich χαρίσματα." (Heinrich Schlier, in *Theological Dictionary of the New Testament*, ed. Gerhard Kittel and Gerhard Friedrich, 10 vols. (Grand Rapids: Eerdmans, 1964-1976), s.v., "βέβαιος," 1(1964):603.

20. Robertson and Plummer, p. 6

21. Ibid., p. 4.

22. Charles Caldwell Ryrie, *The Holy Spirit* (Chicago: Moody, 1965), p. 87.

13

The Unifying Theme of the Epistle of James

D. Edmond Hiebert

The epistle of James is notoriously difficult to outline. This is confirmed by the great diversity of the outlines that have been proposed. They range all the way from two[1] to twenty-five[2] major divisions. The epistle itself does not herald any clear structural plan concerning the organization of its contents. Hendriksen well remarks, "A superficial glance at this epistle may easily leave the impression that every attempt to outline it must fail."[3]

This impression that the epistle lacks any unifying theme for its contents is strengthened by the peculiar practice of James of connecting sentences by the repetition of a leading word or one of its cognates. As an illustration, note 1:3-6: "endurance" (v. 3)*—"endurance" (v. 4); "lacking in nothing" (v. 4)—"if any of you lacks" (v. 5); "let him ask" (v. 5)—"but let him ask" (v. 6); "without any doubting" (v. 6)—"the one who doubts" (v. 6). See also 1:12-15, 21-25; 3:2-8; 4:1-3. The brief paragraphs, the rapid shift of thought, and the

D. Edmond Hiebert
A.B., John Fletcher College; Th.M., Th.D. Southern Baptist Theological Seminary
Professor Emeritus of New Testament
Mennonite Biblical Seminary
Fresno, California

*All Scripture quotations in this article, except those noted otherwise, are from the *New American Standard Bible.*

apparent diversity of themes further support the impression that the epistle is disjointed and lacks a unifying theme.

The disjointed character of its contents is stressed by scholars who view this book as simply another example of "parenesis." "It was characteristic of parenesis," Songer remarks, "to place together in loose organization a series of exhortations without any concern to develop one theme or line of thought in the entire writing."[4] The term *paraenesis* or *parenesis*, derived from the Greek παραίνεσις means "exhortation, advice, counsel" (cf. Acts 27:9, 22). As applied to a written work, the *Oxford English Dictionary* defines it as "a hortatory composition." In modern usage it denotes material characterized by ethical instruction and exhortation.

Those who view the epistle of James as typical parenetic literature hold that no unifying theme should be expected; it should rather be accepted as a collection of miscellaneous exhortations devoid of any intentional unity. Thus Goodspeed describes the epistle as "just a handful of pearls, dropped one by one into the hearer's mind."[5] And Hunter, recalling that the epistle had been called "an ethical scrapbook," concludes that "it is so disconnected, as it stands, that it is the despair of the analyst."[6]

But others, not yielding to despair, discern some measure of organizational unity in holding that James discusses several independent themes. Scroggie asserts that this epistle "has no one subject as have most of the epistles, more than a dozen themes being treated almost disconnectedly," and goes on to remark, "The nature and variety of these subjects suggest that they are abstracts of sermons which James had preached at Jerusalem."[7] Shepherd sees the epistle as consisting of "a series of eight homiletic-didactic discourses" with each discourse developing a principle theme linked together by "skilful use of word-links and thematic recapitulations."[8] Similarly Barker, Lane, and Michaels hold that this epistle is a series of "sermonic expansions of certain sayings of Jesus" and that in it "four brief homilies or messages have been merged into one: on temptation (1:2-18), on the law of love (1:19-2:26), on evil speaking (3:1-4:12), and on endurance (4:13-5:20)."[9]

The suggestion that the contents of this book originally had a sermonic origin is very probable. But the view that James, the dynamic leader of the Jerusalem church, should dispatch such a heterogeneous compilation of sermonic materials as his official message to his readers seems less probable.

Still others hold that all of the epistle of James does indeed relate to a single theme that gives it an unobstrusive unity. This unifying thrust of the epistle is obviously ethical rather than doctrinal. Kee, Young, and Froehlich identify this unifying thrust as follows: "The whole epistle is concerned with one simple truth: It is not enough to 'be' a Christian, if this fact does not show in one's conduct."[10] McNeile identifies this unifying thread of the epistle as "the obvious but important truth that a man's faith, his attitude toward God, is unreal and worthless if it is not *effective,* if it does not *work* practically in life."[11] And Lenski well identifies the unifying theme of the epistle when he asserts, "This entire epistle deals with Christian faith, and shows how this faith should be genuine, true, active, living, fruitful."[12]

The epistle of James has much to say about faith. The noun *faith* ($\pi\iota\sigma\tau\iota\varsigma$) occurs sixteen times[13] and the verb *believe* ($\pi\iota\sigma\tau\epsilon\acute{\upsilon}\omega$) three times.[14] But a glance at the contents of the epistle makes it obvious that James is not concerned with developing a theological exposition of the nature of Christian faith. He holds that a saving faith accepts Jesus Christ as the all-sufficient Savior (1:1; 2:1), but otherwise he says but little about the theological content of such a faith. His purpose is practical rather than doctrinal.

The purpose of James is to goad his readers to recognize and accept their need for a living, active faith and to challenge them to test their own faith by the basic criterion that "faith without works is useless" (2:20). James insists that a saving faith is a living faith, proving its genuineness by what it does. But it is a misconception to assume that his purpose is simply to stress the importance of good works. James is not advocating works apart from faith, but he is vitally concerned to show that a living faith must demonstrate its dynamic character by its deeds.

The contents of the epistle, further, make it clear that James is not content simply to establish the abstract truth that a saving faith is a dynamic, productive faith. His purpose is practical, to present a series of tests whereby his readers can determine the genuineness of their own faith. "The testing of your faith" (1:3) seems to be the key that James left hanging at the front door, intended to unlock the contents of the book. I propose that *tests of a living faith* is indeed the unifying theme of the epistle and that it provides ready access to its contents.

A SURVEY OF JAMES

The opening salutation (1:1) stamps this document as an epistolary communication. Whatever may have been the initial use of this material, the author now employs that material to achieve his epistolary purpose. He is intent on meeting the needs of his readers.

In 1:2-18 James states and discusses his theme. This section is basic to a proper understanding of the thrust of the epistle. For James "faith," the subject of his opening sentence (1:2-3), is central to the Christian life and its true energizing principle. It is essential, therefore, that its genuineness be tested. "The testing of your faith" (1:3) marks the basic thrust of the message. The Greek noun πειρασμός has a double meaning, "testing" and "temptation." Since in human experience the two aspects are often related, James discusses both in this opening section. In verses 2-12 he deals with the tests and trials of believers, whereas in verses 13-16 he discusses the nature of temptation and then shows that it cannot come from God in view of His beneficient activities in human experience (1:17-18).

In order to profit from the testings of their faith, believers must rightly evaluate their testings (1:2-4). Prayer makes available to them the needed wisdom to profit from their testings (1:5); but such prayer must be unmixed with doubt and hesitancy (1:6-8). The testing of their faith equalizes believers (1:9-11), and successful endurance assures future reward (1:12).

In human experience testing and temptation are often closely related. Temptation has its source in lustful human nature and must not be blamed on God (1:13-14). Its nature and results (1:15-16) prove that it is not from God who acts beneficently in human experience (1:17-18). His greatest gift to man is His work of regeneration through His Word.

Having identified and discussed his theme, in the remainder of the epistle James develops a series of tests whereby the readers may seek to purify their own faith.

FAITH TESTED BY ITS RESPONSE TO THE WORD OF GOD
(1:19-27)

Since God's Word is the means of regeneration (1:18), a right response to the Word is appropriately presented as the initial test of a vital faith. For the believer to accept regeneration through the Word is one thing; to permit the Word to work spiritual maturity in him is another.

The necessary response is threefold: eagerness to hear it, restraint on any premature reaction, bridling of any angry rejection (1:19-20). Before the Word can have full sway in the believer's life, he must remove all that hinders its operation (1:21).

Acceptance of the Word must be followed by persistent obedience to the Word (1:22-27). Hearing must be followed by active obedience; otherwise the hearing is useless (1:22-25). But obedience to the Word is more than mere observance of outward forms of "religion" (church attendance, rote prayers, participation in the rites of religion), without the development of inner power to control the tongue (1:26). True obedience to the Word must reveal itself in beneficient social activity and stimulate personal self-control and purity in separation from worldly contamination (1:27).

FAITH TESTED BY ITS REACTION TO PARTIALITY (2:1-13)

The second test of a living faith, as an unfolding of "pure and undefiled religion" (1:27), is drawn from the worship services of James's readers. James administers a stinging rebuke for holding "faith in our glorious Lord Jesus Christ with an attitude of personal favoritism" (2:1). Their partiality, vividly pictured in verses 2-3, must be stopped as inconsistent with Christian faith.

The evil consequences of their partiality are expounded in verses 5-11. It is a false reaction toward both the rich and the poor (2:5-7) and is a breach of the law of love (2:8-11). Their act of partiality breaks the law of love and makes them guilty of violating the purpose of the whole law as an expression of God's will.

Their faith demands a life in accordance with "the law of liberty" (2:12-13). They must obey the liberating law of love in word and deed in view of the coming judgment. The practice of mercy, giving a man what he needs and not what he deserves, will reveal that God's grace has produced a transformation in their own lives.

FAITH TESTED BY ITS PRODUCTION OF WORKS (2:14-26)

Faith and works are mentioned together ten times in this paragraph, but the stress throughout is on their interrelationship. The rhetorical questions of verse 14 state the theme of this further test. A saving faith is a working faith, proving its vitality by its production of works.

James insists that an inactive faith is useless (2:14-17). The rendering, "Can faith save him?" (KJV)* confuses the point of this test. The question is literally, "Can that faith save him" (i.e., a faith without works), and the question implies a strong *no* answer. Not faith, but an inoperative faith, is disparaged. Verses 15-16 vividly illustrate such a faith, and verse 17 states the categorical conclusion.

James further insists that even an orthodox creed apart from works is barren (2:18-20). The interpretation of verse 18 is problematic. From the context it is clear that James insists that even an orthodox, monotheistic faith, if it does not motivate conduct, is demonic (2:19). The faith of the demons stirs their feelings but does not change their conduct. James challenges his opponent to recognize that a faith which does not produce works is "useless," barren like a field that produces no crop (2:20).

Verses 21-25 establish from Scripture that saving faith manifests itself in works. The proof is drawn from the stories of Abraham (2:21-24) and Rahab (2:25). James is not teaching that salvation is partly by faith and partly by works. Rather, both were justified by their faith, but their faith demonstrated its living nature in what it enabled them to do.

The analogy in verse 26 states the essence of this test of a living faith. As a body without the spirit of life in it is dead, so a profession of faith without deeds is lifeless. An inactive faith, entombed in an intellectually approved creed, has no more saving power than a lifeless corpse.

FAITH TESTED BY ITS PRODUCTION OF SELF-CONTROL (3:1-18)

In chapter 3, a self-contained unit, James insists that a living faith must operate in the inner life of the believer, pro-

---

*King James Version.

ducing self-control. And this self-control is most readily tested by one's use of his tongue.

Verses 1-2 stress the importance of a controlled tongue. It is of special importance for the teacher; because of his tremendous influence, conveyed through the tongue, he will be held more strictly accountable (3:1). Since all believers stumble, all need self-control (3:2). Perfect control of the tongue is the mark of a mature man, one able to exercise control in all areas of his life.

Verses 3-6 establish the importance of a controlled tongue. Two illustrations demonstrate the importance and need for properly applied control (3:3-4), whereas verse 5a applies the principle to the boasting tongue. Verses 5b-6 illustrate the damage of an uncontrolled tongue. It is an aggressive and destructive force if left uncontrolled.

Man's natural inability to control the tongue is illustrated and affirmed in verses 7-8. Human nature has asserted control over all kinds of creatures, but effective control of the tongue is an impossible human achievement. Its restless nature and deadly impact make this so tragic.

James rebukes the inconsistency of an uncontrolled tongue (3:9-12). It is a veritable Dr. Jekyll and Mr. Hyde. Such inconsistent usage is utterly unfit for believers (3:10b). The world of nature is not guilty of such duplicity (3:11-12).

The tongue of man does not operate independently; its use reveals the inner spirit in control. Verses 13-18 discuss the two types of "wisdom" competing for control of man's tongue. "Wisdom" is more than intellectual apprehension; it is a moral quality, enabling man to make moral evaluations and decisions in life.

Challenging his readers to identify a "wise and understanding" man in their midst (3:13), James identifies the nature and results of the two spirits seeking to control the inner man. Verses 14-16 describe the marks, nature, and results of the false "wisdom" in control; by contrast verses 17-18 delineate the results when heavenly wisdom is in control of the believer's tongue. Its seven characteristics (3:17) as well as its fruit (3:18) establish that a saving faith must be controlled by such a heavenly wisdom.

FAITH TESTED BY ITS REACTIONS TO WORLDLINESS (4:1-5:12)

Since faith is a matter of trust or dependence on something or someone outside oneself, one's center of dependence in actual life is of crucial importance. Worldliness places self or the things of the world at the center of his aspirations and activities. "The worldly person is the self-centered person."[15] Worldliness manifests itself in various and often subtle ways among believers. Four specific manifestations of worldliness are treated by James.

Worldliness manifested through strife and faction (4:1-12). The quarrels and conflicts of believers are evidence of their worldliness (4:1-3). Their self-centered pleasures are like soldiers going to war against those who thwart the fulfillment of their selfish desires. Two parallel sets of consequences delineate the outcome of their worldliness (4:2a). The two series are clearly marked by the punctuation in the *New American Standard Bible*. Two incriminating reasons, standing side by side as alternative explanations, explain their turbulent relations (4:2b-3).

In verses 4-6 worldliness is sharply rebuked. It is in reality spiritual adultery (4:4). Cultivation of the "friendship with the world," the masses of unredeemed humanity in their self-centered indifference or hostility to God, proves that God does not have the believer's undivided allegiance. It is a position of acting as an enemy of God. Such an attitude violates the teaching of Scripture (4:5a) and evokes God's jealousy (4:5b). He jealously yearns for the believer's undivided attention and in grace desires his return (4:6).

Verses 7-12 are a ringing exhortation to worldly-minded believers. They must resume a right relationship to God (4:7-10). Verse 7 states the basic requirement, while verses 8-10 elaborate the specific demands for a return to a right relationship with God. They must also resume a right relationship to their brethren by terminating their censoriousness toward one another (4:11-12).

Worldliness manifested through presumptuous planning (4:13-17). The worldliness here censured is that of presumptuous planning in independence from God. James is not condemning intelligent planning for the future; he is rebuking that arrogant planning which formulates its course of action in disregard of God. "Come now" (4:13) calls for attention to what follows. Verses 13-14 rebuke the wrong attitude. It is the picture of the self-confident businessman projecting his course of action for a whole year in advance. He arrogantly assumes that the unknown future is under his control.

Verse 15 points out the proper attitude: There must be a willing submission to God's will, involving not only one's continued life but also one's future planned activities.

The present attitude of James's readers is evil because of their arrogance (4:16). They presume to control the future in independence of God. It is a failure to conform their conduct to their professed relationship to God. Knowledge of what is right and the ability to do it involves obligation; failure to do it is sin (4:17).

Worldliness manifested in wrong reaction to injustice (5:1-11). The two parts of this section stand in remarkable contrast. In verses 1-6 James utters a stinging prophetic denunciation of the cruelty and oppression of the world, while verses 7-11 aim at safeguarding believers against a worldly reaction to such experiences of injustice. James strongly denounces social injustices but is concerned that believers maintain a proper attitude and perspective amid such injustices. They test the believer's faith.

The denunciation of the oppressive rich (5:1-6) is in the spirit of the Old Testament prophets. James gives no indication that he regards these rich persons as being Christians. He gives no call to repentance but simply an announcement of impending doom.

Verse 1 announces the fact of impending judgment and the resultant emotional reactions. The impact of the judgment is described in verses 2-3. Their wealth in its various forms will have lost its value and will be a means of torment for their possessors. Three charges are made against them: their oppression of the laborers (5:4), their self-indulgence (5:5), and their violent treatment of the unresisting righteous individual (5:6).

James next counsels and encourages his afflicted brethren (5:7-11). He urges patience and inner stability in view of the expected return of the Lord (5:7-8), warns against unjustified complaints and irritability against fellow believers (5:9), and encourages them with examples of past suffering and endurance under affliction (5:10-11).

Worldliness manifested in self-serving oaths (5:12). Those who see no unifying theme in this epistle find "not the remotest connection between this verse and the section that has gone just before."[16] Minear would explain this lack of connection as due to the fact that "we are dealing with an unor-

ganized jumble of oral tradition which the editor felt no pressure to reorder into a smoother literary sequence."[17] But those
who reject the view that its contents constitute "an unorgan-
ized jumble"and accept a unifying theme for the whole epistle
find there is reason and significance in the inclusion of this
exhortation at this point.

The words "but above all" seem best understood as mark-
ing the conclusion of a line of thought which James has been
pursuing and call for attention to this important concluding
matter. Having censured three different manifestations of
worldliness (4:1-5:11), this exhortation deals with the spirit of
worldliness in one of its most reprehensible forms. The Jews
had learned the fine art of concealing the truth under an oath
with their hair-splitting distinctions between binding and
nonbinding oaths (Matt. 5:33-37; 23:16-22). Such self-serving
oaths, used to hide the truth by appearing to appeal to God to
establish the truth, were totally inconsistent with Christian
honesty. The truthfulness of their word must stand open and
unquestioned.

FAITH TESTED BY ITS RESORT TO PRAYER (5:13-18)

James brings his tests of a living faith to a logical conclusion by insisting that Christian faith finds its center and
power in a vital relationship with God in prayer in all the
experiences of life (5:13). Prayer constitutes the very heart of a
vital Christian faith.

In verses 14-16a this response is specifically applied to
the experience of physical sickness. The "sick," the one physically weak, is to take the initiative by summoning "the
elders," the recognized leaders of the local church. Their
prayer for the sick is to be offered in connection with an act of
anointing with oil, probably as an aid to faith. From verse 15
it is clear that the prayer, not the oil, is viewed as the healing
means. "The prayer offered in faith" (5:15) apparently
denotes a prayer prayed in the Spirit-wrought conviction that
it is God's will to heal the one prayed for. The sickness may be
due to sin, but the construction in the original makes it clear
that this is not always the case. The results of prayer
encourage the practice of mutual confession and prayer
(5:16a). This practice removes any possible hindrance to the
free operation of God's power.

In verses 16b-18 James encourages the practice of prayer

through his positive assertion of its power (5:16b) and his illustration of its mighty impact (5:17-18).

The last two verses (5:19-20) seem best viewed as forming a conclusion to the entire epistle. "If any among you strays from the truth" (5:19) seems to take a final look at the various evils James has censured in the entire epistle. The verb "turns him back" (ἐπιστρέφω) seems best understood as relating to a believer who has erred from the path of God's truth. Such straying is a serious matter. The one acting to restore the erring one is assured that he has saved his erring brother and thereby a multitude of sins are covered, rather than exposed to open judgment (5:20).

SUMMARY

This survey of James suggests that the key found hanging at the front door is indeed the proper key to unlock the structure of the epistle. The use of the key, tests of a living faith (1:3), has readily unlocked the door and given ready access to its various chambers. Not only does it give ready access to all parts of the house but it also brings into conscious display the fact of the underlying unity of the whole. Its use gives unity and coherence to the entire epistle. It displays the full harmony of this epistle with the rest of the New Testament. James, like Paul, fully believed in "faith working through love" (Gal. 5:6).

This understanding of the epistle of James heightens its practical and timely message. The author's stern insistence on Christian practice consistent with Christian profession, his open contempt for all sham, and his stinging rebukes of worldliness in its varied forms are notes that are urgently needed in Christendom today. As long as there are professed Christians who are prone to separate profession and practice, the message of this epistle will continue to be relevant.

NOTES

1. Robert G. Gromacki, *New Testament Survey* (Grand Rapids: Baker, 1974), p. 341.
2. Burton Scott Easton and Gordon Poteat, "The Epistle of James," in *The Interpreter's Bible*, ed. George Arthur Buttrick, 12 vols. (New York: Abingdon, 1957).

3. William Hendriksen, *Bible Survey: A Treasury of Bible Information* (Grand Rapids: Baker, 1949), p. 329.
4. Harold S. Songer, "James," in *The Broadman Bible Commentary*, ed. Clifton J. Allen, 12 vols. (Nashville: Broadman, 1972), 12:102.
5. Edgar J. Goodspeed, *An Introduction to the New Testament* (Chicago: U. of Chicago, 1937), p. 290.
6. A. M. Hunter, *Introducing the New Testament* (Philadelphia: Westminster, 1946), p. 96.
7. W. Graham Scroggie, *The Unfolding Drama of Redemption: The Bible as a Whole*, 3 vols. (Grand Rapids: Zondervan, 1970), 3:290.
8. Massey H. Shepherd, Jr., "The Epistle of James and the Gospel of Matthew," *Journal of Biblical Literature* 75 (January-March 1956):41.
9. Glenn W. Barker, William L. Lane, and J. Ramsey Michaels, *The New Testament Speaks* (New York: Harper & Row, 1969), p. 329.
10. Howard Clark Kee, Franklin W. Young, and Karlfried Froehlich, *Understanding the New Testament* (Englewood Cliffs, N.J.: Prentice-Hall, 1965), p. 379.
11. A. H. McNeile, *An Introduction to the Study of the New Testament* (Oxford: Clarendon, 1927), p. 189.
12. R. C. H. Lenski, *The Interpretation of the Epistle to the Hebrews and of the Epistle of James* (Columbus, Ohio: Lutheran Book Concern, 1938), p. 538.
13. 1:3, 6; 2:1, 5, 14 (twice), 17, 18 (thrice), 20, 22 (twice), 24, 26; 5:15.
14. 2:19 (twice), 23.
15. J. A. Moyter, *The Tests of Faith* (London: Inter-Varsity, 1970), p. 82.
16. W. E. Oesterley, "The General Epistle of James," in *The Expositor's Greek Testament*, ed. W. Robertson Nicoll, reprint, 5 vols. (Grand Rapids: Eerdmans, n.d.), 4:472.
17. Paul S. Minear, "Yes or No: The Demand for Honesty in the Early Church," *Novum Testamentum* 13 (January 1971):7.

14

Fellowship and Confession in I John 1:5-10

Zane C. Hodges

It would be difficult to find any single passage of Scripture more crucial and fundamental to daily Christian living than 1 John 1:5-10. For here, in a few brief verses, the "disciple whom Jesus loved" has set forth the basic principles that underlie a vital walk with God. It is always worthwhile, therefore, to examine those principles afresh in order that their truths might be more effectively applied to daily life.

VERSE 5

*"This then is the message which we have heard of him, and declare unto you."** With these words, the apostle John embarks on his first specific exposition of truth in fulfillment of the expressed intention of his prologue (1:1-4). Moreover, he has already stated there that the epistle is based on firsthand knowledge—"that which was from the beginning, which we have heard, which we have seen with our eyes, which we have looked upon, and our hands have handled, of the Word of life" (v. 1). It is therefore in keeping with this guarantee that what he now unfolds is *"the message which we have heard of*

Zane C. Hodges
A.B., Wheaton College; Th.M., Dallas Theological Seminary
Professor of New Testament Literature and Exegesis
Dallas Theological Seminary

*All Scripture quotations in this article are from the King James Version.

[from] *him.''* In other words, the apostle speaks of truth directly communicated to the apostolic circle by the same Savior whom he had heard, seen, and touched.

It will be observed in this connection that verse 5 clearly perpetuates the first-second-third person relationships so plainly visible in verses 1-4. The "we," of course, both in verse 5 and 1-4, can only be an apostolic "we," since the experiences claimed in verse 1 are such as were only enjoyed by those who had direct, personal contact with the Lord Jesus.[1] In particular, the experience of touching Him is most fittingly mentioned since John was himself the one who, at the Last Supper, reclined in Jesus' bosom and leaned back onto His breast to ask the identity of his Lord's betrayer (John 13:23-25). The "you," however, have not themselves had such intimate experiences and must therefore rely on apostolic communication about them. The words, "that which we have seen and heard, declare we unto you, that ye also may have fellowship with us" (v. 3) clearly establish the dependence of the readers on the message of the writer. The "he" of verse 5 is either the Father or the Son, who are mentioned in verse 3, without any effort really being made in verse 5 to distinguish them. Undoubtedly, John thinks of truth that has been disclosed by Christ, but his conception of the unity of Father and Son is too dynamic to allow the "he" to refer exclusively to the one or to the other.[2] Whatever John has heard from the Son, he has heard from the Father as well.[3] Thus, "the message which we have heard from him, and declare unto you" is an apostolic communication to the epistle's readership that has its source in the truth of God as unfolded by the Lord Jesus. This at once establishes its transcendent authority.

"That God is light, and in him is no darkness at all." The precise content of the message is now stated. It is, of course, entirely possible that this profound assertion about the nature and character of God was made in exactly this form by the Lord Himself. After all, there is but a fraction of His ministry recorded in the gospels (cf. John 21:25), and John's insistence in this passage on the theme of *hearing* (vv. 1, 3, 5) would be appropriately carried out if verse 5 recorded a specific utterance of Christ. But in any case it is evident that the Lord's claim to be "the light of the world" (John 8:12; 9:5; 12:46) lies at the foundation of this conception. And since the Son is in

His own person the unique revealer of the Father (John 1:18; 14:9-11), whatever He has disclosed about Himself becomes the basis of a predication about God. If the Son is light, it follows irresistibly that "God is light."

Moreover, the further observation that "in him is no darkness at all" is a consistent development of the strong antithesis between light and darkness that the fourth gospel portrays in the teaching of Jesus (John 3:19, 20; 8:12, 12:35, 46). Indeed, it is so consistent a development that it is hard to think that it was not actually uttered by the Lord at some point in His ministry. Clearly, John is imparting truth that was, at the very least, perfectly at home in the doctrine of his Master.

As has often been pointed out, the light-darkness motif was widely prevalent in the Hellenistic conceptual world of John's day.[4] Moreover, more recently, scholars have learned also of its presence in the thought patterns of the Jewish sectaries of Qumran.[5] But the apostle is not concerned with the analogies and parallels available in contemporary society, but with the divine origin of this affirmation. It was "the message which we have heard of him." And for John, the concepts of light and darkness are, above all, ethical concepts. The truth, which he associates with light, is not merely something to know but also something to do (cf. v. 6; John 3:21). By contrast, darkness is linked with the doing of evil deeds (John 3:19-20). Hence, to affirm that "God is light, and in him is no darkness at all" is to affirm God's absolute holiness and His complete freedom from any taint of evil. It is, in short, a restatement of Jesus' own claim to sinlessness: "Which of you convinceth me of sin?" (John 8:46). And this truth has profound implications for all who claim a personal association with Him.

VERSE 6

"If we say." Here begins a series of three possible affirmations (cf. vv. 8, 10) which, in view of the message just enunciated (v. 5), are false on the lips of those who make them. It is particularly striking and impressive that the writer continues the "we" of verse 5 and of the prologue itself. Taken at face value, the continuation of this "we" demonstrates the intensely personal way in which the truth "we have heard of him" is applied by the apostolic writer to his own and his fellow apostles' experience. Of course, he intends the readers to apply it to themselves as well—the message is something the apostles "declare into you"—but there are no grounds for denying the applicability of the "we" statements to the circle that originally received the message.[6] Verse 6 cannot be divorced from verse 5.

Naturally, the apostle does not affirm that he has made or will make the false statement of this verse. But he does not deny to himself the possiblity. The form of the Greek conditional clause rendered "if we say" is one that expresses a contingency that is, at least theoretically, capable of realization. It is true that some forms of theology regard it as *a priori* impossible that any Christian, much less an apostle, could ever make an assertion like this. But such theology finds no support in the straightforward statement of the text and, indeed, is guilty of an unrealistic view of human nature. But the apostle John was surely a realist, and as one of the disciples who had confidently affirmed unfailing loyalty to their Lord on the eve of His passion (Mark 14:31), he had undoubtedly long since surrendered the facile notion that there were spiritual failures of which he was somehow quite incapable. As a matter of fact, when correctly understood, the false claim of this verse is one of the easiest for even real Christians to make.

"If we say that we have fellowship with him, and walk in darkness." The Greek word for "fellowship" used here, signified most simply some form of mutual sharing or participation by two or more parties.[7] It is clear that, in this context, it is by no means a mere synonym for salvation because already John has stated, in verse 3, that the aim of the apostolic declaration to the readers is that "ye also may have fellowship with us." John is perfectly clear in this epistle that his readership consists of people already converted (cf. 2:12-14; 2:21, 27), yet the goal of the truth he sets before them is "fellowship"—first with the apostles, and, as a result of that with the Father and the Son. "And truly our fellowship is with the Father, and with his Son Jesus Christ" (v. 3). It follows therefore that, for John, "fellowship" must be something more than what his readers have automatically acquired as a result of their new birth. It is, in fact, something that is predicated on apostolic instruction—the things the apostles have seen and heard concerning "the Word of life" (v. 1) and are "sharing" now with their fellow believers (v. 3). Moreover, this connection of "fellowship" with apostolic teaching is a theme that may be traced back to the earliest days of the Christian church. For, on the day of Pentecost, the initial converts of that day are first declared to have "continued stedfastly in the apostles' doctrine" and next in "fellowship" (Acts 2:42). Thus John's thought here has its roots in primitive Christianity. Those who have come to faith in Christ must be taught by the apostles of Christ in order that they may have fellowship with them and with God Himself. It may be laid down, then, as an axiom of Christian experience, that all true "fellowship" is predicated on apostolic doctrine. Today, of course, the Scriptures preserve this apostolic voice and continue to furnish the instruction on which such fellowship is founded.

What precisely is shared in the *fellowship* John speaks of here is not at this point defined. (It will become clearer in v. 7) But the apostle is, however, concerned to show that this *fellowship* cannot occur for us in the darkness. Inasmuch as "God is light, and in him is no darkness at all," it follows inevitably that darkness must be a sphere where God is not, and where the sharing John speaks of is an impossibility.

"If we say that we have fellowship with him, and walk in darkness, we lie, and do not the truth." Should the claim be made—John says, "if *we* should make it!"—that a man moving in the realm of darkness is engaged in an experience of *sharing* with God, two things may be laid down about that claim. First, it is false ("we lie"), and second it exposes a pattern of life inconsistent with divine revelation "we . . . . do not the truth." Thus darkness is revealed to be a sphere where the light of God is inoperative in the life of him who walks there. He insists (whether sincerely or insincerely is not stated) that he is sharing with God, but this does not conform with reality and is consequently a lie. Moreover, the truth of God, which it is obviously the function of light to disclose, is not being actualized in the life. Hence, as to both words and deeds, the individual who makes this claim is devoid of the effective influence of the light on his personal experience. He is accordingly out of touch with Him who is the Light. But since negatives are best understood in the presence of positives (even in the physical world, darkness is simply the absence of light!), verse 6 is best comprehended by comparison with verse 7.

VERSE 7

"But if we walk in the light, as he is in the light, we have fellowship one with another." This verse has often been mis-understood. It is not a statement about the way in which believers may have fellowship with each other.[8] It is transparently the converse of verse 6, in which the subject is fellowship with God. Of course, John has spoken in verse 3 of having fellowship with his readers (the "we-you" relationship), but he has also spoken there of the "we-He" relation: "and truly our fellowship is with the Father, and with his Son Jesus Christ." Plainly, verse 7 deals with this "we-He" relationship, just as did the previous verse. The point is simple: "if we walk" where He is (in Greek, the pronoun "he" is emphatic), then "we" and "he" both share something in common. To put it crisply, believers share the light with Him, and He shares the light with us. "We have fellowship one with another" (better, "with one another").

Thus, the light becomes the foundation of a life ("walk") of sharing with God. Since "God is light" (v. 5), and since "he is in the light" (v. 7), if we do not share this with Him, our Christian experience will be devoid of real fellowship with the One who saved us. There should be no difficulty with this conception. A son may have in him the life of an earthly father because his father begat him, yet if he makes his home at a distance from his father, they will not be able to have shared expereinces. In the same way, a Christian who lives at a moral distance from his heavenly Father loses the privilege of shared experience with God. Walking in the light brings Father and spiritual child into the same moral realm, and that realm itself becomes the foundational experience that they have in common. All other mutual experiences must be built upon this.

It must be noted that John does not say, "if we walk *according to* the light," but "if we walk *in* the light" (italics added). If conformity to the light were the issue, fellowship would be impossible for any except those who were perfectly sinless. For "God is light, and in him is no darkness at all!" It follows, then, that where one is walking in relation to God is the paramount consideration. Another way of putting this is to say that when "we walk in the light," we expose ourselves to God and to His truth. We allow the light to shine on our hearts and lives, and we do not shrink from it into the dark.

The man who walks in darkness, on the other hand, has withdrawn himself from the presence of God and from the luminous reality of His holiness, as the apostles have proclaimed it.

It is precisely for this reason that it becomes easy for a Christian to make the false claim of verse 6. When a believer is consciously doing evil that is contrary to the light of divine truth apostolicly communicated, he may undertake to hide from himself, as well as from others, the intolerable reality of the breach in his communion with God. The psychological defense he attempts to erect may be precisely that of denying that the breach exists. Yet at the same time he is not comfortable in God's presence. Indeed, every Christian knows from experience how difficult it is to pray or read the Word of God when there is a consciousness that we are violating His revealed, specific will. We may claim fellowship, but we are hiding—walking—in the dark!

On the other hand, when our hearts are completely open to God and to all that His Word has, or may, reveal to us or about us—it is then that we are transparently moving in the sphere of light. Apostolic truth—God's truth—thus illumines our lives. This does not involve sinlessness, of course, but a willingness to see sin and to treat it for what it really is. John is quite clear, in fact, that walking in the light does not involve the total absence of failure from our lives. For, after declaring that "if we walk in the light, as he is in the light, we have fellowship with one another," he adds a crucial concomitant reality.

"And the blood of Jesus Christ his Son cleanseth us from all sin." It is of the greatest moment to observe that the verbal statements, "have fellowship" and "cleanseth us," are the same tense and exist as coordinate fulfillments of the condition, "if we walk in the light."[9] That is, while the believer exposes himself openly to God and to God's truth, he experiences both a sharing with God and a cleansing by God. The latter makes the former both reasonable and right, for given the sinfulness of even the best of men—the apostles themselves, in fact—fellowship with a sinless God—in whom "there is not darkness at all"—could only occur if man's unholiness were constantly under the efficacious influence of "the blood of Jesus Christ his Son." This has nothing to do with our initial salvation, which is fully guaranteed to us at the moment of our faith. Rather, it has to do with the righteousness of God in permitting His far-from-perfect children to live in His presence and to share the light where He is. Nothing less than the *blood* of Christ could make this possible, and no Christian has ever enjoyed so much as a single moment of fellowship to which the Savior's sacrifice, in all its value, has not been contemporaneously applied!

VERSE 8

"If we say that we have no sin, we deceive ourselves, and the truth is not in us." The second false assertion now becomes evident. And it is appropriate that it should follow at once John's claim that "the blood of Jesus Christ" is being applied to our sin, even while we "have fellowship" with Him and with His Father. For ironically, while the assertion of verse 6 is most readily made by a man consciously out of fellowship, verse 8 is a tempting claim for the man who has hitherto been walking in the light. For if to walk in the light is to open our hearts to God for whatever He may show us about ourselves, when we for the moment see nothing wrong we may foolishly believe that there is nothing wrong![10] But, says John, that would be a mistake, a self-deception. "We deceive ourselves." The truth itself should teach us our error, for who can contemplate the holiness of a God who is light, and the awfulness of the sacrifice our sin made necessary, without being overwhelmed by the desperate depths of man's unholiness. If then, in the absence of conscious sin, one is able to deduce the absence of any sin, the cross has not gripped him as it ought. When we feel that way, says John—be it ever so briefly—"the truth is not in us." Not that we have not believed the truth, but rather that it is not interwoven into the fabric of our thoughts as it ought to be. It is not *in us* as a controlling force. For no man, in whom God's truth is fully at home, can say even for an instant, "I have no sin." To say that would be to make oneself, for that same instant, without need of "the blood of Jesus Christ his Son."

VERSE 9

"If we confess our sins, he is faithful and just to forgive us our sins, and to cleanse us from all unrighteousness." If it is true, according to verse 8, that one may never at any time claim sinlessness without at the same time deluding himself, it follows quite naturally that he should be ready to acknowledge his sins whenever they appear. It is equally clear that this readiness to confess sin is an integral part of walking in the light. After all, light is the sphere where things appear ("for whatsoever doth make manifest is light"—Eph. 5:13), while darkness is the realm in which reality is hidden. Indeed, the longer one walks exposed to God's character and God's Word, the more one sees by contrast the failures that mar his earthly life. A newly converted believer will not have anywhere near the same sensitivity to sin as one who has walked for years in the presence of God, for the new Christian has just emerged, blinking as it were from a lifetime's experience in the dark. But the longer we are in the light the more we become accustomed to that light, and the more plainly we see the reality it increasingly exposes to our gaze. Not that sin is our major preoccupation there—God is!—but God cannot be truly known apart from an extended, concurrent process of self-discovery. And it is that very self-discovery that forces us to confront our sin and to acknowledge it.

"It we confess our sins, he is faithful and just to forgive us our sins." Strangely, it has recently been denied that this verse could apply to Christians at all on the grounds that Christians are already forgiven and need not ask for what they already have.[11] But this point of view directly contradicts the teaching of our Lord Jesus Christ. Indeed, the writer John himself was among the disciples to whom the Master taught His model prayer. And the Savior had prefaced that prayer with the words "whenever you pray,"[12] and had instructed His followers, after their "day by day" petition for had daily bread, to say: "And forgive us our sins; for we also forgive everyone that is indebted to us" (Luke 11:4). John knew clearly, therefore, that one of the corollaries to that message "we have heard of him, and declare unto you," was his Lord's insistence on the need for daily forgiveness in the lives of His disciples.

Of course forgiveness, on the level at which John is discussing it, must be distinguished clearly from the doctrine of justification. Justification by faith imparts to the believing sinner a perfectly righteous standing before God at the moment he receives Christ (see Rom. 3:21-26; 4:5; etc.), and nothing can be added to this or subtracted from it. But this legal and forensic issue is not the same as the question of fellowship with God within His family. Though the believer in Christ is promised that he "shall not come into judgment" (this is a better rendering than "condemnation" in John 5:24), it should be obvious that the question of family discipline is something different. The familiar illustration of the judge who paid a fine for his own son in court, but was perfectly free to discipline that same son once they got home, carries the point. Every sin of which the believer is guilty has been paid for by the cross of Christ, and thus he can never be summoned before the bar of eternal justice to answer for this, since the Savior has already atoned for it. But as a Father, God is free to set the terms on which His children shall commune with Him and His refusal to commune with the sinning child until confession has occurred is transparently a diving prerogative. Hence, forgiveness, in this context of thought, relates to the restoration of broken fellowship within the household of God.

It is also true that there is a sense in which the believer enjoys a continuing and perfect forgiveness "in Christ" already, so that, for example, Paul could write *"in whom* we have redemption through his blood, the forgiveness of sins" (Eph. 1:7, italics added). But this is a part of a characteristicly Pauline conception whereby he see believers "blessed . . . with all spiritual blessings in heavenly places in Christ" (Eph. 1:3). In this sublime spiritual relationship, God "hath raised us up together, and made us sit together in heavenly places in Christ Jesus" (Eph. 2:6), and there can be no question of sin there as a barrier between ourselves and Him. But John is not talking about our session in "heavenly places," but about our walk on earth. And down here sin is an undeniable reality in our lives, capable of erecting a true spiritual and psychological barrier between us and our heavenly Father. And the removal of sin's estrangement of the soul from God must still be called what the Christian consciousness has always called it—forgiveness.[13] That this is indeed the correct terminology, "the Lord's prayer"—the disciple's model whenever he prays—confirms.

John couples the necessity of forgiveness, however, with the certainty of forgiveness. "He is faithful and just to forgive us our sins." In other words, when the believer acknowledges his sin to God, his heavenly Father is both *reliable* and *righ-*

teous in extending His remission. And though a Christian immediately after confession sometimes may not feel forgiven, he must not rely on feelings but on facts. God can be counted on, John affirms, to grant the forgiveness we seek. Moreover, there is no unrighteousness in His doing so. For, as John will shortly point out, our heavenly "advocate with the Father" is "Jesus Christ the righteous: and he is the propitiation for our sins: and not for ours only, but also for the sins of the whole world" (1 John 2:1-2). And if the propitiatory work of Christ is large enough in scope to cover even the sins of a world that never applies to Him for the benefits of His cross, it is transparently sufficient for those of us who do! No, says John, count upon it. It is right that God should grant you forgiveness, whenever you acknowledge your need thereof.

But, of course, it is obvious in all this that one can only acknowledge what the light shows him. There can he no question of confessing unknown sins, since a man cannot confess what he does not know. And not surprisingly, John shows an awareness of this reality. "If we confess our sins," John says, "he is faithful and just to forgive us our sins, and to cleanse us from all unrighteousness." And it must be observed that the word *our*, printed in italics by the King James Version, is not present in the original Greek. Indeed the phrase should be read, *he is faithful and just to forgive us the sins*, that is, *the sins we confess.* But then John adds, "and to cleanse us from all unrighteousness." The point is very clear, for the contrast lies between *the* "sins" and *all* "righteousness." In a word, when we make a clean breast of the sins the light discloses, not only are these known faults forgiven, but *all* else that is not right in our lives—however ignorant we may be about it—is at the same time thoroughly cleansed away. But in reality, the provision is not greatly different from that laid down for us in verse 7 as well. The honest, open walk in the presence of divine light is accompanied by a cleansing "from all sin" through the blood of Christ. It follows therefore that, as honest acknowledgment of our failures takes place in that light, the same kind of cleansing "from all unrighteousness" must likewise take place. Everything hinges on our integrity before God. If we are willing to keep ourselves exposed to what He is (for He is light), even when this exposure compels us to acknowledge sin in our lives, we will always have His perfect cleansing. The moment we begin to dissemble, to equivocate, to excuse our evil, that moment "we lie, and do not the truth." We are then hiding—hiding in the dark.

Verse 10

"If we say that we have not sinned, we make him a liar, and his word is not in us." This is the third and final false assertion. John's train of thought runs smoothly, and each of these false claims flows out of an immediately preceding truth the claim contradicts. Thus, verse 6, with its claim to fellowship with God by one who is actually walking in the dark, contradicts the reality of verse 5, that "God is light, and in him is no darkness at all." Thus also verse 8, with its claim to being without sin, clashes with the reality of verse 7, that even while "we walk in the light" we are not faultless, for "the blood of Jesus Christ his Son" even then is cleansing us "from all sin." Accordingly, as might he expected, the spurious assertion of verse 10 is the opposite of the truth of verse 9. If a Christian discovers sin in the light, he can confess it and thus agree with God concerning the true nature of what he has done.

But there is another option. He can disagree with God! Although God's Word tells him he has done wrong, he may justify himself and rationalize his sin away. In short, he can say—on any given occasion of failure—not "I confess" but "I have not sinned"![14] But, says John, "If we say we have not sinned," we are contradicting God—"we make him a liar." And "his word"—which exposes sin—"is not in us." for no man, true Christian though he may be, is genuinely under the influence of God's Word when in fact he contradicts it. That dynamic indwelling of the Savior's words in the life of His followers, of which He spoke elsewhere (cf. John 15:7), cannot exist unless those words can bend our consciences to their truth. And when we deny the sin those words plainly disclose, it is evident that they are not "in us" in any vital, transforming sense.

Conclusion

There is nothing complicated about John's conceptions, though the depths of those conceptions challenge a lifetime of careful thought. But in their essence they are simple. God is perfect light, perfect purity. To share anything with Him as Christians, we must at least share the light where He is. There is much else we can share with Him *besides* that, but nothing else *without* it! To share the light is to be in it, to be exposed to it, and to refuse to hide in the dark from any reality it discloses. And if, in fact, it discloses our sin, we must acknoledge that reality too; we must confess it, and then continued sharing of the light will go on. We are never perfect, even while we are in the light, but if we stay in that light we are perfectly clean! The blood of Jesus Christ his Son provides for that. And God will always faithfully apply the value of that blood to the honest heart.

What then is the principle of fellowship with God!? Succinctly stated, it is openness to God and full integrity in the light of His Word. Indeed, the psalmist sensed it long ago and captured its essence in these lovely words: "Search me, O God, and know my heart: try me, and know my thoughts: and see if there be any wicked way in me, and lead me in the way everlasting" (Ps. 139:23-24).

NOTES

1. This interpretation has been denied by C. H. Dodd, *The Johannine Epistles* (London: Hodder & Stoughton, 1966), pp. 9-16. His arguments are effectively rebutted by John R. W. Stott, *The Epistles of John: an Introduction and Commentary* (Grand Rapids: Eerdmans, 1964), pp. 26-34.
2. In fact, John's pronouns so easily glide back and forth between references to the Father and the Son, that it is clear that precise distinctions are out of harmony with his thought. See esp. 2:28-3:2.
3. See, e.g., John 14:9-10, 24; 17:8, 14; and so forth.
4. See Dodd's succinct survey in *The Johannine Epistles*, pp. 18-19.
5. For example, in "The Manual of Discipline," there are phrases like "the children of light" and "the children of darkness"; "on paths of light he sees but darkness"; "the true light of life"; and "the spirits of light and darkness." Theodor H. Gaster, *The Dead Sea Scriptures: in English Translation with Introduction and Notes*, rev. ed. (New York: Doubleday, 1964). pp. 46, 49-51.
6. This, however, has nevertheless been done. In *Love Is Now* (Grand Rapids: Zondervan, 1970), Peter E. Gillquist writes: "John in this section writes with a style called the 'editorial we.' By saying 'we' instead of 'you,' he can readily identify with his readers without sounding as though he is preaching at them" (p. 62). But this is inaccurate and misleading. An "editorial we" is not a "we" used in place of a "you," but a "we" used for an "I." The fact is that the kind of "we" Gillquist wants here has no recognized place in Greek grammar, and is without analogy in the New Testament.
7. Friedrich Hauck, in *Theological Dictionary of the New Testament*, ed.

Gerhard Kittel and Gerhard Friedrich, 10 vols. (Grand Rapids: Eerdmans, 1964-1976), s.v., "*κοινός, κοινωνός, κοινωνέω, κοινωνία*," 3(1966) : 797-98.

8. Despite the prevalence of the "Christian fellowship" view among modern commentators, R. E. O. White, in siding with Augustine and Calvin, is surely right when he says, "Nevertheless it is essential to the coherence of the passage, and to the meaning of the next phrase, that the idea of fellowship with God who is light remain the fundamental one. John has already emphasized his desire to promote fellowship among Christians, and stressed that this is a common fellowship with the Father: doubtless this motive shapes his language here. To be out of fellowship with God, through sin, is to be out of fellowship with each other, and vice versa" (*Open Letter to Evangelicals: A Devotional and Homiletic Commentary on the First Epistle of John* (Grand Rapids: Eerdmans, 1964), pp. 235-36 (italics his).

9. This is certainly the most natural way to read the text with the verbs *ἔχομεν* and *καθαρίζει* forming a compound apodosis for the conditional sentence. The other option, to place a major mark of punctuation after *μετ' ἀλλήλων*, destroys the rhythm of the passage. (This option is not even offered in the punctuation apparatus of the UBS edition of the Greek text.)

10. The interpretation that to "have no sin" is a reference to the sin nature cannot be harmonized with John's usage elsewhere of the phrase *ἔχειν ἁμαρτίαν*. See John 15:22, 24; 19:11. The view given above accords fully with these other uses, and also fits the immediate context better.

11. Gillquist, p. 64

12. The Greek phrase is *ὅταν προσεύχησθε* (Luke 11:2). Of the use of *ὅταν* with the present subjunction, Arndt and Gingrich point out: "Preferably in (regularly) repeated action *whenever, as often as, every time that . . .*" (William F. Arndt and F. Wilbur Gingrich, *A Greek-English Lexicon of the New Testament and Other Early Christian Literature* [Chicago: U. of Chicago, 1965], p. 592).

13. Estrangement between the offender and the offended is the lowest common denominator in unforgiven sin, whether on a human or a divine level. Punishment may or may not be involved. On an earthly level, when one person extends forgiveness to another, the personal barrier between them is removed and "fellowship" can begin again. In personal relationship, the remission of penalty is usually not involved—unless the estrangement itself is regarded as a penalty. Within the family of God, the experience of forgiveness may be understood in precisely these terms. Indeed, "forgiveness" as extended to a sinning saint may not at all undo the necessary consequences of his failure (as in the case of David in 2 Sam. 12:13-14), but harmonious relationships with God are always renewed thereby (see Ps. 51!).

14. The perfect tense of the verb here (*ἡμαρτήκαμεν*) is no objection to this interpretation. Note the use of the perfect tense in reference to specific cases of sin in 2 Corinthians 12:21 and 13:2; and James 5:15. The thought of a total denial of sin, as though the person had never done any at all, is not germane to the context, and is most certainly not implied merely by the use of a perfect tense.

15

The Rapture in Revelation 3:10

Jeffrey L. Townsend

Equally sincere and devout students of the prophetic Scriptures hold differing views on the time of the rapture of the church in relation to the tribulation. This is due in large measure to the fact that no verse of Scripture specifically states that relationship. But Revelation 3:10 comes close: "Because you have kept the word of My perseverance, I also will keep you from the hour of testing, that hour which is about to come upon the whole world, to test those who dwell upon the earth."* Consequently, as Gundry has stated, "Probably the most debated verse in the whole discussion about the time of the Church's rapture is Revelation 3:10."[1]

In Revelation 3:10 the church at Philadelphia is promised protection from the hour of testing. The great pretribulational/posttribulational debate over this verse concerns the nature of the protection promised. Pretribulationists maintain that the church is here promised preservation *outside* the hour of testing by means of the rapture (external preservation). Posttribulationists, on the other hand, argue that the church is preserved *in* the hour of testing (internal preservation). The solution to the problem of the nature of the protec-

---

Jeffrey L. Townsend
A.B., University of Northern Iowa; Th.M., Dallas Theological Seminary; graduate study toward Th.D., Dallas Theological Seminary
Assistant Director of Alumni and Church Relations
Dallas Theological Seminary

*All Scripture quotations in this article are from the *New American Standard Bible.*

tion promised the church is bound up in the phrase σε τηρήσω ἐκ τῆς ὥρας τοῦ πειρασμοῦ ("I will keep you from the hour of testing").

THE MEANING OF "KEEP FROM"

Although τηρέω is often translated "keep," a better rendering in Revelation 3:10 would be "preserve" or "protect," since great trials are in view in the hour of testing.[2] Whatever the promise involves, its great fruit will be the genuine preservation and protection of the church during the hour of testing.

This presents an immediate problem for posttribulationism, since it holds that the church will be preserved on earth during the hour of testing. Yet verses such as Revelation 6:9-10; 7:9, 13, 14; 13:15; 14:13; 16:6; 18:24; and 20:4 present a time of unprecedented persecution and martyrdom for the saints of the tribulation period. Gundry identifies these saints as members of the church.[3] One wonders with Sproule, "If multitudes of Christians are going to die under the fierce persecution of Antichrist, Satan, and the wicked, then *in what way* has God preserved them through the tribulation?[4] Moreover, it must be questioned whether this kind of "preservation" would be of any comfort and encouragement to the persecuted Philadelphians. In effect, the posttribulational scheme denies the meaning of preservation in τηρέω.[5]

The preposition ἐκ is the focal point of the debate over whether Revelation 3:10 promises internal or external preservation from the hour of testing. The standard lexicons and grammars are in agreement on the basic meaning of the preposition. According to Robertson, "The word means 'out of,' 'from within,' not like ἀπό or παρά.[6]

Applying this meaning to Revelation 3:10, posttribulationists interpret the verse in two ways. Reese states both views: "The use of *ek* in Rev. iii. 10 distinctly implies that the Overseer would be in the hour of tribulation; the promise refers, either to removal from out of the midst of it, or preservation through it."[7] Posttribulationists who hold the latter view tend not to see any reference to the rapture of the church in Revelation 3:10 but only to preservation of the church during the hour of testing.[8] This is an untenable position because the idea of preservation in and through the hour of testing would normally have been expressed by ἐν or διά.[9]

This leaves Reese's first view which, in modified form, is the view of Gundry. In a rather lengthy study of ἐκ Gundry makes the following assertions:

> Essentially, ἐκ, a preposition of motion concerning thought or physical direction, means *out from within*. 'Εκ does not denote a stationary position outside its object, as some have mistakenly supposed in thinking that the ἐκ of Revelation 3:10 refers to a position *already* taken outside the earthly sphere of tribulation. . . . If ἐκ ever occurs without the thought of emergence, it does so very exceptionally.[10]

These statements pose a very real problem for pretribulationism for it appears that τηρέω ἐκ must look at "protection issuing in emission," a concept in line with posttribulationism.[11]

However, sufficient evidence exists throughout the history of the meaning and usage of ἐκ to indicate that this preposition may also denote *a position outside its object with no thought of prior existence within the object or of emergence from the object.*

'EK IN CLASSICAL LITERATURE

Liddell and Scott list several examples of ἐκ, chiefly in the early writers, with the heading, "of Position, *outside of, beyond.*"[12] For example, in the following quotation from Murray's translation of *The Iliad*, the italicized portion is the translator's rendering of ἐκ βελέων: "Thereafter will we hold ourselves aloof from the fight, *beyond the range of missiles*, lest haply any take wound on wound . . . ."[13] In this and other references listed by Liddell and Scott[14] the meaning of ἐκ is clearly *not* motion "out from within." Gundry notes this evidence, but relegates it to early classical writers and certain lingering frozen forms of expression.[15] However, these writers have the effect of establishing that from the earliest times ἐκ can denote outside position (as well as motion "out from within").

'EK IN THE SEPTUAGINT

Proverbs 21:23 exemplifies the fact that the idiom of outside position expressed by ἐκ continued into the era of the Septuagint: "The one who guards his mouth and tongue *keeps* (διατηρεῖ) his soul *from* (ἐκ) trouble."[16] This verse is significant not only because it provides an example of ἐκ meaning outside position, but also because it does so by using διατηρέω with the preposition. Although there are no examples of τηρέω with ἐκ in the Septuagint. διατηρέω with ἐκ has a very similar meaning. The preposition διά in composition with τηρέω simply intensifies the idea of keeping (hence, "to keep continually or carefully"[17]). Thus the Septuagint contains a very comparable idiom to that found in Revelation 3:10, and the meaning in the Septuagint is not "keep by bringing out from within," but rather "keep outside of." The ideas of prior existence in the object and emission from it are missing.[18]

Proverbs 21:23 is not an isolated case. Ἐκ with the idea of outside position is also found in expressions employing synonyms of τηρέω (cf. ἐξαιρέω with ἐκ in Josh. 2:13; ῥύομαι with ἐκ in Ps. 33:19 [Septuagint, 32:19]; 56:13 [Septuagint, 55:13]; Prov. 23:14).[19] Abbott notes that "Ps. lix. 1-2 σῶσον ἐκ, ἐξελοῦ ἐκ, ῥῦσαι ἐκ, may mean, not 'Bring me safe *out* after I have fallen *in*,' but 'Save me [*by keeping me*] out (of the hands of my enemies who surround me)."[20] In summary, the Septuagint offers examples of expressions that are not frozen forms and where ἐκ has the idea of outside position.

'EK IN JOSEPHUS

The works of Josephus also provide examples of ἐκ used to express outside position rather than motion out from within. In perhaps the clearest example, the italicized portion is Thackeray's translation of ῥύομαι with ἐκ: "He *delivered* them *from* those dire consequences which would have ensued from their sedition but for Moses' watchful care."[21] The idea here is preservation rather than removal, since the judgment of God was prevented by Moses' intercession.

'EK IN THE NEW TESTAMENT

Examples of ἐκ carrying the idea of outside position have thus been found in each period of the development of the Greek language. Acts 15:29 establishes the fact that this meaning of ἐκ is also found in the New Testament. In Acts 15:28-29 the brethren in Jerusalem concluded their letter to the Gentiles in Antioch with instructions to abstain from certain practices that would be especially offensive to Jewish brethren. Their concluding remark is found at the end of verse 29: "If you *keep* yourselves *free from* (ἐξ ... διατηροῦντες) such things, you will do well." The expression employs διατηρέω in the form of a circumstantial participle with ἐκ. Like the expression with διατηρέω and ἐκ in Proverbs 21:23, the idea is outside position, not motion out from within.[22] The thrust of verses 28 and 29 is a request for future abstention (cf. ἀπέκεσθαι, v. 29a) from certain practices (outside position), not an accusation of current vices from which the brethren in Antioch must desist (motion out from within). As noted previously, διατηρέω differs from τηρέω only in the strength of the idea of keeping (hence "keeping . . . free" rather than simply "keeping"). Consequently, Acts 15:29 provides another construction very similar to τηρέω ἐκ in Revelation 3:10, and again the meaning is not keeping out from within, but keeping outside the object of the preposition.

In addition to Acts 15:29 at least four other verses in the New Testament contain verbal constructions with ἐκ in which ἐκ seems to indicate a position outside its object.[23] Each of these verses needs to be examined in some detail.

John 12:27. The use of ἐκ in John 12:27 is important because this verse, written by John, can shed light on his usage of the same preposition in the book of Revelation.[24] Whether or not Jesus' words, "Father, save Me from this hour," express a question or a petition is relatively unimportant to the present discussion. The question at hand is whether Jesus was speaking about preservation from the coming hour of His death (ἐκ meaning outside position) or deliverance out of an hour which had already come to pass (ἐκ meaning motion out from within). The verb σώζω is capable of either idea.[25] Robertson is certain that Jesus had already entered the hour.[26] However, John 7:30 and 8:20 along with the immediate context of 12:23 seem to use "the hour" in reference to Jesus' betrayal and death, which would be followed by His glorious resurrection. Evidently the request of the Greeks in 12:21 vividly brought to mind the hour of the Lord's impending death, but the actual occurrence of the hour was yet future. This is the conclusion of Smith, who writes a helpful appendix on the significance of John 12:27 in relation to the rapture question in Revelation 3:10:

> That Jesus' suffering at this time was proleptic and anticipatory that the "hour" spoken of was in reality still in the future is evident in that He Himself declares a few days later, "With desire I have desired to eat this passover with you before I suffer" (Luke 22:15), and later still, just previous to His arrest, "Behold, the hour is at hand [Greek: *near*], and the Son of man

is betrayed into the hands of sinners" (Matthew 26:45). The phrase "is at hand" always denotes proximity and never total arrival.[27]

It appears that Jesus was referring to preservation rather than deliverance with regard to the hour of His death. Thus John 12:27 provides an example (which is parallel in many respects with Rev. 3:10) in the Johannine literature where the meaning of ἐκ is position outside the object of the preposition.

Hebrews 5:7. A second example of ἐκ indicating outside position is found in Hebrews 5:7, in which the Lord is said to have prayed "to the One [who was] able to save Him from death" (σῴζειν . . . ἐκ θανάτου). The description of His prayers as being made "with loud crying and tears" and the reference to the Father as "able to save Him from death" indicates that the Gethsemane prayer is in view (Matt. 26:39; cf. Mark 14:36; Luke 22:42). This connection is significant for the present discussion, since, as Hewitt points out, "If the prayer which Christ offered *with strong crying and tears* was a prayer to be saved 'out of' death, it cannot easily be reconciled with another request made in the Garden —'Father, if thou be willing, remove this cup from me' (Lk. xxii. 42)."[28] In order to reconcile Hebrews 5:7 with the gospel accounts, which stress preservation from death and not resurrection out of death, ἐκ must have the idea of position outside its object rather than emergence from the object.[29]

James 5:20. This passage presents yet another use of σῴζω with ἐκ where the meaning of the preposition is outside position. James writes, "He who turns a sinner from the error of his way will save his soul from death" (σώσει . . . ἐκ θανάτου). This sinner is defined in 5:19 as a brother who has strayed from the truth he once held (either doctrinal or moral) and who needs to be turned back (ἐπιστρέφω) to his former direction of life. The most natural way of understanding the context is to see this sinner as a true believer who has embraced erroneous doctrine or practice. The death in 5:20 then must be physical death. Wessel comments, "Since the NT teaches the security of the believer in Christ, it is best to take the reference to death as physical death. The early church believed and taught that persistence in sin could cause premature physical death (cf. 1 Cor. 11:30)."[30] This interpretation is supported by the context of 5:15-16 where sin is linked with the loss of physical health. If physical death is in view in James 5:20, then ἐκ cannot mean out from within. Instead it must mean position outside its object.

This study of ἐκ throughout its linguistic history and especially its usage in the New Testament has shown that the preposition may sometimes indicate outside position (whereas other times it means removal out from within). In relation to the interpretation of τηρέω ἐκ in Revelation 3:10, this finding establishes the pretribulational position as a bona fide grammatical possibility. To understand τηρέω ἐκ as indicating preservation in an outside position is well within the bounds of the linguistic history and usage of ἐκ.[31]

John 17:15. In order to determine the most probable meaning of τηρέω ἐκ in Revelation 3:10, its usage in John 17:15 must be considered. This is the only other occurrence of τηρέω with ἐκ in either biblical or classical Greek.[32] It is significant that both verses are Johannine and in both cases Jesus speaks the words. Hench much can be learned from John 17:15 about the meaning of τηρέω ἐκ in Revelation 3:10.

John 17:15 begins with a negative petition using αἴρω and ἐκ. Jesus uses these words to express His prayer that the disciples not be physically removed from the earth. Removal would be one way of preserving them spiritually in His absence, but it would violate their commission as witnesses (cf. John 15:27). It is significant that in the case of αἴρω with ἐκ the idea of motion in the verb naturally lends itself to the idea of taking ἐκ in the sense of motion out from within (cf. οἱ ἐρχόμενοι ἐκ, Rev. 7:14). This points up the necessity of considering the verb and the preposition together and not simply isolating the components of the expression. The context is also an important determining factor in deciding the exact force of the phrase. The disciples were in the world (17:11), so ἐκ must mean "out from within" in John 17:15*a*.

In 17:15*b* the Lord contrasts (using ἀλλά) His first petition with a petition using τηρέω and ἐκ for preservation from the evil one.[33] Gundry asks, "How then can τηρέω ἐκ [in Rev. 3:10] refer to the rapture or to the results of the rapture, when in its only other occurrence the phrase opposes an expression [αἴρω ἐκ] which would perfectly describe the rapture?"[34] The answer lies in the combined effect of the verb and the preposition in the context—factors that Gundry tends to overlook.

Regarding the context, the disciples were in the world physically. This combined with the idea of motion in αἴρω demands that αἴρω ἐκ in John 17:15a be understood as removal out from within. However, John 17:15b *describes an entirely different situation.* The disciples were *not* in the evil one spiritually when Jesus prayed. This combined with the fact that τηρέω demands not the idea of motion but rather the idea of preservation indicates that τηρέω ἐκ in John 17:15b be understood as preservation in an outside position.[35] This is in line with the pretribulational understanding of Revelation 3:10—just as the disciples were not in the evil one, so the Philadelphians were not in the hour of testing and the promise is that Jesus Christ will keep them outside that hour.

Gundry interprets John 17:15b as a prayer for the preservation of the disciples *in* the moral sphere of Satan, since they are to be left in the world (John 17:15a).[36] However, both the immediate context and John's other writings argue against this interpretation. In the context of John 17:11-16, the idea of keeping is related to salvation and the possession of eternal life, not preservation from the moral assaults of Satan. The issue is the keeping of salvation (i.e., the perseverance of the saints), not progression in sanctification (which is taken up in 17:17).

First John 5:18-19 is also against Gundry's premise. In 1 John 5:18 the evil one does not touch (ἅπτω) the one who has been born of God, because the One who was born of God (Jesus Christ) keeps (τηρέω, cf. John 17:11) him. In 1 John 5:19 the apostle wrote, "We know that we are of God, and the whole world lies in the power of the evil one." Gundry's interpretation of John 17:15b as preservation *in* the moral sphere of Satan does not square with the Johannine emphasis on the separation of believers from the spiritual realm of the evil one.

Thus the idea in John 17:15b is not the moral sphere of the evil one (i.e., the world system), as Gundry and most post-tribulationists suppose, but the spiritual realm of the evil one (i.e., spiritual death). The disciples were not in Satan's realm spiritually and Christ prays, using τηρέω ἐκ, that the Father would keep them so. Hence τηρέω ἐκ, in John 17:15 is an expression for preservation in an outside position. Applied to Revelation 3:10, this evidence indicates that the pretribulational position is not only possible, but is also probable.

Revelation 3:10 may then be paraphrased, "Because you have held fast the word which tells of My perseverance, I also will preserve you in a position outside the hour of testing. . . ."

This paraphrase points up an important nuance of meaning that must be recognized. Τηρέω ἐκ in Revelation 3:10 does not describe the rapture as such. Instead it describes the position and status of the church during the hour of testing. It describes the results of the rapture, not the rapture itself. Revelation 3:10 does not state directly how the church will be preserved outside the hour of testing. However, the remainder of the verse indicates that the proper logical deduction is preservation by means of a pretribulational rapture of the church.

THE MEANING OF "THE HOUR OF TESTING"

THE MEANING OF "THE HOUR"

The object of the preposition ἐκ in Revelation 3:10 is "the hour of testing" (τῆς ὥρας τοῦ πειρασμοῦ). The preservation promised the Philadelphians is in relation to *a specific period of time*. This is indicated by the inclusion of τῆς as an article of previous reference. Jesus is speaking of *the* well-known hour of testing, which is a reference to the expected time of trouble, the Tribulation period, before the return of the Messiah (Deut. 4:26-31; Isa. 13:6-13; 17:4-11; Jer. 30:4-11; Ezek. 20:33-38; Dan. 9:27; 12:1; Zech. 14:1-4; Matt. 24:9-31).[37] This period is graphically portrayed in Revelation 6-18 (cf. "the great tribulation," 7:14; and "the hour of His judgment," 14:7).[38]

In relation to the rapture question, it is significant that the Philadelphian church is here promised preservation outside the *time period* of the Tribulation. The combination ἐκ τῆς ὥρας thwarts the posttribulational view of the church being kept from trials while on earth during the hour of testing. As Thiessen notes, the promise "holds out exemption from the period of trial, not only from the trial during that period."[39] Ryrie comments, "It is impossible to conceive of being in the location where something is happening and being exempt from the time of the happening."[40]

Gundry attempts to "undercut stress on the term 'hour' "[41] in three ways. First, he claims that the hour will elapse in heaven as well as on earth. But the verse claims that this hour is coming on the οἰκουμένη (the "inhabited earth") and thus is related to the earthly time continuum. This was certainly John's perspective.

Second, Gundry claims that "the hour of testing" does

not emphasize a period of time, but rather the trials during that period. Although Delling notes this possibility in his article on ὥρα, he gives Revelation 3:10 as an example of ὥρα in the general sense of " 'the divinely appointed time' for the actualisation [sic] of apocalyptic happenings."[42] Gundry's view errs in failing to square with the use of the definite article τῆς which indicates that a well-known hour (fixed in length by Dan. 9:27) is in view. A careful evaluation of the evidence seems to prove all the more that both time and event are inextricably linked.

Third, Gundry notes that in Jeremiah 30:7 (Septuagint, 37:7) Israel is given a similar promise of being saved from (σώζω with ἀπό in the Septuagint) the "time of Jacob's distress" (cf. "hour of testing"). Even though ἀπό denotes separation more strongly than ἐκ, Israel is preserved within the time of trouble, not outside it. Gundry concludes his argument by stating, "If a pretribulational rapture was not or will not be required for deliverance from the time of Jacob's distress, neither will a pretribulational rapture be required for preservation from the hour of testing."[43] This appears to be a strong argument until one considers the context of Jeremiah 30:7. Jeremiah 30:5-6 indicates that the nation is already in the great day of trouble when salvation comes. This is confirmed in Matthew 24 where the Jews are told to flee the persecution of the one who desecrates the Temple and in Revelation 12 where the dragon persecutes the woman and her offspring. From this trouble, the nation is promised rescue in Jeremiah 30:7. Thus the promises are different and not comparable. Israel is promised rescue within the time of trouble,[44] the church is promised preservation from the hour of testing. Only the latter case demands rapture from earth to heaven.

THE SCOPE OF "THE HOUR"

The qualifying phrase, "which is about to come upon the whole inhabited earth," further describes the hour as imminent and worldwide in its impact. Τῆς μελλούσης ἐρχεσθαι goes beyond conveying future tense. It carries a note of imminency, as indicated by ἔρχομαι ταχύ which begins Revelation 3:11. Both the coming of the hour and the coming of the Lord are imminent. This connection indicates a relationship between the promise of keeping in 3:10 and the coming of the Lord in 3:11. There will be preservation outside the imminent hour of testing for the Philadelphian church when the Lord comes. This, in turn, indicates that, although τηρέω ἐκ in 3:10 does not refer directly to the rapture of the church, rapture as the means of preservation is a proper deduction from the context.

The whole inhabited earth will be overtaken by this hour (cf. Rev. 2:10 where local persecution is in view). Since the church is to be preserved outside a period of time which encompasses the whole world, preservation by a pretribulation rapture is again seen to be a logical inference from the context. Only a rapture to heaven removes the church from the earth and its time continuum.[45]

THE PURPOSE OF "THE HOUR"

"To test those who dwell upon the earth" gives the purpose of the coming hour. In both secular and biblical Greek, πειράζω has the root idea of a test that is applied in order to expose the true character of someone.[46] Usually πειράζω denotes negative intent—to test in order to break down, to demonstrate failure.[47] Hence the hour of testing will come on the whole world with the specific purpose of putting earth-dwellers to the test, which will demonstrate their utter failure before God. In other words, the tribulation period will provide condemning evidence for the judgments the Lord will carry out when He returns to the earth (cf. Matt. 25; Rev. 19:19-21; 20:4).

According to Johnson, τοὺς κατοικοῦντας ἐπί τῆς γῆς corresponds to the Hebrew idiom יֹשְׁבֵי הָאָרֶץ which, in Isaiah 24:1, 5, 6; 26:9, becomes a technical term for people on the earth during the time of Jacob's trouble.[48] The term is not all-inclusive, since in each of its seven other uses in Revelation the reference is to unbelievers, and both pretribulationists and posttribulationists agree that there will be many saints in the Tribulation period. The question is whether these saints are the preserved church (which is unlikely since many are martyred) or people who come to salvation during the tribulation and are martyred for their faith. In Revelation 13:8 and 17:8 an earth-dweller is further defined as one "whose name has not been written in the book of life from the foundation of the world." These are the nonelect of the tribulation period, and as a result they worship the beast (cf. Rev. 13:8, 14). On these earth-dwellers will come judgments that have the purpose of demonstrating openly their absolute and utter depravity (cf.

Rev. 6:15-17; 9:20-21; 16:21). McClain notes, "In that hour the physical judgments will generally fall upon saved and unsaved alike."[49] But the special objects of testing and wrath will be the earth-dwellers.

CONCLUSION

In seeking a solution to the pretribulational/posttribulational debate over the nature of the preservation promised the church in Revelation 3:10, the preposition ἐκ was traced throughout its history in order to establish the fact that ἐκ may at times indicate outside position as well as at other times indicating motion out from within. This brought the pretribulational interpretation of Revelation 3:10 within the realm of possibility. In addition, John 17:15—the only other occurrence of τηρέω ἐκ in either biblical or classical Greek—was studied. Pretribulationists and posttribulationists alike note the similarity in meaning between John 17:15 and Revelation 3:10. Hence when it was determined that τηρέω ἐκ in the context of John 17:15 demanded the idea of preservation outside the evil one, this had the effect of making outside preservation the preferred (or most probable) interpretation of Revelation 3:10.

The preservation promised in Revelation 3:10 relates to a specific, well-known hour of trial, the future seven-year Tribulation that is to precede the Messiah's return and which is described in detail in Revelation 6-18. Revelation 3:10 teaches that the coming of this hour is imminent, that it is worldwide in its scope, and that the purpose of the hour is to put the ungodly earth-dwellers of the Tribulation period to the test to reveal evidence of their wickedness in preparation for the Lord's judgments when He returns to the earth.

Although Revelation 3:10 describes the result of the rapture (i.e., the position and status of the church during the Tribulation) and not the rapture itself, the details of the hour of testing just mentioned establish the pretribulation rapture as the most logical deduction from this verse. The promise of preservation is from a period of time which will envelope the whole world. Only a pretribulation rapture would remove the church completely from the earth and its time continuum. Thus the pretribulation rapture is found to be a proper logical deduction from the data found in Revelation 3:10.

NOTES

1. Robert H. Gundry, *The Church and the Tribulation* (Grand Rapids: Zondervan, 1973), p. 54.
2. Gundry claims that "where a situation of danger is in view, τηρέω means *to guard*," and that "throughout the LXX and the NT τηρέω always occurs for protection within the sphere of danger . . ." (Ibid., p. 58). Although "to guard" does not differ much from "to protect," Gundry's second statement is questionable. In 2 Peter 2:9 and Jude 21, for example, the idea of protection within the sphere of danger is inappropriate.
3. Ibid., p. 80.
4. John A. Sproule, "A Revised Review of *The Church and the Tribulation* by Robert H. Gundry" (paper delivered at the Postgraduate Seminar in New Testament Theology, Grace Theological Seminary, Winona Lake, Ind., May 15, 1974), p. 32 (italics his).
5. Gundry's comment that "were the Church absent from the hour of testing, keeping would not be necessary" (Gundry, p. 58) looks at the situation from a posttribulational viewpoint within the tribulation where keeping seems necessary. There is also the viewpoint of the Philadelphians prior to the hour of testing. To them, protection from that hour definitely necessitated some form of keeping. In relation to a worldwide judgment, it would seem that keeping in heaven would be a necessity.
6. A. T. Robertson, *A Grammar of the Greek New Testament in the Light of Historical Research*, 4th ed. (New York: Doran, 1923), p. 596.
7. Alexander Reese, *The Approaching Advent of Christ: An Examination of the Teaching of J. N. Darby and His Followers* (London: Marshall, Morgan, & Scott, 1937), p. 205.
8. As Ladd puts it, "This verse neither asserts that the Rapture is to occur before the Tribulation, nor does its interpretation require us to think that such a removal is intended" (George Eldon Ladd, *The Blessed Hope* [Grand Rapids: Eerdmans, 1956], p. 86).
9. Cf. E. Schuyler English, *Re-Thinking the Rapture: An Examination of What the Scriptures Teach as to the Time of the Translation of the Church in Relation to the Tribulation* (Travelers Rest, S.C.: Southern Bible, 1954), p. 89.
10. Gundry, pp. 55-56.
11. Ibid., p. 59.
12. Henry George Liddell and Robert Scott, *An Intermediate Greek-English Lexicon* (Oxford: Clarendon, 1968), pp. 498-99.
13. Homer, *The Iliad*, 2.14,130 (italics added).
14. Cf. ἐκ καπνοῦ, "out of the smoke" (Homer, *The Odyssey*, 2.19.7); ἐκ μέσου κατῆσατο, "stood aside" (Herodotus, 2.3.83).
15. Gundry, p. 55.
16. Old Testament citations are based on the Masoretic text. Variations in the Septuagint are indicated in parentheses.
17. Joseph Henry Thayer, *A Greek-English Lexicon of the New Testament* (Grand Rapids: Zondervan, 1962), p. 142. Cf. Harald Riesenfeld, in *Theological Dictionary of the New Testament*, ed. Gerhard Kittel and Gerhard Friedrich, 10 vols. (Grand Rapids: Eerdmans, 1964-1976), s.v., "τηρέω," 8(1972):151.
18. Preservation in an outside position is also found in Psalm 12:8 (Septuagint, 11:7), using διατηρέω with ἀπό Thus, ἐκ in the Septuagint is capable of the idea of separation normally found in ἀπό.
19. Also compare ἐκκλίνω with ἐκ in Proverbs 1:5 and ἀνέχω with ἐκ in Amos 4:7.

20. Edwin A. Abbott, *From Letter to Spirit: An Attempt to Reach Through Varying Voices the Abiding Word*, Diatessarica, part 6 (London: Adam & Charles Black, 1903), p. 311. In the Septuagint the reference is Psalm 58:1-2.

21. Josephus, *The Antiquities of the Jews*, 4.2.1 (italics added). Cf. ῥύομαι ἐκ in Antiquities, 12.10.5; 13.6.3.

22. In a similar context of keeping from idols, 1 John 5:21 employs τηρέω with ἀπό, indicating that, as in the Septuagint, ἐκ and ἀπό are difficult to distinguish as to meaning in the New Testament. Both may mean "separation from." (Compare John 17:15 with James 1:27; Mark 1:10 with Matthew 3:16; and 1 Thessalonians 1:10 with Romans 5:9.)

23. In addition to the verbal constructions with ἐκ, the nonverbal expression ἐλεύθερος . . . ἐκ πάντων ("free from all") in 1 Corinthians 9:19 seems to use ἐκ in a way that indicates a position outside its object.

24. Smith notes a further correlation with Revelation 3:10. "It is significant that Jesus is the speaker and John the writer just as is the case in the Revelation [3:10] text, and that in each case mention is made of a coming hour of suffering. In all probability, therefore, the meaning of the phrase *from the hour* is similar in both instances" (J. B. Smith, *A Revelation of Jesus Christ: A Commentary on the Book of Revelation*, ed. J. Otis Yoder [Scottdale, Pa.: Herald, 1961], p. 331).

25. William F. Arndt and F. Wilbur Gingrich, *A Greek-English Lexicon of the New Testament and Other Early Christian Literature* (Chicago: U. of Chicago, 1957), pp. 805-6.

26. Robertson, p. 598.

27. Smith, p. 331.

28. Thomas Hewitt, *The Epistle to the Hebrews: An Introduction and Commentary*, Tyndale New Testament Commentaries (Grand Rapids: Eerdmans, 1960), pp. 99-100.

29. Both Bruce and Lenski are correct in answering the question of how the Lord's prayers were answered since He went to the cross in spite of His prayers. "While Gethsemane provides 'the most telling illustration' of our author's words, they have a more general reference to the whole course of our Lord's humiliation and passion" (F. F. Bruce, *The Epistle to the Hebrews: The English Text with Introduction, Exposition and Notes*, New International Commentary on the New Testament [Grand Rapids: Eerdmans, 1964], p. 100).

   "Jesus prayer for deliverance from death only with an 'if': 'if it be possible' (Matt. 26:39): 'if this cup may not pass away from me, except I drink it' (v. 42). The real burden of His prayer was: 'Nevertheless, not what I will, but what thou wilt' (Mark 14:36). So also Matt. 26:39, 42, 'thy will be done,' and this prayer of Jesus' was fully and truly granted" (R.C.H. Lenski, *The Interpretation of the Epistle to the Hebrews and the Epistle of James* [Minneapolis: Augsburg, 1943], p. 164).

30. Walter W. Wessel, "The Epistle of James," in *The Wycliffe Bible Commentary*, ed. Charles F. Pfeiffer and Everett F. Harrison (Chicago: Moody, 1962). p. 1439.

31. As Morris puts it: " 'Keep thee from (ek) the hour of temptation' might mean 'keep thee from undergoing the trial' or 'keep three right through the trial.' The Greek is capable of either meaning" (Leon Morris, *The Revelation of St. John: An Introduction and Commentary*, Tyndale New Testament Commentaries [Grand Rapids: Eerdmans, 1969], p. 80). Cf. Henry Alford, *The Greek Testament: with a Critically Revised Text, a Digest of Various Readings, Marginal References to Verbal and Idiomatic Usage, Prolegomena, and a Critical and Exegetical Commentary*, rev. Everett F. Harrison, 4 vols. (Chicago: Moody, 1958), 4:585;

James Moffatt, "The Revelation of St. John the Divine," in *The Expositor's Greek New Testament*, ed. W. Robertson Nicoll, 5 vols. (London: Hodder & Stoughton, 1900-10), 5(1910):368.

32. Riesenfeld, 8:142.
33. Although τοῦ πειρασμός may be either masculine or neuter, it is most likely masculine and a reference to Satan, according to Johannine usage (cf. John 12:31; 14:30; 16:11; 1 John 2:13-14; 3:12; 5:18-19).
34. Gundry, p. 59.
35. Evidently, combining τηρέω with ἐκ modifies the meaning of the preposition from the primary meaning of motion out from within to the secondary meaning of outside position (S. Lewis Johnson, Jr., class notes in 228, "The Revelation," (Dallas Theological Seminary, Fall 1976).
36. Gundry, p. 59.
37. For evidence that πειρασμός was associated with θλῖψις in the New Testament, compare Luke 8:13 with Matthew 13:21 and Mark 4:17.
38. Mounce thinks that the hour is "three and a half years of rule by Antichrist in Revelation 13:5-10. In fact, all the judgments from 6:1 onward relate to this final hour of trial" (Robert H. Mounce, *The Book of Revelation*, New International Commentary on the New Testament [Grand Rapids: Eerdmans, 1977] p. 119). However, it seems better in the light of the seventieth week concept of Daniel 9:27 to see the hour as a seven-year period of time. Cf. Henry C. Thiessen, "Will the Church Pass Through the Tribulation?" *Bibliotheca Sacra* 92(January-March 1935):45-50.
39. Thiessen, 92:202-3.
40. Charles Caldwell Ryrie, *A Survey of Bible Doctrine* (Chicago: Moody, 1972), p. 170.
41. Gundry, p. 60.
42. Gerhard Delling, in Kittel and Friedrich, s.v. "ὥρα," 9(1973):677.
43. Gundry, p. 60.
44. That it is possible for ἀπό to indicate prior existence in its object (as ἐκ normally does) is demonstrated by its use in Psalm 69:14 (Septuagint, 68:14) and Psalm 140:1, 4 (Septuagint, 139:1, 4). According to Turner, in both the Septuagint and the New Testament ἀπό encroaches on ἐκ Nigel Turner, "Syntax," in James Hope Moulton, *A Grammar of New Testament Greek*, 4 vols. (Edinburgh: T. & T. Clark, 1906-76), 3(1963):250-51.
45. Some posttribulationists insist that οἰκουμένη limits the hour of testing to the Roman world of John's day. Bell writes, "The seemingly universal terms are used elsewhere in the New Testament to mean the civilized world of that day, i.e., the Roman Empire. . . . The several empire-wide persecutions of Christians could easily satisfy the universal terminology" (William Everett Bell, Jr., "A Critical Evaluation of the Pretribulation Rapture Doctrine in Christian Eschatology" [Ph.D. diss., New York University, 1967], p. 304). But as Johnston notes, "οἰκουμένη may have a very wide reference. . . . Sometimes it is synonymous with αἰών and κόσμος. . . . Hence, oecumenē may mean also mankind as a whole . . ." (George Johnston, "Οἰκουμένη and Κόσμος in the New Testament," *New Testament Studies* 10 [April 1964]:353). This is exemplified by the use of Οἰκουμένη in Matthew 24:14 and Acts 17:31. Commenting on the use of οἰκουμένη in the Matthew passage, Michel writes, "It is certainly not to be linked here with political imperial style. The reference is simply to the glad message which is for all nations and the whole earth" (Otto Michel, in Kittel and Friedrich, s.v." ἡ οἰκουμένη," 5(1968):158. In both Acts 17:31 and Revelation 3:10 οἰκουμένη is set in an eschatological context that also seems to demand the widest possible reference. Furthermore,

the next phrase in Revelation 3:10, τοὺς κατοικοῦντας ἐπὶ τῆς γῆς ("those who dwell upon the earth"), is used only pejoratively in Revelation (cf. 6:10; 8:13; 11:10; 13:8; 14; 17:8), thus indicating that unbelievers are designated by the phrase. This is fatal to Bell's view because, as Brown points out, "If the enemies of the Christian religion are to be affected . . . by the 'hour of trial,' it is clear that the author cannot be thinking of a persecution directed against Christians" (Schuyler Brown, "The Hour of Trial" (Rev. 3:10), *Journal of Biblical Literature* 85 [Summer 1966]:310).

46. Cf. Heinrich Seesemann, Kittel and Friedrich, s.v., "πεῖρα κτλ," 6:(1969):23; and Thayer, p. 646.
47. Richard Chenevix Trench, *Synonyms of the New Testament* (New York: Redfield, 1854), p. 281. Cf. Kittel and Friedrich, s.v., "πεῖρα κτλ," 6(1969):23.
48. Johnson, class notes.
49. Alva J. McClain, *The Greatness of the Kingdom* (Grand Rapids: Zondervan, 1959), p. 465.

Ministerial Studies

16

Priorities for the Local Church

Raymond C. Ortlund

Peter Drucker, management expert, has consulted with many churches and Christian organizations. He says the first question he always asks them is this: "What are you trying to accomplish?" And often he finds that they are in a crisis of objectives, not a crisis of organization.[1]

The problem most churches face is not that they do not do anything; they do plenty. The problem is that they are not doing the right things.

A pilot announced to his passengers over his intercom system, "Ladies and gentlemen, I have good news and bad news. The good news is that we have a tail wind, and we are making excellent time. The bad news is that our compass is broken, and we have no idea where we are going." A similar situation is true of many churches.

The issue is not that God's promises to the church are inadequate. Dods expands on God's statement, "I am the Almighty God," with these words:

> I am the Almighty God able to fulfill your highest hopes and accomplish for you the brightest ideal that ever My words set before you. There is no need for paring down the promise until it squares with human probabilities, no need of adopting some interpretation of it which may make it seem easier to fulfill, and

Raymond C. Ortlund
B.S., University of Puget Sound; B.D., Princeton Theological Seminary; D.D., Talbot Theological Seminary
Pastor, Mariners Church
Newport Beach, California

no need of striving to fulfill it in any second-rate way. All possibility lies in this: I am the Almighty God.[2]

God's promises to His church are vast. The church is equipped with the power to fulfill every objective God has for it. Certainly its expectation should be to accomplish every goal carved out by God.

Spurgeon said to a young preacher, "Young man, you don't really expect to see high and wonderful things happen in your life, do you?" The fellow said, "Well, no . . . ." And Spurgeon almost exploded, "Then you won't see them happen, either!"

Genuine expectation is part of the key. But for the church today perhaps a problem greater than low expectation is simply not knowing what its goals should be.

BIBLICAL PRIORITIES

What should be a church's biblical priorities? What should its overall objectives include?

Unless these questions are asked, churches will aim at nothing and hit it every time! Many a pastor thinks he has served a church five years or ten years, when actually he has repeated a one-year pastorate five times over, or ten times over. He has no sense of direction for himself or for his people.

Churches must have a philosophy of ministry, a direction, a sense of where they are going. "What is needed today are congregations that understand their unique purpose as a church and concentrate on fulfilling that function."[3]

A decade ago I asked the leaders of the congregation I was pastoring, "What should be a church's biblical priorities? What is a church basically to be, whether it is in Africa or South Dakota, whether existing in the year A.D. 200 or 2000?"

After working on a philosophy of ministry for several months, the congregation concluded that it is to be committed first to Jesus Christ, then to one another in Christ, and then to the world Christ died to save.

These three priorities must be kept in proper order. A church must not let its ministry to the world—its evangelism and good works—become of first importance.

Some churches are primarily "evangelistic centers." Most of

what is done during the week and on Sunday mornings leads up to one exciting moment: the altar call. That is the focus of the entire life of the church; and it is wonderful to see people walk the aisle to the altar and acknowledge a decision of some kind. But that is not to be the *primary* focus of the church.

Some churches consider themselves "mission centers." These churches raise an extensive amount of money for missions, they have world maps in prominent places with lights twinkling on them, and the people talk a lot about "fifty-fifty budgets" and hear numerous missionary reports from their pulpits. It is wonderful that local churches can help spread the good news in far-off places. But that is not to be the *primary* focus of the church.

Some churches, as "information centers," have as their main purpose the pouring out of biblical material. The people eagerly fill their notebooks, and the one with the fullest notebook and the fullest head is often considered the most spiritual. The pastor of this kind of church is primarily a dispenser of information. But that is not to be the *primary* purpose of the church. Other churches are "program centers." They present one extravaganza after another—gospel magicians, singing groups, ventriloquists, etc. Some churches are "building centers," acquiring an "edifice complex." Their distinctive is only in their buildings. But none of these ought to be the *primary* purpose of the church. Still other churches are primarily "fellowship centers," where the emphasis is on "body life," relational theology, discipling, small groups, and the function of gifts. Relationships are exciting and beneficial, but they are not to be the *primary* purpose of the church.

Primarily—first and foremost—the church is to be for the Lord. He is the Head, and He must be the focus, the first priority.

Churches—and individual believers—are to be committed first to Christ, then to one another in Christ, and then to the world. These three are not to be "done" chronologically, one at a time, but they are to be part of churches' and believers' lives all at the same time.

The Bible repeatedly spells out these three priorities, both generally and specifically. In John 15 Jesus weaves these into His teaching on the vine and the branches. Verses 1-11 stress the admonition, "Remain in Me." That is the first priority. Verses 12-15 focus on the command, "Love each other." That is the second priority. And verses 16-27 say, in essence, "Testify about Me." That pertains to the third priority.

In John 17 the prayer of the Lord Jesus to His Father reveals His own personal priorities. In verses 1-5, the emphasis is on God the Father. "Glorify Thy Son, that the Son may glorify Thee."* Then in verses 6-19, He prayed for "the men whom Thou gavest Me out of the world" (v. 6). He prayed for their protection (vv. 11, 15) and their joy (v. 13). And in verses 20-26 His praying extended to the world ("that the world may believe," [v. 21], "that the world may know" [v. 23]).

In Jesus' ministry on earth, these three priorities are clearly evident. He often withdrew from the disciples to be alone with His Father. But then He also gave much time to His inner circle of followers. And He gave Himself in preaching and healing to the people at large.

The epistles also are heavily loaded with these three elements. In Colossians, for instance, Paul announced that Christ is preeminent (1:16-18). And "therefore," he wrote, since Christ is supreme over all believers, His lordship is to be evident in loving relationships with each other (3:12—4:2). And based on the preeminence of Christ and believers' family relationships with each other Paul gives these urgent words: "And pray for us, too, that God may open a door for our message, so that we may proclaim the mystery of Christ, for which I am in chains. Pray that I may proclaim it clearly, as I should. Be wise in the way you act toward outsiders; make the most of every opportunity. Let your conversation be always full of grace, seasoned with salt, so that you may know how to answer everyone" (4:3-6, NIV).†

One should not suppose that these three priorities are always given in this order throughout the Scriptures, for they are not. But they *are* in these passages cited, and they help to provide balance for church ministries.

THE FIRST PRIORITY—THE LORDSHIP OF CHRIST

The Scriptures cry out that at the top, at the center, in the front, and underneath, all that believers are and have is

---

*All Scripture quotations in this article, except those noted otherwise, are from the *New American Standard Bible.*

†*New International Version.*

Christ. Paul told the Christians in Colossae that Jesus Christ is supreme (Col. 1:18). All creation is His work and exists for Him (1:15-17a). He holds it all together (1:17b). He is the Head and source of the church (v. 18).

The lordship of Christ, however, is not some elementary truth that a Christian can leave as he goes on to deeper teaching. No believer ever outgrows this relationship to Christ. Every aspect of life is to be lived—and lived continually—in the light of this truth.

Many churches state in some way in their doctrinal statement that Christ is Lord and Head over all that the people are and do. But often there is a gap between a church's theology and its practice because of a failure to discern fully the implications of His lordship. Believers must learn to acknowledge Him "in all [their] ways" (Prov. 3:6).

Acknowledging the lordship of Christ takes constant attention (and an entire lifetime) to live out and experience. Christians are to be humble enough to admit the possibility that in some areas of their lives He indeed is not preeminent. Thus they need to spend time adjusting to Him and His supremacy. With Christ at the center there is movement, rearrangement, empowerment.

Christ is in a class by Himself. Believers are to worship *Him.* They are to bow in reverence to *Him*—and no other. "God was pleased to have all his fullness dwell in *him*" (Col. 1:19, NIV). Christ is Lord!

How easy it is to let someone or something else become central. But nothing else works well at the center of a Christian's life. One's wife or husband cannot be central. At death a husband and wife must let go of each other's hands; they must each move into eternity alone. He or she can only be a companion on the way. Nor can one's children be first in life. Eventually, they will bolt from home to escape that kind of pressure. Scholarship cannot be central. Some have made the symbols of scholarship—the degrees and letters after their name—so important that almost all of life is absorbed in and for scholarship. Nor should a believer make himself preeminent. Each believer was regenerated in order that Jesus might be exalted. "Seek [continually] first His kingdom and His righteousness, and all these things shall be added to you" (Matt. 6:33).

Fromke expressed this point when he wrote, "Believers may not often realize it, but even as believers we are either centered on man, or centered on God. There is no alternative. Either God is the center of our universe and we have become rightly adjusted to Him, or we have made ourselves the center and are attempting to make all else orbit around us and for us."[4]

Balance in one's life comes from making sure that Christ is supreme. This is equally true in the corporate lives of churches. If a church is centered on any person, any doctrine, any project, or anything but Christ, it is off balance. Such churches are prone to rush here and there after every new program or gimmick that comes along. Eventually, such patterns of behavior become deeply entrenched, and the church focuses on activities rather than Christ.

The truth that Jesus Christ must be central may seem trite; but if it is taken seriously, its ramifications in a local church will be exciting, creative, and fresh.

> I have learned that there is only one truth that can motivate man simply through life: Christ. Before we can consider ourselves Christians we must have believed in Christ and accepted all the consequences of a radically altered life. Without this first basic commitment, growth in Christ through any church structure is impossible.[5]

Andrews prayed so beautifully,

> Be, Lord,
> within me to strengthen me,
> without me to guard me,
> over me to shelter me,
> beneath me to establish me,
> before me to guide me,
> after me to forward me,
> round me to secure me.[6]

THE SECOND PRIORITY—THE BODY OF CHRIST

People come to Christ individually; but as soon as they are inside the door of faith, they are surrounded by spiritual brothers and sisters. And this new family of God is to be held in high regard.

Paul was amazed that the Macedonian churches had their priorities right. "And they did not do as we expected, but they gave themselves first to the Lord and then to us in keeping with God's will" (2 Cor. 8:5, NIV). Christ was first, but that was not the end of it. They also loved and cared for others in Christ.

The epistles command believers to unite together on the basis of their new family relationship in Christ. Over and over come the instructions: suffer together (1 Cor. 12:26), rejoice together (Rom. 12:15), carry each other's burdens (Gal. 6:2), restore each other (Gal. 6:1), pray for each other (Rom. 15:30), teach and admonish each other (Col. 3:16), refresh each other (Rom. 15:32), encourage each other (Rom. 1:12), forgive each other (Eph. 4:32), confess to each other (James 5:16), be truthful with each other (Eph. 4:25), spur each other to good deeds (Heb. 10:24), and give to each other (Phil. 4:14-15).

The great emphasis of the New Testament epistles clearly states that believers are to give themselves generously to each other—in building up each other, caring for each other, loving each other, and keeping peace among themselves. The last phrase of Galatians 6:10 spells out this priority: "So then, while we have opportunity, let us do good to all men, and especially to those who are of the household of the faith." Fellow believers are to have a higher priority than those outside of Christ.

How should this second priority be carried out? Certainly, Christ's followers are to love the entire church by the power of the Holy Spirit's gift of love (Rom. 5:5). They must never make fun of any segment of the church or disparage it in any way. The church is God's redeemed, and each believer is a member of Christ's body. This truth is strongly affirmed in Christ's rebuke to Saul for persecuting believers. "I am Jesus, *whom you are persecuting*" (Acts 9:5, italics added). Christ, as Head of the universal church, is intimately associated with it. Believers should thus speak well of the church, and should praise God for the whole Body of Christ and all of its parts.

All believers need to associate with and come under the authority of a local body of Christians. Younger Christians need to learn from older believers who have a wealth of experience in Christ. Adults need the vitality and vision supplied by children and youth. To be well acquainted with the whole spread of ages in a local church is a joyful experience.

Beyond his participation in a local church, the believer should be related to a select number of Christians in a deeper fellowship. Christ loved all the world and all His many hundreds of followers, but He spent much of His time with His inner circle of Twelve.[7] Paul always traveled with and had around him a small group of encouraging brothers. He included several of them in the greetings with which he opened many of his epistles: "Paul . . . and Sosthenes our brother" (1 Cor. 1:1); "Paul . . . and Timothy our brother" (2 Cor. 1:1); "Paul and Timothy, bondservants of Christ Jesus" (Phil. 1:1); "Paul . . . and Timothy our brother" (Col. 1:1); "Paul and Silvanus and Timothy" (1 Thess. 1:1; 2 Thess. 1:1).

Both the Lord Jesus and the apostle Paul, as they were leaving this life, were careful to say, in essence, "Now don't be the end of the line!" Jesus sent His disciples, saying, "Go . . . and make disciples . . . teaching them to observe all that I commanded you . . ." (Matt. 28:18-20).

Likewise, Paul said, "The things which you have heard from me . . . these entrust to faithful men, who will be able to teach others also" (2 Tim. 2:2). In other words, they both encouraged others to keep the chain of discipling going.

My life was enriched and deeply changed when in the pastorate I began to meet with a small group of men. I had always had groups around me; but some years ago, as my local church was seeking to take more seriously the models of Christ and of the apostle Paul, I realized my need to be obedient to the biblical pattern. I called in a few close friends in the church and stressed that I was exhausted because I had not been ministering in full accord with biblical methods. I pointed out, "Jesus worked through a small band of men, and for at least a year I would like you to become that group within our church. I would like two hours a week of your time for us to be together as a fellowship group."

They all with one accord began to make excuses! Understandably they were busy men. Finally one of them said, "This is not a discussion group. This is an altar call." And he went from one to the other saying, "Will you? Will you? Will you?" They all said yes, and that year of fellowship with those brothers provided a new beginning in my life. I learned that I could not live without contact with other believers, at close range.

THE THIRD PRIORITY—THE WORLD

Out of one's commitment to Christ and to the church must flow a concern for the world that Christ died to redeem. This logical sequence is seen in John 15: "Remain in me" (v. 4), "love each other" (v. 12), and "go and bear fruit" (v. 16).

If believers put their ministry to the world above their ministry to each other, they are likely to injure each other in the process. This writer has often seen missionaries—certainly dedicated to God (priority one) and certainly dedicated to their work (priority three)—who have completely overlooked priority two and are lonely Christians, bottled up with their fears and frustrations, not deeply knowing or being known. And this is true of many Christians in this country as well.

If followers of Christ look at their local church as basically an *organization*, they will see the people in it according to their *function*. There is George the choir director, and there is Mrs. Murphy who keeps the Sunday school attendance records. There is Charlie who does not teach his third-grade boys very well, and there is Susie, a student behind in paying her tuition. When people in the church are seen as workers, as producers, they quickly begin to judge each other.

On the other hand, if believers look at the local church as basically an *organism*, they will see the people in it as brothers and sisters, as members of the Body of Christ, as what they *are* more than what they *do*.

Out of commitment to each other must come commitment to the world. This eliminates the mindset of "God-bless-us-four-and-no-more" exclusivism. Together, in teams, in cooperative strategy, through prayer and through tears, believers are to reach out to the world.

Jesus said that the unity or togetherness of believers is in itself a witness to the world. It proves that they are genuine and that their faith is valid.[8] "A new commandment I give to you, that you love one another, even as I have loved you, that you also love one another. By this all men will know that you are My disciples, if you have love for one another" (John 13:34-35).

With those words, Jesus began His Upper Room discourse. And after that discourse He prayed in a similar vein: "I . . . ask . . . for those also who believe in Me through their word; that they may all be one; even as Thou, Father, art in Me, and I in Thee, that they also may be in Us; that the world may believe that Thou didst send Me . . . may [they] be perfected in unity, that the world may know that Thou didst send

Me, and didst love them, even as Thou didst love Me" (John 17:20-21, 23).

In a sense, the unity of believers in Christ is evangelistic, for it gives proof to the world that Christ is the Son sent from God and that God loves them as much as He loves His Son. Love for each other actually helps to teach unbelievers the gospel.

Immediately before His ascension, the Lord Jesus said, "As the Father has sent Me, I also send you" (John 20:21). Jesus had come to bring to the world the full-orbed compassion of the Father. He commissioned the twelve, and He has commissioned all believers with that same ministry.

The early church quickly got the picture. The Christians went out in compassion to the needy world, and they went out in teams. As Jesus had sent out the twelve and the seventy, so the first believers went out—two by two, or in small groups.

Peter and John teamed up, showing their unity in Christ. Such an unlikely pair! It is interesting that their names were frequently linked in the early chapters of Acts, in service and in preaching (Acts 3:1, 3-4, 11; 4:13, 19; 8:14).

Paul, Barnabas, and John Mark teamed up. On other occasions Paul was joined by Silas, Timothy, Luke, or others. Only in an emergency situation because of persecution did Philip minister alone in Samaria (Acts 8:4-13), but the apostles in Jerusalem heard about it and quickly sent along Peter and John (8:14-17).

These three priorities form a measurement by which Christians can test whether they are balanced. Is Christ being put first? Or is His preeminence merely a theological truth? Is there joy in fellowshiping with God's family as a local church, and with a few select believers on a deeper level? And is there a genuine, heartfelt reaching to the world? Only when these three priorities are operative and in their proper order is a believer—and a local church—balanced, whole, and biblical.

NOTES

1. Peter Drucker, "The Art of Doing the Important," *The Christian Ministry*, September 1972, p. 6.
2. Marcus Dods, "The Book of Genesis," in *The Expositor's Bible* (London: Hodder & Stoughton, 1907), p. 131.
3. Ezra Earl Jones, *Strategies for New Churches* (New York: Harper & Row, 1978), p. 17.

4. De Vern F. Fromke, *Ultimate Intention* (Mount Vernon, Mo.: Sure Foundation, 1962), p. 10.
5. Paul W. Witte, "Can Catholics Learn Anything from Evangelical Protestants?" *Christianity Today*, 18 December 1970, p. 14.
6. Alexander Whyte, *Lancelot Andrews and His Private Devotions* (London: Oliphant, Anderson, and Ferrier, 1896), p. 103.
7. See Robert Coleman, *The Master Plan of Evangelism* (Old Tappan, N.J.: Revell, 1963) for amplification of these ideas.
8. See Raymond C. Ortlund, *Lord, Make My Life a Miracle* (Glendale, Calif.: Gospel Light, Regal, 1974), and Raymond C. Ortlund, *Intersections* (Waco, Tex.: Word, 1979), pp. 69-87.

17

A Biblical View of the Marital Roles: Seeking a Balance

A. Duane Litfin

Should husbands and wives maintain distinct gender-based roles in marriage? Twenty years ago this question could scarcely have been raised in conservative Christian circles. Today it leaps out again and again from the pages, pulpits, and podiums of the evangelical world, and has become a major bone of contention even among those who claim allegiance to an authoritative Bible.

A quick survey of the battlefield seems to indicate that those who would answer the above question with a no (the feminists) have gained a current advantage against their well-entrenched opponents by a bold and daring foray into the realm of the Bible and theology. The most notable leaders of this attempt to gain the initiative are Letha Scanzoni and Nancy Hardesty[1] and Paul King Jewett.[2] Their books were listed high on *Eternity* magazine's 1975 list of most significant books[3] and have received a wide reading.

Those who would answer the question with a yes (the traditionalists) seem to have been caught off guard by this attack and have perhaps not yet regained their composure. Some angry reprisals have been given in book reviews and articles,

A. Duane Litfin
B.S., Philadelphia College of Bible; Th.M., Dallas Theological Seminary; Ph.D., Purdue University; graduate study toward Ph.D., Oxford University
Associate Professor of Pastoral Ministries
Dallas Theological Seminary

but a comprehensive counterattack has yet to be mounted. The fact is that the traditionalists have not shown themselves eager for battle in this particular arena. Some of their reservation may be attributed to a desire to avoid another battleground whereon evangelicals spill each other's blood. There are too many of these already. Others may be holding back, simply because to advocate the traditional, hierarchical view in the current climate of opinion is unpopular. For espousing such a "heresy," ministers are being denied ordination in some groups. Few relish being viewed as "against women."

Yet it seems that the deep concern of the traditionalists over the feminists' handling of the Scriptures will eventually crystallize into some sort of significant response. Hopefully, this response will involve not only an argument-by-argument refutation of alleged feminist errors, but a positive, balanced treatment of a hierarchical view of the marital roles. Perhaps the key word here is "balanced," for in refuting an opponent's position the tendency is often to allow the pendulum to swing past midpoint to an opposite extreme. The point of equilibrium, where both sides of the issue are held in tension, is often elusive. This article is an initial attempt to locate that important point of balance in an understanding of what the Bible says about gender-based roles in marriage.

VIEWS OF THE BIBLICAL ROLES

The traditional understanding of biblical roles in marriage is essentially this: the husband and wife function together in a "symbiotic" relationship. The word *symbiosis* is a biological term referring to two different organisms living in close association or union, especially where such an arrangement is advantageous to both. The opposite of symbiosis is *parasitism*, which refers to a relationship in which one organism lives off another organism and derives sustenance and protection from it without making compensation. God never intended that marriage partners should be leeches on one another; rather, He intended that they should live together in the closest possible harmony, fulfilling complementary and mutually edifying roles, so that both partners might conjointly grow and mature into their full potential. Traditionally the essence of these complementary, symbiotic roles has been defined in terms of the wife's submission to the authority of her husband, and the husband's selfless care for the needs of his wife.

Unfortunately, such an understanding of the marital roles has long suffered at the hands of misdirected males who have failed to grasp the inherent symbiotic balance God intended for marriage. Choosing to emphasize only the wife's responsibility to live under the authority of her husband, many have somehow come to the conclusion that the wife is secondary or even inferior in some essential way and therefore relatively unimportant. She exists, in this view, only to meet the needs of her husband. This is her purpose in life. She lives out her existence for and through her husband and submerges all of her individuality, intellect, feelings, opinions, dreams—indeed, her very potential as a human being—into her husband so that they are lost in him. She becomes subsumed under him, living her life almost vicariously through him, never attaining her full potential as a person who exists in her own right, for her own sake.

Such an aberrant view of the wife's role has too often characterized the church's teaching on marriage. Fortunately, this view is becoming increasingly untenable as the developments in contemporary secular society force Christians back to their biblical foundations. The church seems to be realizing anew that where marriages like this have existed or do exist, the husband has too often become like a parasite on his wife, drawing her very life from her and offering very little in return. Such marriages are neither biblical nor healthy, for either partner, and the church must not condone them even implicitly.

Similarly, there is another, more contemporary misunderstanding of the roles of the husband and wife that must also be resisted. The feminists argue that the marital roles of husband and wife as traditionally understood are themselves outdated and less than the biblical ideal—that, in other words, there ought to be no such thing as roles for husband and wife at all. The Bible clearly portrays man and woman as equal, says this view, and therefore any teaching that holds that the husband is the head of the wife in the sense of being in authority over her must be unbiblical. The underlying assumption here is that the woman's subordination automatically and inevitably implies her inferiority.[4] Since the female is clearly not inferior to the male—a premise evident from both Scripture and experience—it follows, the feminists argue, that there could be no inherent requirement on a wife, simply because she is a woman, to live in submission to her husband, simply because he is a man.

OBSERVATIONS CONCERNING THE FEMINIST VIEW

Several observations may be made about this view. First, it is not surprising that it has emerged. With the history of abuse experienced by the more balanced biblical position, and with the current atmosphere engendered by the secular feminist movement, it is not surprising to find even some evangelicals tending toward such an understanding of marriage.

Second, this view of marriage will probably not commend itself to most evangelicals, since such an interpretation requires feats of exegetical legerdemain most conservatives will be unwilling to perform. For example, the creation account of Genesis 2 must be considered merely a "story" rather than a historical account of the actual taking of woman from man.[5] Also several important texts from the epistles must be viewed as either non-Pauline or at least sub-Pauline passages wherein the apostle expresses embarrassingly sexist opinions that are contrary to his best instincts as reflected in Galatians 3:28.[6] Further, the overall tone of the Scriptures, with the exception of the gospel accounts of the life of Jesus, must be viewed as fundamentally demeaning of women and chauvinistic toward men, reflecting merely the rabbinic, patriarchal biases of the authors.[7] Most evangelicals will probably prefer to judge their culture by the Scriptures, rather than the Scriptures by their culture, and will reject such a handling of the Bible as inadequate. Thus this view of marriage probably has little potential for becoming the position of mainstream evangelicalism.

Third, it is also worth noting that the basic assumption undergirding this interpretation is faulty. Subordination does not automatically or inevitably imply inferiority. It has often been noted that within the Godhead full equality coincides with subordination, without any hint of inferiority being attached to the subordinate members. But there are other analogies even within the human sphere. For example, embedded in the fundamental principles of the society of the United States there exists a similar tension. On the one hand, the President of the United States holds a position of authority over the nation's citizens, and they are required by the Constitution to acknowledge that authority and submit to it. Yet on a more foundational level the Constitution also establishes the ideal that even the President is subject to the law of the land in the same way as the citizens; before the bar of justice they stand together coequal with him in the eyes of the law. Nothing in the President's position implies that all others are inferior to him; instead, their submission to him is purely pragmatic. Under the Constitution every citizen, whether President or pauper, stands equal before the blindfolded maiden of justice, each possessing the same inalienable rights as the other.

Since submission to authority implies nothing about the intrinsic superiority or inferiority of citizens or officials in society at large, why is it so difficult to recognize the same principle at work in the home as designed by God? To argue that the submission of the wife to the husband automatically implies the inferiority of the wife is to erect a straw man (or straw person?). It is perfectly consistent to say, as Paul clearly does on numerous occasions, that God has ordained, for the proper functioning of the home, that the husband is to serve as the head of the home and of the wife, but that in their standing before God in Christ, the two are absolutely equal (Gal. 3:28). To hold that God designed it so does not require one to say that the woman is inferior. The latter need not logically follow from the former, and it is perhaps not unfair to question the objectivity of those who keep insisting that it does.

Fourth, perhaps the most important observation about the view of marriage that would do away with the roles of husband and wife is this: At the heart of the issue this view shares the same shortcoming as that other abuse, which sees the wife as merely an addendum to her husband. Both views seem to suffer from a common misunderstanding of the authority God has given the husband in marriage. The man who attempts to subjugate his wife to himself has certainly missed the biblical balance, and therefore denies his wife her rightful personhood. In response, those who would eliminate the marital roles declare that such an abuse could never be God's design for marriage (and they are right!), and then proceed to throw out the proverbial baby with the bathwater. The important thing to note is that neither side of the issue has grasped the essential nature of the authority given to the husband by God, or of the subjection to that authority urged on the wife.

NATURE OF THE HUSBAND'S AUTHORITY

The New Testament word for "subjection" is the noun ὑποταγή, which is derived from two compound words, ὑπό, meaning "under, below," and τάγμα, meaning "that which is ordered, ranked, or placed in rows." According to the Scriptures, the originator of all rank and order is God, and all of the τάγματα or "orders" of time and creation have their source in Him (Rom. 13:1). Moreover, the New Testament speaks of several τάγματα: citizens are to be subject to civil authorities (Titus 3:1; Rom. 13:1); employees are to be subject to their employers (Titus 2:9); church members are to be subject to their leaders (1 Cor. 16:16) and to one another (Eph. 5:21); children are to be subject to their parents (1 Tim. 3:4); the church is to be subject to Christ (Eph. 5:24); and wives are to be subject to their husbands (Eph. 5:22; Col. 3:18). Ultimately all of these τάγματα or "over" and "under" relationships will find their goal in and be dissolved in God who is all in all (1 Cor. 15:24, 27-28). In the meantime, however, they are designed to preserve for mankind an orderly society in which to live. Thus the New Testament instructs the wife "to place or rank herself under" her husband (ὑποτάσσω, the verbal form of ὑποταγή, Eph. 5:21, 24; Col. 3:18; 1 Pet. 3:1), that is, to recognize his authority over her and to submit herself to it.

But what exactly is the authority of the husband? The New Testament concept of authority is best captured in the Greek term ἐξουσία, which in the King James Version is translated "authority" twenty-nine times and "power" sixty-nine times. This word is regularly used to designate "the power exercised by rulers or others in high position by virtue of their office."[8] In 1 Corinthians 11:10 it is used to speak of the sort of "power" God has given the husband over his wife.

What is often overlooked here is that the husband's "power" or authority in marriage is sourced not in any inherent superiority of the male but rather in the position or "office" God has given the husband within the overall τάγματα of society. Moreover, such authority in reality is only one of several kinds of authority human beings regularly exercise over each other, a fact that has major implications for the way the husband's role is to be viewed. This can be seen more clearly by examining briefly the kinds of authority ordinarily observed in human society.

Researchers in social psychology have designated at least five kinds of "social power," authority, or influence that human beings exercise over each other.[9] The first is called *information power*. A person, or source, exerts this sort of "power" over another when the information he controls influences the thinking or behavior of the recipient. *Referent power* exists when the recipient identifies with the source and desires to be like him. Thus the source influences the recipient by his example. *Coercive-reward power* exists when the recipient believes that the source can and will punish or reward his behavior. *Expert power* is the sort of influence that accrues to the source by knowing more or being able to do something better than the recipient. *Positional power* exists when the recipient accepts a relationship in which the source is permitted or obliged, because of his position, to prescribe behaviors for the recipient, and the recipient is obliged to accept this influence.

In examining the nature of the husband's authority over his wife as spelled out in the Bible, three crucial points emerge. First, of the five kinds of power or authority listed above, only the fifth—positional power—is designated by the New Testament as belonging to the husband; and even this type of "power" is not uniquely the husband's, for there are areas of authority over her husband that a wife holds by virtue of her position as well (see, e.g., 1 Cor. 7:4). Second, the other four types of authority are equally available to the husband and wife alike. Although it is probably true that coercive-reward power should seldom if ever be used by either marriage partner, the Bible clearly encourages the wife to exert several of the other types of power over her husband (e.g., the use of referent power in 1 Pet. 3:1-4, and the use of expert power in Prov. 31). Third, *the type of power delegated by God to the husband is the only one of the five that does not depend on some inherent superiority on the part of the one exerting the authority. Rather, it depends solely on the position God has given the husband in the overall hierarchy of human society.* Thus the wife is urged to submit herself to her husband "as to the Lord" (Eph. 5:22), for her submissive attitude is to be in response not to any intrinsic superiority of her male partner but to the design of a sovereign God who has placed her in that submissive role.

One option at this point, of course, is to question the wisdom of God in designing such an arrangement for the home in the first place. This seems to be what many Christians are doing today. But such an option is a dead-end street, even apart from the lack of faith it involves (Rom. 14:23; Heb. 11:6). It may never be understood why God gives a husband who is inferior to his wife a position of authority over her, any more than one can explain why God gives civil officials who are inferior to most of the populace a position of authority over them. In both cases the Christian's responsibility is to submit "as to the Lord" to those whom God has placed in authority, recognizing that such submission is not because the individual holding the position of authority is necessarily a superior human being, but rather because respect is due to the sovereign wisdom of the God who ordained that relationship of authority and submission (Rom. 13:1-2).

Such considerations ought to provide a much more balanced view of the "authority" of the husband. Those who favor the subjugation of the wife have clearly failed to grasp the fact that God has granted to the husband only a limited type of authority over his wife for the sake of the smooth functioning of the home, and that this authority is always to be exercised in understanding love (1 Pet. 3:7). Indeed, the example the husband is to emulate here is nothing less than the lofty one of Christ's selfless giving of Himself for His bride, the church (Eph. 5:25-30). Likewise, those who advocate the eradication of the biblical roles for husband and wife have seemingly also missed the balance point; otherwise, they would not continue to insist that submission inevitably implies inferiority. What both sides of the issue have failed to realize is that the biblical balance God intended for marriage says nothing about the inherent superiority or inferiority of the male or female, but rather provides both husband and wife with a wide range of opportunities to reach their full potential within the relationship.

Conclusion

The balanced biblical view of the mutually complementary or symbiotic roles of the husband and wife in marriage is an integral part of the overall framework for human society as revealed in God's Word. It must not be allowed to be bent out of shape by abuses from any quarter. The contemporary feminist movement has done the church a favor by forcing it to reevaluate what the Bible actually teaches about the husband-and-wife relationship in marriage, thereby bringing to renewed attention a long-standing abuse of the doctrine by misguided men whose prejudices blinded them to the truth. In working diligently to eliminate this abuse, Christians should not fall prey to another abuse that emerges from an equally twisted and prejudiced understanding of the Bible. For this second abuse, which urges that the roles of husband and wife be eliminated altogether, will no doubt prove equally as bad as the first.

NOTES

1. Letha Scanzoni and Nancy Hardesty, *All We're Meant to Be* (Waco, Tex.: Word, 1974).
2. Paul King Jewett, *Man as Male and Female* (Grand Rapids: Eerdmans, 1975).
3. *Eternity*, December 1975, pp. 44-45.
4. In Virginia Mollenkott's foreword to Jewett, she writes, "To my knowledge [Paul King Jewett], is the first evangelical theologian to face squarely the fact that if woman must of necessity be subordinate, she must of necessity be inferior" (p. 8).
5. See Jewett, pp. 120-28.
6. Cf. Scanzoni and Hardesty, pp. 23-72; and Jewett, pp. 142-47.
7. See Jewett, pp. 86-119.
8. William F. Arndt and F. Wilbur Gingrich, *A Greek-English Lexicon of the New Testament and Other Early Christian Literature* (Chicago: U. of Chicago, 1957), p. 278.
9. Barry E. Collins and Bertram H. Raven, "Group Structure: Attraction, Coalitions, Communication, and Power," in *Handbook of Social Psychology*, ed. Gardner Lindzey and Elliot Aronson, 5 vols. (Reading, Mass.: Addison Wesley, 1969), 4:166-68.

18

Paul, Women, and Contemporary Evangelical Feminism

H. Wayne House

Various approaches have been used in recent years to explain the apostle Paul's statements on the role of women in the church. To today's new feminine consciousness the apostle appears to be a formidable foe. He is not considered an obstacle to the secular feminist, but Paul must be considered by the evangelical Christian before one makes a final statement of conviction. This article examines how the apostle is understood by different interpreters today, and interacts with some recent developments in the interpretation of Paul on women among some feminists who claim to be within evangelicalism.[1]

APPROACHES TO PAUL'S THINKING ABOUT WOMEN

PAUL AS A MISOGYNIST

The apostle is seen by many feminists as one who hates women, or at least as one who accepts the inferiority and debasedness of the female. The contention is that Paul must be interpreted in the light of intertestamental rabbinic misogyny. It is argued that since Paul received his training under

H. Wayne House
A.B., Hardin Simmons College; M.Div., Th.M., Western Conservative Baptist Seminary; Th.D., Concordia Seminary
Assistant Professor of Bible
Le Tourneau College
Longview, Texas

Gamaliel, one of the most famous rabbis, and since he was a man socialized in a very chauvinistic society, it was natural for Paul to believe in the inferiority of women.[2] In line with this idea, Richardson says, "The goal in Paul's exegesis appears to be, without I hope being unduly harsh, greater conformity with the Jewish (or Palestinian) view of subordination of women (1 Tim. 2:11-15; 1 Cor. 11:7-16, especially vv. 10, 12)."[3]

According to this view, Paul must be understood in the light of his training in the Old Testament, which purportedly denigrates women, but the intertestamental writings and rabbinic sources exerted an even greater influence on Paul's low view of women.[4]

PAUL AS A PHILOGYNIST

Rather than considering Paul a hater of women, some have perceived him as one attracted to women. But if that were so, what should we say about those supposed "anti-feminine, pro-subordination-of-women passages"? Walker suggests one solution, in his discussion on 1 Corinthians 11:2-16 as an interpolation:

> This means, of course, that the passage (1 Cor. 11:2-16) cannot be used as a source for determining Paul's attitude toward the proper status and role of women. If the authenticity of 1 Tim. 2:8-15; Tit. 2:3-5; Eph. 5:22-33; Col. 3:18-19; and 1 Cor. 14:33-36 (or 34-35) is similarly rejected on critical grounds, as I am inclined to do, then the genuine Pauline corpus contains none of the passages which advocate male supremacy and female subordination in any form. On the contrary, the only direct Pauline statement on the subject is Gal. 3:28, which insists on absolute equality in Christ.[5]

Walker's assumptions on Pauline philogyny take on primary importance in his rejection of 1 Corinthians 11:2-16.[6] So then, one may excise seemingly conflicting statements and have blissful harmony; Paul is not "the all-time chauvinist," but instead, "the one clear voice in the New Testament asserting the freedom and equality of women in the eschatological community," in the words of Scroggs.[7]

A more positive approach to the Pauline corpus is taken by Leonard, who quotes Holzner as saying that "St. Paul was the first person who saw the value of women as workers in the Church and used them extensively in the development of the missions."[8] He is presented as one who worked with, preached to, and accepted men and women on an equal plane. Examples of this abound: Phoebe carried important papers for Paul (Rom. 16:1-2); the apostle sent equal greetings to men and women (Rom. 16); he urged both to do the work of deacons and deaconesses (1 Tim. 3:11); he had a high regard for Priscilla and Aquila (Rom. 16:3-4); and Paul regarded highly the information he received from Chloe's household at Corinth (1 Cor. 1:11).[9] Where did Paul receive this attitude? It came, according to Leonard, from Paul's interpretation of Christ's message of equality.[10]

PAUL AS A THEOLOGICAL SCHIZOPHRENIC

In contrast to the two foregoing opinions about Paul and women a third option is now being offered by many, among whom are some evangelical feminists whose basic presupposition is as follows: "All of us as Christians are called to forsake the ways of the world which include domination and lording it over others. . . . In Christ there is no chain of command but a community founded by self-giving love."[11] With this basic assumption as the rudder for interpretation, evangelical feminists (or biblical feminists) see a tension in the thinking of Paul who supposedly accepted an equal status for women "in Christ" but at the same time put them in an inferior position. Virginia Mollenkott pointedly says, "There are flat contradictions between some of his theological arguments and his own doctrines and behaviors."[12]

Stendahl recognizes the dichotomy between the social order and one's position before God in the New Testament, but he sees a direct contradiction between the two. The most important breakthrough in the proper attitude toward women is Galatians 3:28. Unlike other Pauline writings, this verse is a theological statement directed against what is called the order of creation, and it creates a tension with those biblical passages used to subordinate women.[13]

Paul is thus viewed as both an enslaver and deliverer of women. He gave the great emancipation theology, it is said, in Galatians, bringing to written and didactic fulfillment the attitudes and actions of Jesus toward women. On the other hand, he is charged with supporting their inferiority throughout his writings. Some feminists view Paul at times as a rabbi and at other times as a Christian.

Paul as a rabbi. In reference to Galatians 3:28 Jewett says that Paul was more cautious in the implementation of his own insight, since he had spoken of women as being subordinate and unequal.[14] But why would Paul act that way? According to Mollenkott this contradiction in the apostle is because of his rabbinical training: "For Bible believers the problem is that the apostle Paul seems to contradict his own teachings and behavior concerning women, apparently because of inner conflicts between the rabbinical training he had received and the liberating insights of the gospel."[15]

Also Jewett accepts this rabbinic spell on Paul. In discussing Paul's teaching in 1 Corinthians 11, Jewett says, "It appears from the evidence that Paul himself sensed that his view of the man/woman relationship, inherited from Judaism, was not altogether congruous with the gospel he preached."[16] He then concludes, "Here we have what may be the first expression of an uneasy conscience on the part of a Christian theologian who argues for the subordination of the female to the male by virtue of her derivation from the male."[17] Thus Paul is viewed by Jewett as having a continual struggle between his programmed rabbinic chauvinism and his new insights in Christ.

Paul as a Christian. In what way did Paul as a Christian differ from Paul as a rabbi? Paul, according to Jewett, accepted the equality of male and female in Christ not simply as a theory but he acted out this truth remarkably, especially for a former rabbi. Though he did not implement this new view completely, he did let it begin to take effect in his own life and in the church.[18]

Galatians 3:28 was the great charter of Christian equality, and to many this passage is the key to the male/female problem. It holds the key to bringing harmony, and removes the clash that necessarily occurs when one sex is viewed as inferior to the other.[19] But what about the other Pauline passages on women and men's relationship? They are all concerned with practical issues of personal relationships or behavior in worship services.[20] The passages in which Paul supposedly contradicts Galatians 3:28 are viewed as a misunderstanding, on Paul's part, of the creation narratives. Paul inappropriately draws the conclusion, it is said, that man is to exercise authority over woman because man was created first (1 Tim. 2:13) and because woman was derived from man (1 Cor. 11:7-9).[21]

How is an evangelical supposed to react to these misinter-
pretations of Paul? Mollenkott gives one asnwer:

> We must open our eyes to these conflicts, demonstrating
> faith in the God who allowed them to appear in the New Testa-
> ment. We must conquer our fear that honest attention to what
> we see in the Bible will undercut the doctrine of inspiration. We
> must allow the facts of Scripture to each us in the way it is
> inspired, rather than forcing Scripture to conform to our own
> theories about it.[22]

Thus the consensus of many feminists within evangelicalism declares that a tension existed within the apostle Paul,
which sometimes caused him to regress to rabbinical misogyny and at other times led him to the higher view of women
that the Lord Jesus possessed. Christians are asked to accept
this contradiction in the writings and teachings of the apostle
and to develop a view of Scripture in line with this conclusion.

SOME PROBLEMS WITH THE CONTEMPORARY EVANGELICAL FEMINIST APPROACH

Two major problems exist in much of the current feminist
argumentation: (1) a low view of inspiration, and (2) an
improper hermeneutic.

ITS LOW VIEW OF INSPIRATION

Scripture is presented by many evangelical feminists as
having erroneous teaching on the role of women. Pinnock, in
a recent work on inerrancy, acknowledges that "moderate"
evangelicals (advocates of limited inerrancy) tend to handle
the Bible like liberals. He avers that Jewett does so in *Man
as Male and Female*, since he attributes to Paul a sub-Christian view on women in Paul's passages that cannot be harmonized with Galatians 3:28. Pinnock argues that if this is
so then God does not always speak in Scripture, and therefore the reader must determine when God does and when He
does not. He observes, "In principle this seems to be liberal,
not firmly evangelical, theological methodology, and therefore a disturbing doctrinal development."[23]

Similar to Jewett, Mollenkott has bodly declared that
Paul contradicted himself in his teaching on women.[24] Interestingly, although she says that Paul misinterpreted the Genesis
2 account, she hesitates to call Paul's position an error in
Scripture. She says that Paul was thinking aloud and trying

to work through his conflicts.[25] (One wonders how broad a meaning the term "error" may have, or exactly who in this discussion is contradictory.) Mollenkott believes that Paul interpreted Genesis 2 the way he did because of what he had been socialized to think is natual.[26]

It appears to me that the aforementioned procedure opens a Pandora's box in regard to biblical interpretation. Whatever one disagrees with in Scripture may be simply relegated to socialization. Could not one consider the holy wars of Joshua cultural? Or were not Paul's views on homosexuality merely socialization? Mollenkott answers that the words "and God said 'Go down and smite them' " are to be regarded as socialization, and therefore the words "God said" were only an assumption of Joshua.[27] In addition, she and Scanzoni have recently written that evangelical opposition to some forms of "legitimate" homosexuality is because of homophobia in present-day society rather than the teaching of Scripture.[28]

What about those evangelicals who reject this line of reasoning about socialization and the de-absolutizing of biblical culture because of their belief in the full inspiration of Scripture? Mollenkott answers that they will come to a more scholarly approach to the Bible and will learn the difference between faith and fear.[29] Mollenkott continues, "Things have come to a bad pass when we have to avoid seeing certain facts of Scriptures (or to avoid *admitting* that we see them) in order to preserve our preconceived notions about inspiration."[30]

There can be little question that the transgression of the above-mentioned feminists in the matter of inspiration goes beyond acceptable limits in evangelical theology. If areas of disagreement may be eliminated merely by an appeal to socialization, then interpretation has no controls, and the idea of limited revelation or degrees of inspiration can hardly be avoided. Are Paul's arguments on the doctrine of sin coming from one man to be discounted in view of contemporary anthropological studies? Or is it to be argued that Paul merely borrowed his ideas on original sin from rabbinical theology? These obviously must be answered in the negative. But the real question is whether one will be submissive to the revealed Word of God.

ITS IMPROPER HERMENEUTIC

Did Jesus contradict the Old Testament? The citation of Scripture against Scripture seems to be characteristic of many feminists. Justification for this is offered by Jewett when he says that Christ is his example in his interpretive method. In Mark 10:3-5 Christ was asked if His view of divorce was in harmony with the Mosaic law. Jesus, Jewett says, in a sense appealed to Scripture against Scripture. Although Jesus acknowledged that the Mosaic legislation allowed for divorce, He recognized that it did not express the true intent of creation in regard to monogamous marriage. Jesus, in citing Genesis 1:27 and 2:24, said that the permission given in Deuteronomy 24:1 was on account of hardness of hearts—a cultural conditioning—and was not the will of God. Jewett then applies this reasoning to his intepretation of Paul on women:

> Such reasoning, we submit, is analogous ... to that which we have followed in seeking to understand the Pauline statement of sexual hierarchy in the light of the creation ordinance of sexual partnership. To say that a man may write a bill of divorce and put away his wife, or to say that the woman by definition is subordinate to the man, is to come short of the revealed intent of the Creator; it is to break the analogy of faith.[31]

Severe fallacies are present in Jewett's presentation: (a) Jesus was not contradicting the passage in Deuteronomy 24 by His appeal to the creation narrative. He expressed God's original intention over and against God's concession. God inspired the Deuteronomic legislation (Deut. 12:1, 26:16—27:1); it was not merely a socialization apart from God's direction. In reality this case-law gave women protection that would not necessarily have been so generous if it originated purely from a male-dominated society. Jewett seems to recognize the tenuousness of his argument when he uses the phrase "in a sense" when referring to Jesus' appeal to Scripture against Scripture. However, Jesus really did not contradict Scripture. It is a non sequitur to say that one Scripture passage may be cited against another. (b) To assert that Paul must be interpreted against himself is to assume that he misinterpreted the Old Testament in practically all of his writings on women (with Galatians 3:28 being the one exception). The reason this latter passage becomes all-important to feminists is that it is the only real passage in epistolary literature that is amiable (*prima facie*) with their desired teaching on women. However, it is not at all certain that Galatians 3 is concerned with the question of the social equality of male and female. Nor is it self-evident (as will be discussed later), that tension exists between this text and the other Pauline teachings on the subject.[32]

Did Paul contradict himself? Evangelical feminists contend that Paul was divided in himself about his view of women and was not faithful in bringing proper completion to the teachings of Christ, and that he misinterpreted the second creation narrative to propagate the inferiority of women. Mollenkott writes, "Each of these Pauline contrasts reinforces the impression that according to his rabbinical training Paul believed in female subordination but that according to his Christian vision he believed that the gospel conferred full equality on all believers."[33] My contention, however, is that there was no contradiction in Paul, that he was in perfect harmony with Jesus' view on the equality and role of women, and that he correctly understood the presentation of man and woman in Genesis 1 and 2 and deduced proper implications from those narratives for the responsibilities of man and women in the church and the home.

Those feminists who see a contradiction in Paul make several false assumptions that lead them to wrong conclusions.

First, it is assumed that equality between persons requires interchangeability of roles. Since Paul regarded women as equal with men (Gal. 3:28), but did not let them teach or exercise authority over men (1 Tim. 2:12), he was contradictory. But this assumption is without support both in experience and in the Scriptures. Parents and children, employers and employees, the President and citizens of the United States are all equal as persons, but they have definite role differences. Also, although church members are equal in Christ, some members are in positions of authority in the local congregation (1 Thess. 5:12; Titus 1:5; Heb. 13:17; 1 Pet. 5:1-5).

Second, evangelical feminists assume that Paul borrowed his views on feminine subordination from rabbinic sources rather than the Old Testament, or that when he did go to the Old Testament he interpreted it in a rabbinical fashion, which caused him to arrive at wrong conclusions.[34] Rabbinic influence on the New Testament writers is very debatable, since most of the sources were written centuries later, and even isolated talmudic statements may only represent individual thought and not a generally held opinion. Whether talmudic ideas were influential on Paul is not part of this debate. The point is that if they were influential, they were not necessarily wrong, nor was the apostle Paul wrong in using them under the guidance of the Holy Spirit.

Third, evangelical feminism's position on Paul leads to a rejection of his authority as an apostle. In writing to the Corinthians about his authority, Paul spoke of his own teaching and that which is based on oral tradition from Jesus. But he did not consider the acceptance of his teachings as optional (1 Cor. 11:1-2; 14:33b-38). Thus modern-day feminism falls into the Corinthian error of attempting to consider some of Paul's teachings optional.

Fourth, evangelical feminists insist that all the other passages on women are in practical contexts whereas Galatians 3:28 is the only theological one. "Of all the passages concerning women in the New Testament, only Galatians 3:28 is in a doctrinal setting; the remainder are all concerned with practical matters."[35] They are saying, then, that Galatians 3:28 is a more important passage for this issue in the Pauline epistle than his others. Whether this is true or not, their major fallacy is that they distinguish between the theological and the practical in Paul's argumentation, as Dunham so aptly says:

> The fact is, that Galatians is not completely doctrinal and 1 Corinthians and 1 Timothy completely practical. Anyone who knows the style of the apostle Paul ... will remember that he characteristically sets forth his doctrine, then brings the practical implications out of that. Further, his reason for writing the letter to the Galatians was a practical and a theological one. Our practice is solidly built upon our theology, and so was his. The problem of circumcision—practical, arose because of the misunderstanding of the relationship between Law and Grace, and the new covenant versus the old—theological.[36]

Fifth, it is wrongly assumed that Galatians 3:28 teaches the elimination of hierarchical structure because all are one in Christ. Such an interpretation is beside the point in the passage at hand. Rather than doing away with societal distinctions, this verse concerns the subject of justification and the believer's relationship to the Abrahamic covenant. Paul was not seeking to demonstrate social equality relationships among the classes he mentioned; instead he wished to show that all, regardless of standing in society, may participate by faith in the inheritance of Abraham, to be sons of God. To draw social implications from Galatians 3:28 is to go beyond the text. Boucher says that "the ideas of equality before God and inferiority in the social order are in harmony in the New Testament. To be precise, the tension did not exist in first century thought, and it is not present in the texts themselves. The tension arises from *modern man's* inability to hold these two ideas together."[37] If Boucher is correct in her analysis, there is an implicit admittance of female subordination on the apostle's part even in this text usually marshalled for an egalitarian view of sexual relationship.

Did Paul contradict Christ? There can be little argument against the fact that Jesus had a high view of womanhood. Albrecht Oepke has written: "We never hear from the lips of Jesus a derogatory word concerning woman as such. In holding out the prospect of sexless beings like that of angels in the consummated kingdom of God . . . He indirectly lifts from woman the curse of her sex and sets her at the side of man as equally the child of God."[38] Also Jewett recognizes Jesus' high view of woman, when discussing His actions recorded in Luke 10:38-42.

> What Jesus did in this case must have been absolutely incomprehensible to them. They would never dream of entering a house occupied by two unmarried women, let alone discoursing with them, especially concerning spiritual things. Jesus is here showing an utter disregard for custom in order that he might do his kingdom work. And so he fellowshipped with these women who were his disciples even as he fellowshipped with men who were his disciples. He showed the same intimacy and esteem toward Mary and Martha as he showed toward men.[39]

Is Paul to be seen as the betrayer of Christ in reference to women? Some view Paul as seeking greater conformity with the Jewish view of women rather than following Christ's new freedom. For example, Richardson states that Paul "has not pushed Jesus' new view of women any further, but has rather retreated, in the face of local factors that threaten the stability of the struggling community of believers, to a more Judaic and rigidly Pharisaic view."[40] Mollenkott adds that "Jesus doesn't seem to matter much to traditional evangelicals; Paul is the one who counts."[41]

Was Christ's perception of women really contradictory to Paul's? Though Jesus did treat women with kindness and respect[42] and considered them equal before God, the biblical records say nothing at all about His considering women equal to men in ministerial leadership or spiritual headship. There is no evidence that any woman was commissioned as one of the seventy or the twelve.[43] Women are not represented among the apostles to head the heavenly rule of Christ to come in the New Jerusalem. No amount of argument or rhetoric can change these facts.

How does Paul compare to Christ? The book of Acts and Paul's epistles reveal the tender heart Paul had toward women and his appreciation for their help in the gospel ministry.[44] But nowhere did he ordain them as overseers, nor did they serve as apostolic representatives to the churches. Richardson is correct; Paul has gone no further than Jesus—and neither should believers today. Christ and Paul have no tension between equality and hierarchy as based on creation.

Did Paul misunderstand the Old Testament? The last problem posited by feminists concerns the apostle's supposed misinterpretation of the creation narrative in his counsel on women in 1 Corinthians 11; 14; and 1 Timothy 2. Some think that God originally intended an egalitarian social relationship among men and women but that the curse (Gen. 3:16) brought women into enslavement. Acceptance of Christ brings about an abrogation of this curse. Genesis 1:27 is viewed as teaching the simultaneous creation of male and female, with the result that the two are functionally and ontologically equal, whereas Genesis 2 presents woman created after man. Though Paul correctly interprets Genesis 1 in Galatians 3:28, it is argued, he draws improper conclusions on the subordination of the female from Genesis 2. Scanzoni and Hardesty assert this position in their discussion of 1 Corinthians 11:8-9: "The second creation narrative does say that woman was made from and for man, but the theological leap from this to woman's subordination is a traditional rabbinic . . . understanding that is not supported by the text."[45]

Who has misinterpreted Genesis 1 and 2—Paul, or some modern feminists? First, Genesis 1:26-28 has nothing to say about social relationships between male and female. It speaks of the ontological unity of male and female with both being image-bearers of God. From this passage Paul concludes that both have an equal right to the grace of God (Gal. 3:28). Moreover, the text does not say they were created simultaneously as some have claimed.[46] There is no time frame given in Genesis 1 as there is in Genesis 2.

Second, Genesis 2 indicates that Yahweh created male, and then created female. This is true whether one takes the details literally or figuratively. The woman was to be a helper (not slave) to the man, corresponding to him. Since Adam named her, a prerogative in the Old Testament to the one having authority,[47] he demonstrated his authority over her. This priority in Paul's teaching proved man's responsibility for the woman, which is to be carried out with sacrificial love (Eph. 5:22-33). Her responsibility is to follow his leading willingly. These roles stem from God's creation, not from man's Fall (1 Cor. 11:8-9; 1 Tim. 2:12-14).[48]

Third, Genesis 3:16 does not introduce the hierarchical structure of male and female. That structure is found in the creation narrative of Genesis 2. The Genesis 3 passage reveals the distortion of the original pattern. Rather than man lovingly ruling and woman willingly being submissive, the war of the sexes had begun. Man would seek dominance, with woman vying for his position.[49] This conflict, not the hierarchical structure, is gradually to be done away in Christ (Eph. 5). Man is to love as he leads, and woman is to submit herself to her husband. In Christ the creation intentions for male and female are restored. Paul understood this; unfortunately the feminists do not.

CONCLUSION

The preceding material has been presented to draw attention to underlying presuppositions and methods of arguments by many influential feminists in evangelicalism. Whether these individuals have a proper right to the term *evangelical* is a difference of opinion, but that they have weakened the walls is undeniable. They have developed an obviously inadequate view of inspiration and an unacceptable hermeneutic. In seeking to cause the biblical text to speak their language, rather than learning its language, these feminists have often eisegeted the Scriptures and fabricated inconsistencies and tensions in Paul of which he was unaware.

NOTES

1. In this article evangelical feminists are not to be considered a stereotype of all feminists, but only of those who follow the thinking of those interacted with in this article. The author recognizes many legitimate grievances of some feminists.
2. Virginia Mollenkott, "A Conversation with Virginia Mollenkott," *The Other Side*, May-June 1976, p. 26. Mollenkott would also consider Paul to have a philogynist side to his nature, so her views will be discussed later in this article.
3. Peter Richardson, "Paul Today: Jews, Slaves, and Women," *Crux* 8 (1970): 37.
4. Tosefta Berakoth reads, "One should not trust a woman's virture or intelligence, since sin came about through her. They are all more or less given to witchcraft. Men who let themselves be led by women are ridiculed. Every pious Jew repeats the prayer of R. Judah: 'Blessed be He who has not made me a woman' " (vii. 18, cited by Joseph Bonsirven, *Palestinian Judaism in the Time of Jesus Christ* [New York: Holt, Rinehart and Winston, 1964], p. 100).
5. William O. Walker, "1 Corinthians 11:2-16 and Paul's Views Regarding Women," *Journal of Biblical Literature* 94 (March 1975): 109. See the rebuttal to Walker's arguments by Jerome Murphy-O'Connor, in his article, "The Non-Pauline Character of 1 Corinthians 11:2-16?" *Journal of Biblical Literature* 95 (December 1976):615-21.
6. Walker, "1 Corinthians 11:2-16," p. 104.
7. Robin Scroggs, "Paul and the Eschatological Woman," *Journal of the American Academy of Religion* 40(1972):302.
8. Joseph Holzner, cited by Eugene Andruss Leonard, "St. Paul on the Status of Women," *Catholic Biblical Quarterly* 12(July 1950):317.
9. Ibid., pp. 315-19.
10. Ibid., p. 320.
11. Letha Scanzoni and Nancy Hardesty, *All We're Meant to Be* (Waco, Tex.: Word, 1974), p. 22.
12. Mollenkott, "A Conversation," p. 22.
13. Krister Stendahl, *The Bible and the Role of Women*, trans. Emilie T. Sander (Philadelphia: Fortress, 1966), p. 32.
14. Paul Jewett, *Man as Male and Female* (Grand Rapids: Eerdmans, 1975), p. 145.
15. Virginia Mollenkott, *Women, Men, and the Bible* (Nashville: Abingdon), p. 96. One example of this dependence on rabbinical thought that she cites is 1 Corinthians 14:34 where women"are not allowed to speak, but must be submissive, as the Law says," which law she curiously interprets as being not the Old Testament, but as a reference to the social custom of first-century Judaism (ibid.).
16. Jewett, p. 113.
17. Ibid.
18. Jewett illustrates this radical change of attitude on the part of the former rabbi: (a) In rabbinic usage a woman was designated only as the wife of another man, whereas Paul in Romans greets the women by name; (b) Priscilla's name is mentioned before her husband's; (c) Paul calls Phoebe, who delivered the epistle to the Romans, a sister; (d) as a rabbi he hardly would address a group of women with no man present, yet he did this at Philippi without any hesitation (Acts 16:13); (e) he accepted the invitation of Lydia without the slightest scruple (Acts 16:15) (Jewett, pp. 145-46).

19. Scanzoni and Hardesty, p. 15.
20. Ibid., pp. 18-19. Mollenkott writes, "All those passages are addressed to very specific cases. But Galatians 3 which says there is no male or female is in a fully theological context. So that context tells us that Galatians is normative while the others are cultural" ("A Conversation," p. 73).
21. Jewett, p. 142; Scanzoni and Hardesty, pp. 27-28.
22. Mollenkott, *Women, Men, and the Bible,* p. 105
23. Clark Pinnock, "Three Views of the Bible in Contemporary Theology," in *Biblical Authority,* ed. Jack Rogers (Waco, Tex.: Word, 1977), pp. 69-70. Similarly Lindsell sounds an alarm, "At stake here is not the matter of women's liberation. What is the issue for the evangelical is the fact that some of the most ardent advocates of egalitarianism in marriage over against hierarchy reach their conclusion by directly and deliberately denying that the Bible is the infallible rule of faith and practice" (Harold Lindsell, "Egalitarianism and Scriptural Infallibility," *Christianity Today,* 26 March 1976, p. 46).
24. Mollenkott, "A Conversation," p. 25.
25. Ibid., pp. 27-28.
26. Ibid.
27. Ibid., p. 30.
28. Virginia Mollenkott and Letha Scanzoni, "Homosexuality: 2 Perspectives," *Daughters of Sarah,* Nov./Dec. 1977, pp. 6-7.
29. Mollenkott, "A Conversation," p. 75.
30. Mollenkott, *Women, Men and the Bible,* p. 103 (italics hers).
31. Jewett, pp. 136-37.
32. If one were to follow the reasoning used by feminists cited in this article, it could be suggested that "male and female" in Galatians 3:28 is an early interpolation by a rare feminist scribe. Or it might be argued that the verse was written by a less experienced and mature apostle (late A.D. 40s). Sensing the radicalism of some first-century Christian feminists, based on this type of teaching found in Galatians 3:28, he excluded it from his subsequent writings. Colossians 3:11 (late A.D. 50s or early 60s) has a similar listing but omits the phrase "male and female." Also the difference in 1 Corinthians (middle A.D. 50s) and 1 Timothy (middle A.D. 60s) may be noted.
33. Mollenkott, *Women, Men, and the Bible,* p. 103.
34. The idea that Paul is referring to rabbinic traditions when he uses "law" in 1 Corinthians 14:33b-35, as Mollenkott has suggested (Ibid., p. 98), is pure conjecture.
35. Scanzoni and Hardesty, p. 71.
36. Duane Dunham, "Women in the Ministry, Ephesians 5 and Galatians 3," chapel lecture (Portland, Ore.: Western Conservative Baptist Seminary, 1968), p. 8.
37. Madeline Boucher, "Some Unexplored Parallels to 1 Cor. 11:11-12 and Galatians 3:28: The NT on the Role of Women, " *Catholic Biblical Quarterly* 31(1969):57-58 (italics hers). In her article she compares the "pairs" in Galatians 3:28 with that of rabbinical materials.
38. Albrecht Oepke, in *Theological Dictionary of the New Testament,* ed. Gerhard Kittel and Gerhard Friedrich, 10 vols. (Grand Rapids: Eerdmans, 1964-1976), s.v., γυνή, 1(1964):785.
39. Jewett, p. 99.
40. Richardson, p. 37.
41. Mollenkott, "A Conversation," p. 26.
42. One must recognize that the attitude of Christ to women was not unique in the Mediterranean world. The Epicureans had a high regard for

women in their school; women were treated as equals. Even in Jewish society the common label of Jewish misogyny must be tempered. Epstein has demonstrated that women, before talmudic times, were given access to worship in Judaism approaching that of men and there is some evidence they could read the Torah in mixed crowds. Certainly many rabbis had a high regard for women, even teaching them the Torah (Louis M. Epstein, *Sex Laws and Customs in Judaism* [New York: KTAV, 1968], pp. 78-85).

43. Since culturally one would expect the seventy to be men, and since the twelve were men, the burden of proof is on the one who wants to find women among the seventy commissioned by Jesus.

44. See fn. 18.

45. Scanzoni and Hardesty, p. 28.

46. Mollenkott, "A Conversation," p. 28.

47. Umberto Cassuto, *A Commentary on the Book of Genesis*, 2 vols., trans. Israel Abrahams, Part I: *From Adam to Noah* (Jerusalem; Magnes, 1961), p. 130.

48. Some argue against priority as a basis for man's leadership. Scanzoni and Hardesty say, "Man was made from dust but this does not make him subordinate to the earth" (p. 28). However, the Genesis narrative is discussing male as prior to female as uniquely created by God; it is not simply discussing the question of priority in general.

49. See the excellent article by Susan T. Foh, "What Is the Woman's Desire?" *Westminster Theological Journal* 27(Spring 1975):376-83.

19

Integrating Faith and Learning: Principles and Process

Kenneth O. Gangel

On September 20, 1912, the great Christian apologist J. Gresham Machen addressed the convocation exercises at the opening of Princeton Theological Seminary's one hundred and first year. The address stands to the present hour as one of the great classics on what is now called "the integration of faith and learning." Perhaps Machen tipped his hand that day regarding the caliber of his address when he added these words in the very first line: "One of the greatest of the problems that have agitated the Church is the problem of the relation between knowledge and piety, between culture and Christianity."[1] The gauntlet was laid, the banner was raised, and over more than six decades later Christian educators are still attempting to practice what Machen said in that hour.

And yet most educators are able to talk about the integration of faith and learning better than they can practice it. Indeed, in some quarters it becomes almost a symbol, a shibboleth to be uttered but not demonstrated. Invariably it is a rallying cry that will bring nods of approval from the faithful multiplied hundreds of teachers in Christian classrooms at all

Kenneth O. Gangel
A.B., Taylor University; M.Div., Grace Theological Seminary; S.T.M., Concordia Theological Seminary; Ph.D., University of Missouri at Kansas City; Litt.D., Mercy College
Professor and Chairman, Department of Christian Education
Dallas Theological Seminary

levels of education as they continue to grope for evasive implementation of the ideal.

The phrase "integration of truth" refers to *the teaching of
all subjects as a part of the total truth of God, thereby
enabling the student to see the unity of natural and special
revelation*. Though this may seem simplistic, it requires a lifetime of effort and the best possible education a teacher can
bring to his task in order to achieve what Machen challenged
educators to do that September evening.

PRINCIPLES FOR INTEGRATING FAITH AND LEARNING

The cardinal essential for the achievement of the integration of truth in the Christian classroom is *a commitment
to the authority of the Bible*. Gaebelein identifies several reasons why the Word of God "must be central in Christian
education":

> 1. The sheer, unapproachable greatness of the written Word of
> God ... to take as the center of the curriculum the one book
> among all the other great books to which alone the superlative
> "greatest" can without challenge be uniquely applied — this is
> neither narrow nor naive. Rather it is simply good judgment to
> center on the best rather than the second best.
>
> 2. Its authority as the inspired, inerrant Word of God.
>
> 3. Its indispensable critical function. In a day of debased values
> and satisfaction with the second and even third rate, education
> requires a standard and point of reference by which the cheap-
> ened standards of our day may be judged.
>
> 4. It relates to the all-important matter of knowing and finding
> the truth.[2]

Quite obviously any one of Gaebelein's points could be
expanded into a full treatise of theological and pedagogical
implications. The essential issue here, however, centers on the
word *authority*. It is one thing to verbalize a commitment to
the inspiration of Scripture; it is quite another to accept the
inerrant authority of Scripture as the centerpiece for contemporary education.

And that leads to a second principle: The integration of
faith and learning demands *a recognition of the contempora-
neity of the Bible and the Holy Spirit*. Here the authoritative
and inerrant Bible is related to the student's life where he is.
To borrow an idea from Korzybski, the great general semanti-

cist, the "here and now" depends greatly on the "then and there." The Bible, as God's special written revelation, is an accurate and absolute record of the "then and there" which in most cases continues to the "here and now." But the Bible alone is insufficient to develop a distinctively evangelical view of the teaching-learning process. The educator must also recognize the role of the Holy Spirit in interpreting God's truth in accordance with the words of the Lord Jesus who said to His disciples,

> When He, the Spirit of truth, comes, he will guide you into all truth. He will not speak on his own; he will speak only what he hears, and he will tell you what is yet to come. He will bring glory to me by taking from what is mine and making it known to you. All that belongs to the Father is mine. That is why I said the Spirit will take from what is mine and make it known to you (John 16:13-15, NIV). *

A third principle for the integrative process is a *clear understanding of the nature, source, discovery, and dissemination of truth.* How can one deal with this vast conceptualization without a full epistemological essay? The classic banner many have raised a thousand times continues to fly over the castle: All truth is God's truth. But what does it mean to say that all truth is God's truth? Simply that wherever truth is found, if it is genuine truth, it is ultimately traceable back to the God of the Bible. And since the God of the Bible is also the God of creation, the true relationship between natural and special revelation begins to emerge at the junction of a Christian epistemology. Another reference from this writer's former mentor speaks eloquently to the subject:

> Now Christian education, if it is faithful to its deepest commitment, must renounce once and for all the false separation between secular and sacred truth. It must see that truth in science, and history, in mathematics, art, literature, and music belongs just as much to God as truth in religion. While it recognizes the primacy of the spiritual truth revealed in the Bible and incarnate in Christ, it acknowledges that all truth, wherever it is found, is of God. For Christian education there can be no discontinuity in truth, but every aspect of truth must find its unity in the God of all truth.[3]

Let it be said that the thinking Christian does not fear research and experimentation. He understands that, since all

---

New International Version.

truth is God's, the more honest effort put forth by any man, regenerate or unregenerate, must ultimately result in an uncovering of more of God's truth. Such is the design of common grace.

A fourth principle on which the integrative process is based has to do with *designing a curriculum that is totally constructed on the centrality of special revelation.*

As seen in Figure 1, special revelation — taught formally in Bible and theology classes in the curriculum — forms the foundation for curriculum design. This is surrounded in the next concentric circle by natural revelation — science, mathematics, literature, music, and so on. Many Christians tend to think of natural revelation only as the study of God's creation, but in reality all beauty is God's beauty just as all truth is God's truth. Consequently, God's revelation comes in the humanities as well as in the hard sciences, though it is more easily corrupted the further one moves away from the study of hard-core, measurable sciences such as chemistry or mathematics.

The third level of curriculum development at secondary or

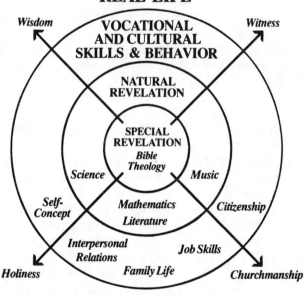

Figure 1
THE CENTRALITY OF SPECIAL REVELATION IN
A CHRISTIAN COLLEGE CURRICULUM

higher education levels is what may be called "vocational and cultural skills and behavior." The student learns about himself, interpersonal relations, family life, job skills, citizenship, and a host of other things that produce the well-rounded Christian gentleman or lady — the holistic view of life in the world.

When properly implemented, such a Christian curriculum designed around the centrality of special revelation produces a student who is able, at the end of his educational pattern, to demonstrate commensurate levels of wisdom, witness, holiness, and churchmanship as representative ideals. At the end of his secondary educational experience the student in the Christian institution ought to demonstrate a maturity level in these and similar virtues, which is parallel with the educational pattern he has achieved at that point.

The arrows in figure 1 indicate that special revelation not only forms a rallying banner for the curriculum, but also represents a permeation. If there is a God (and there is), and if He has spoken in history (and He has), then *the most important thing about education is to learn what God has said*. And having begun to learn it, God's revelation will then form the frame of reference for everything else learned.

What happens then is that each subject is related to special revelation and no area remains untouched. In a very real sense, integration takes place like the two cells of a battery — negative and positive. Christian educators integrate faith and learning by recognizing basic ways in which the subject fits into or is congruent with God's revelation. Statisticians would call this "positive correlation."

But educators also integrate by noting and demonstrating for students how the facts, theories, and implications of any given subject matter have been *negatively* affected by sin and thereby distorted. Quite obviously this may be called "negative correlation."

Another figure may be helpful in showing how various subject matter fields or areas of learning relate in different ways to the issue of integration with respect to both necessity and potential. Figure 2 shows an arrangement of the areas of knowledge in relation to their distortion because of sin, adapted from Emil Bruner and also appearing in a slightly different form in Gaebelein's journal article documented earlier. Indeed, another paragraph from Gaebelein is of value in rela-

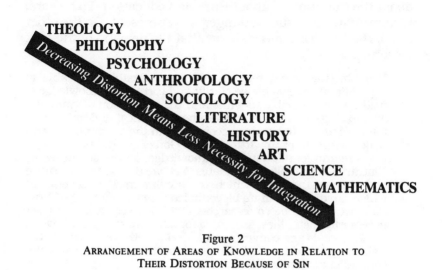

Figure 2
ARRANGEMENT OF AREAS OF KNOWLEDGE IN RELATION TO
THEIR DISTORTION BECAUSE OF SIN

tion to the diagram, although the diagram illustrated here differs slightly from his.

> At the top are those subjects where there must be the greatest integration, or re-integration, with God's truth. Being the most personal subjects in relation to God and man, in them the distortion through the fall and through sin is greatest. As the subjects become less personal and humanistic, the distortion lessens, until in mathematics, the most objective subject, it is almost nil. So it may be that Christian teachers may try too hard to integrate science and mathematics with Biblical truth. The very nature of these subjects — precise, comparatively unaffected by sin (two times two is four for the villain and the saint alike) is its own testimony, so plainly that, like the basic postulate of the Bible — "In the beginning God" — it is self-evidently true.[4]

A fifth principle dealing with the integration of truth in Christian education is *a demand for the development of a Christian world and life view*. There is no dichotomy between the sacred and secular for the thinking Christian. And the teacher who understands what Christian education is all about will work courageously at developing an internalization of God's truth, not just a cognitive knowledge.

Some have feared that the development of a Christian world and life view will produce a spirit of "worldliness" about the Christian or about Christian education. To be sure, history shows that such a danger is ever present. On the other hand, the New Testament shows that the demand of the task is worth the risk.

> The Christian mind must be dynamic, flexible, and able to expand and develop as we clarify and correct our knowledge of truth. It must be able to withstand the temptation of gradually acquiescing to what we know to be un-Biblical and anti-Christian. We must not become accomplices in the secular enterprise which wittingly or unwittingly robs God of His rightful place at the core and foundation of all knowledge, and which develops contrary to the biblical mandates. Yet, we do want to recognize and salvage the truth which the secular mind uncovers but which are distorted in its pigeonholed view of reality. As Christians we need to be co-researchers with the secularists but not necessarily their allies, searching for and confirming truth when it corresponds and converges with God's truth, yet reserving the right to question man's findings when they appear or actually contradict and contest God's truth.[5]

A sixth principle demands that *bibliocentric education extend to all areas of student life.* Just as there is no divorce of the sacred and the secular in the genuinely Christian life, so there is no divorce between faith and learning, for faith is related to every other activity on the distinctively Christian campus. The student who is able to memorize Bible verses for personal evangelism or offer a profound explanation of the Westminster Shorter Catechism is not a positive product of the system unless that knowledge affects his life in the dormitory, on the football field, and in relationships with his parents at home. The Christian school that speaks openly of its integration of faith and learning has the accompanying responsibility to demonstrate how that philosophical posture is implemented in the lives of students at all times and in all places.

PRACTICING THE INTEGRATION OF FAITH AND LEARNING

How can faith and learning actually be integrated? That is the constant and legitimate cry of all who earnestly yearn to treat Christian higher learning as a sacred trust. The following are six suggestions for this integration process.

First, *the teacher who would integrate faith and learning must constantly be about the all-important task of theo-*

logical sieve-building. As depicted in Figure 3, each student may be thought of as having a funnel in his mind and life into which there will be poured during the years of his education a great deal of information — some good, but much of it bad. Some educators in educational institutions within the Christian world have opted to close off the top of the funnel, not allowing information to enter that is not consonant with what the institution or the educator wishes the student to hear.

Unfortunately (or perhaps, fortunately) such an approach is no longer possible in today's mass-media global village, for any student with an ounce of awareness will be picking up impressions from his culture unless his institution is a modern-day replica of medieval monasticism. And even if educators *could* somehow keep the lid on, they would live with that nagging fear that perhaps some day the students might blow the lid seeking to discover all those things that were never allowed through the cracks.

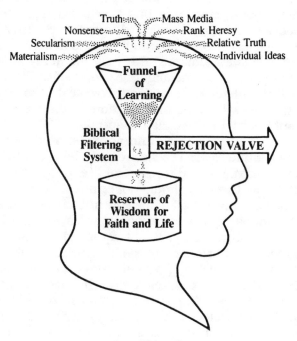

Figure 3
BIBLICAL FILTERING SYSTEM FOR
INTEGRATING FAITH AND LEARNING

The alternative is to build into the funnel what may be called a theological sieve. Insofar as a certain student at a given level of education understands and internalizes the absolute truth of God and makes it his own through the applicatory power of the Holy Spirit, to that extent he is able to cope cognitively and affectively with other kinds of information that bombard his mental processes.

When such information makes it through the filtering system, it can be tucked away for use in a reservoir of truth for faith and life. When, however, it is shown by the theological sieve to be inconsistent with biblical teaching, it is labeled "untruth" and the computer spits it out the ejection valve.

To be sure, the diagram and its explanation are an oversimplification at best. But it is one way of identifying specifically what a teacher does in a given subject matter in order to practice integrating faith and learning.

This is made possible by a second suggestion: *Every teacher must be at least an amateur theologian.* The word *amateur* is used here not in a sense of inadequacy or inability, but to suggest that a person who has specialized in mathematics or science should not be expected to write scholarly criticisms on theological subjects nor to make his living by teaching theology. He is an amateur. But just like many amateur golfers and tennis players, he might be very good at his avocation. Indeed, the better he is at his theological pursuits, the more effective he will be at his vocation in the teaching of whatever subject matter he calls his specialty.

The implication for boards and administrators of Christian schools is quite clear: Teachers at any level of Christian education who have not had a respectable exposure to formal study of Bible and theology should not be hired. To be specific, a person who has traveled all of his educational path within a secular educational system and has now earned the Ph.D. degree in, say, anthropology, is not equipped to teach such subject matter in a Christian college because his inability to work in the area of theology prohibits him from carrying out the practice and process of integration. The fact that he is a Christian, has attended church and Sunday school all his life, and has read a few books on theology is not sufficient compensation for his lack of preparation to be that "amateur theologian."

A third suggestion is that *teachers must help students*

"get it all together" in a Christian world and life view. This is simply the implementation stage of principle number 5 enunciated above. Holistic Christian thinking does not just happen but is deliberately designed by the effective Christian teacher. Machen calls Christian educators to bring culture and Christianity into close union without feeling that culture will destroy Christianity. He asks and answers a most important rhetorical question:

> Is it not far easier to be an earnest Christian if you confine your attention to the Bible and do not risk being led astray by the thought of the world? We answer, of course it is *easier.* Shut yourself up in an intellectual monastery, do not disturb yourself with the thoughts of unregenerate men, and of course you will find it *easier* to be a Christian, just as it is easier to be a good soldier in comfortable winter quarters than it is on the field of battle. You save your own soul — but the Lord's enemies remain in possession of the field.[6]

Fourth, the practice of integration can only go forward if *teachers stop confusing the integration of truth with classroom devotions.* Indeed, chapel and classroom devotions in the Christian college are most praiseworthy. But they are not to be compared in value to the total awareness created in the mind of the student by the alert teacher who facilitates the informal experiencing of truth by digging fertile furrows across the minds of his students. Classroom devotions may be worship, and worship is important, but the integration of faith and learning is truth-searching in depth.

A fifth step in the process of integration is the procedure of *learning to walk a carefully balanced line between open-mindedness and unchallengeable doctrine.* Christian teachers, particularly at the college level, tend to err in one of two extremes with respect to classroom attitude toward truth. Quite obviously, one extreme is an unwarranted dogmatism that offers regimented indoctrination as a religious sop to a student who really comes for rational inquiry and learning. Such a practice may be historically equated with the colonial schoolroom in the time of the Puritans, but not with the Christianity of the New Testament as practiced and taught by Jesus and Paul.

But the other extreme is also dangerous, namely, an open-mindedness that does not lead the student to consider that one or two alternatives of interpretation may be better than others because they are more biblical. Note the qualifying phrase — they could only be better *because they are more biblical*, not because they are more closely related to the teacher's point of view. There is a world of difference between having an inspired Bible and an inspired interpretation of that Bible. As James has warned, "Not many of you should presume to be teachers, my brothers, because you know that we who teach will be judged more strictly" (James 3:1, NIV).

Sixth, it may be helpful to remember that *the task of integration should be approached with reverence, relevance, and relaxation.* Sometimes teachers try too hard, as Gaebelein suggests regarding the subject matter in mathematics. To be sure, integration of faith and learning will not automatically fall into place. Learning unrelated to life is as dead as faith without works. The goal of the integrative process is to develop Christian minds, and to have a Christian mind is to think "Christianly."

NOTES

1. J. Gresham Machen, "Christianity and Culture" (an address delivered at the opening of the 101st session of Princeton Theological Seminary, September 20, 1912), p. 1.
2. Frank E. Gaebelein, *A Varied Harvest* (Grand Rapids: Eerdmans, 1967), pp. 41-44.
3. Frank E. Gaebelein, "Towards a Christian Philosophy of Education," *Grace Journal* 3(Fall 1962):13.
4. Ibid., p. 15.
5. David Carlson, "Thinking Christianly about Academic Subjects," mimeographed (Deerfield, Ill.: Trinity College, n.d.).
6. Machen, p. 6.

20

Untold Billions: Are They Really Lost?

J. Ronald Blue

Planet earth now strains under the weight of four and one-half billion people. Like some dusty tennis ball, the globe wobbles its way through space in an erratic but carefully designed course around God's unrivaled source of energy, the sun. With each spin some of earth's people die and others are born. The net increase each day is about 200,000. Every morning there are 200,000 more mouths to feed![1]

In the year 2000 the world must make room for an additional two billion people and, within the lifetime of many reading this article, the globe will be packed with what demographers are now calling the world's *projected ultimate population size*—close to ten billion people![2]

It is hard to grasp the magnitude of the word "billion." Government budgets and world bank transfers have made billions seem like so many buttons lined up behind a lone needle. It is easy for a meticulous accountant to record the figures "1,000,000,000" in the neat columns of some ledger. Easier yet is it for a congressman to add a few billion to an already fat "pork barrel" project.

A billion takes on more realistic value when it is divorced from the shifting value of dollars and is applied to the more

J. Ronald Blue
A.B., University of Nebraska; Th.M., Dallas Theological Seminary; Ph.D. cand., University of Texas at Arlington
Associate Professor and Chairman, Department of World Missions
Dallas Theological Seminary

constant measure of time. One billion days ago the earth may not yet have been created. One billion hours ago Genesis had not yet been written. One billion minutes ago Christ was still on earth. One billion seconds ago the first atomic bomb had not yet exploded. Yet, one billion dollars ago, in terms of governmental spending, was yesterday!

Neither dollars nor days can adequately measure the significance of the growing billions of people who comprise the global village. It is imperative that Christians visualize the multiplied billions as individual people. It is not a matter of billions but of beings. The calculations and statistics must be interpreted with a concern for souls. Every life is of eternal worth. The billions must be portrayed in terms of individual spiritual needs on a stage as broad as the earth and in a time span as long as eternity.

A CHALLENGE

Of the four and one-half billion beings presently residing on planet earth, about one-third are nominally Christian, one-third are unresponsive to Christ, and the remaining third have not so much as heard the name of Christ.[3]

The one-third "nominally Christian" are of course Christian in name only. The number of true Christians in the New Testament sense is probably a minimal part of that total.[4] The Lord alone maintains access to the exclusive record of true Christians: The Lamb's book of life. The estimates of genuine born-again believers may be more accurately portrayed in the unique guide to intercession entitled *Operation World*. Johnstone indicates that the ratio of true Christians to the total population of the Middle East stands at 1 in 3,600, Communist Asia at 1 in 1,000, and Roman Catholic Europe at 1 in 900.[5] Much of God's earthly real estate is all too sparsely populated with those who can be rightfully called Christians.

Of an even greater challenge, however, is the vast expanse where there is *no* viable Christian witness. Attention must be given to that one-third of the world's population who have not so much as heard of Christ. McGavran numbers these unevangelized at two billion.[6] Winter indicates that they include as many as two and one-half billion.[7] Whatever their number, these people are not only unreached but are living where there is no Christian contact. They are sometimes called "hidden peoples."[8] Just as one side of the globe is always turned from the sun's rays, so one half of the world's peoples remains in spiritual darkness. Masses are hidden from God's light of the gospel.

The challenge to the church is immense. The chorus still sung in some missions conferences, "untold millions are still untold" is out of date. There are now untold *billions*, with thousands added every day, who will never hear of Jesus Christ unless someone crosses the cultural and linguistic barriers and penetrates that dark half of the globe with the good news. It is estimated that there are between 25,000 and 30,000 "people groups" in the world[9] of which about 3,000 "unreached peoples" are identified and cataloged.[10] Some 10,000 languages and dialects are said to exist in the world[11] of which only 1,500 have even a part of the Word of God.[12]

As impressive as it may seem, the present number of missionaries is not adequate. Winter states that only five percent of the total missionary force is involved in cross-cultural evangelistic activity in the three major blocs of unreached peoples—the Chinese, Hindus, and Muslims. Ninety-five percent of all missionaries work among peoples who have already been evangelized.[13] Unless present missionaries are redeployed and new missionaries are directed to the unreached, the dark side of the globe will not only continue in darkness but will continue to multiply in that darkness.

Interestingly enough, one of the reasons for the rather restrained response to the overwhelming need to evangelize these neglected masses lies in a basic theological issue: Are these people who have not heard of Christ really lost?

A CONTROVERSY

In the midst of the challenge for world evangelization, the church is faced with an unending controversy over the spiritual state of those billions who have never heard of Christ.

It is not only the university intellectual who asks the burning question, "Are the heathen lost?" Well-meaning Christians face the question with sincere interest. This is as it should be. Those who have received new life in Christ are the ones who should care most about the state of the unevangelized.

Are the unevangelized billions really on their way to a

place so fearfully described in the Bible as *hell?* It is awesome enough to ask the question: to answer affirmatively is considered by some people as an affront to the loving nature of God.

There is disagreement on the state of the unevangelized even among those who appear vitally interested in missions. At one of the Urbana conferences, out of five thousand replies to over eight thousand questionnaires distributed, only 37 percent believed that "a person who doesn't hear the gospel is eternally lost." Only 42 percent believed that "unbelievers will be punished in a literal hell of fire," and 25 percent believed that "man will be saved or lost on the basis of how well he followed what he *did* know."[14]

A Complexity

Though it may appear to be a rather peripheral question designed for heated debates among theologians or stimulating discussions in college dorm rooms, the fate of the unevangelized is of utmost importance. Inherent in the seemingly simple question, "Are the heathen lost?" are several more basic and exceedingly critical questions:

The character of God is questioned: "Is God just?" This is a challenge to theology proper.

The sufficiency of Christ is questioned: "Is Christ the only way?" This is a challenge to Christology.

The necessity of the Cross is questioned: "Did Christ have to die?" This is a challenge to soteriology.

The depravity of man is questioned: "Is man inherently sinful?" This is a challenge to biblical anthropology.

The judgment of sin is questioned: "Is not evil relative?" This is a challenge to hamartiology.

The role of the church is questioned: "Is the church God's unique witness?" This is a challenge to ecclesiology.

The culmination of history is questioned: "Is there a future reckoning?" This is a challenge to eschatology.

The seemingly innocent question strikes at the very foundations of theology.

A Confusion

"Are the heathen lost?"

The diverse reactions to this question are an indication of its importance. Some react strongly to the mere suggestion that those who have never heard might be eternally lost. They contend that all religions are basically the same. One theologian argues that "Christ came not to destroy but to fulfill the strivings of mankind everywhere throughout the ages. . . ." He concludes, "To discover the reality of Christ in all the religions of the world is the essence of the ecumenical approach."[15] Christianity becomes simply another ingredient in a universal religious succotash. "God does not condemn anybody . . . ," writes Pannikan, "God is at work in the 'pagan' religions. . . ."[16]

Although it is true that the religions of the world may embody man's thoughts about God, Christianity is founded on God's revelation to man. Reason must give way to revelation; religious ritual to a righteous relationship. Biblical Christianity is centered on the God who in times past spoke "by the prophets" and in these last days has spoken "by his Son" (Heb. 1:1-2, KJV).* To consider Christianity as but one more commodity on the world religion market is to deny the biblical authority and God's clear revelation.

Certain scholars attempt a more orthodox position with appeals to Scripture to avoid the fate of the unevangelized billions. They suggest some kind of second chance after death citing 1 Peter 3:19-20, Christ's "proclamation to the spirits . . . who once were disobedient"† Pinnock contends that this "second chance" is more accurately a first chance at death. He sees the exegetical possibility of Christ's proclamation to the spirits now in prison as "the occasion when the unevangelized have an opportunity to make a decision about Jesus Christ."[17] The "exegetical possibility" is both inconsistent with the whole tenor of Scripture and with the immediate context. First Peter 3:19 simply states that Christ, by the Spirit, spoke through the prophet Noah to the ungodly prior to the Flood, whose spirits are now locked in the prison of eternal separation from God. (Compare 1 Peter 3:20 with 1 Peter 1:11 and Genesis 6:3.) There is no hint of a chance for salvation after death. "It is appointed for men to die once and after

---

*King James Version.

†All Scripture quotations in this article, except those noted otherwise, are from the *New American Standard Bible*.

this comes" not a chance for salvation, but "judgment" (Heb. 9:27).

A third position taken to skirt the reality of the finality of death for the unevangelized of the world is centered in the apparent sincerity of the so-called heathen. "They will be judged according to the light which they have received," they say. Espousing this view, Salmond states, "We need nothing beyond Paul's broad statement that those who have the law shall be judged by law, and that those who are without law shall be judged without law."[18] However, the verse Salmond quotes, Romans 2:12, actually teaches that those who have sinned without the Law will *perish* just as surely as those who have sinned with the Law. The verb ἀπόλλυμι is not "be judged" but "perish," "be destroyed," or "be lost." The argument of the passage is not to excuse men but to show that they have no excuse. They will all perish before God's righteous and impartial judgment. The focus is on the verdict of destruction regardless of the revelation given.

Although Kane takes the position that the heathen are indeed lost, he hints at some benevolent conclusions.

> The heathen on the other hand will have a much easier time. But he will not go scot free. He had the light of creation, providence, and conscience and will be judged by that light. If he is finally condemned it will . . . be . . . because he failed to live up to the light he had.[19]

Pinnock combines his erroneous arguments from Romans 2 and 1 Peter 3 discussed above to conclude:

> Of one thing we can be certain: God will not abandon in hell those who have not known and therefore have not declined His offer of grace. Though He has not told us the nature of His arrangements, we cannot doubt the existence and goodness of them.[20]

As comfortable as Pinnock's conclusion may appear, it is dead wrong on two counts. First, Scripture confirms that God indeed *does* abandon or give up those who, not knowing of Christ's redemption, have suppressed divine truth; and second, God *has* revealed the nature of His arrangements in Scripture.

A RESOLUTION

The only valid resolution to the seeming dilemma over the

state of the unevangelized is to be found in God's Word. All other solutions are mere conjecture. Man's attempt to bridge the gap between a holy God and a depraved human race is a part of that continuing conjecture. The average unbeliever makes God a little less "hard and judgmental" and thereby a little less righteous and just than He really is. The average Christian makes man a little more "sincere and searching" and thereby more righteous than he really is. These futile attempts to bring God down or to lift man up are shattered by Scripture.

Paul makes it very clear in the opening section of his letter to the Romans that all men are by nature sinners and *all* stand under God's just retribution. Already under condemnation, no one has any rights before an almighty God. This is not some new truth. Paul quotes the Old Testament to show that "THERE IS NONE RIGHTEOUS, NOT EVEN ONE . . . THERE IS NONE WHO SEEKS GOD"(Rom. 3:10-11). From Adam condemnation has come on all men (5:18). The question of the lostness of mankind is not so much a question of God's sovereign justice as it is man's sinful nature.

Nonetheless the just judgment of God on the unevangelized is not irrational. God can be shown fair, even by standards of reason. To say that God sends people to hell because they have not trusted a Person of whom they have never heard seems unjust. Regardless of the divine standard, by human standards such action would be declared unfair. Paul makes it clear as he develops his argument in his letter to the Romans that God neither sends people to hell, nor does He judge them on the basis of their response to Christ of whom they have not heard.

JUDGMENT BASED ON GOD'S REVELATION

The judgment of God in relation to the untold billions of the world is based not on their response to unrevealed truth but to revelation they *have* received. Although the righteousness of God is only revealed to those who believe in the gospel of Jesus Christ (Rom. 1:16-17), God's wrath is revealed against all unrighteousness of those who suppress the truth they have both received and understood. In other words, if a person in this present age has not been drawn by God's grace and mercy to salvation through faith in Christ's atonement, he faces God's wrath. That might seem harsh and unfair were it not for Paul's clear explanation.

Man is not said to face God's wrath because he has failed to accept a gospel he never heard, or because he failed to put his faith in a Savior he has not known. God's wrath is on "all ungodliness and unrighteousness" (Rom. 1:18). Some confusion has existed because of the faulty translation of this verse in the King James Version. The verb χατέχω is not merely "to hold" the truth but "to hold down" the truth, or as Lenski puts it, "to suppress the truth, to prevent the truth from exerting its power in the heart and the life."[21] Calvin writes, "to hold down the truth is to suppress or obscure it."[22] Chalmers identifies those who face God's wrath as individuals "who stifle the truth."[23]

Paul continues his argument by giving just cause for God's wrath. He makes it clear that God's revelation has been both penetrating and persistent. He explains that the truth of God has been revealed to all men in two ways.

First, the truth or "reality" (ἀλήθεια) of God is an integral part of every person's *conscience* (Rom. 1:19). Those who have never heard of Christ nonetheless know of God. That knowledge, by the way, is not as superficial as some would make it. Paul uses the second aorist active participle of γινώσκω, "to know by personal experience."

Not only do they know of God, but also they instinctively know of His law. God's law is written in their hearts, "their conscience bearing witness, and their thoughts alternately accusing or else defending them" (Rom. 2:15). DeHaan writes, "Even though the light of conscience has been dimmed because of deliberate wickedness, it still exists everywhere."[24]

Second, the truth of God's eternal power and divine nature has been clearly seen and has been understood through *creation*. One Greek article combines δύναμις with θειότης (Rom. 1:20). There is no eternal power apart from divinity and no divine nature apart from supernatural power. God's nature and power are together clearly revealed in nature. The Maker is known through what has been made. Barnhouse explains, "No man can truly ask, 'Who is God?' 'What is God?' 'Where is God?' 'What does God want?' The creation 'round about us is witness that there is a supreme Being."[25]

Paul concludes that man is without excuse. The truth of God is revealed to all men through conscience and creation. In unrighteousness men everywhere suppress that revealed truth. Consequently, man is held inexcusable (Rom. 1:20). The Greek εἰς τό with the infinitive, an expression of purpose, came to signify *result*. Here it is not "that they *may be* without excuse" but "so that they *are* without excuse." As Archer explains, "There is sufficient knowledge for each person after the fall to be criminally liable for sin."[26]

The issue, therefore, is not that the unevangelized have not put their trust in a Person of whom they have never heard, but that they have suppressed the truth they have both received and understood.

Paul then continues with an explanation of what the natural man does with God's revelation. In fact the apostle does more than merely explain. He gives the reason for God's wrath and man's inexcusable state. In Romans 1:21 Paul does not use γαρ ("for"), but διότι ("because"). The cause is clear." "Even though they knew God [γνόντες τόν θεὸν, a concessive aorist participle], they did not honor Him as God, or give thanks."

Man starts his descent down a sin-slick staircase to destruction. The first two of the seven steps downward are convicting. They might be labeled "no praise" and "no thanks." To move down those two steps requires little effort. In fact it requires *no* effort. The person who does nothing is not standing still; he is sliding from God. Even the Christian needs to be reminded that the day he fails to honor God and fails to thank God, he may well be in a tailspin.

The natural man has but begun the descent. Failure to honor or thank God brings futile, empty speculations and foolish, darkened sensitivities. The mind puffs up while the heart shrinks (Rom. 1:21).

"Professing to be wise," man becomes a fool (Rom. 1:22). Pride becomes the precipice from which the sinner falls into perdition. Fully confident of his own capabilities, like some puffed-up toad, the individual jumps to his destruction.

The basement of the sordid seven-step descent is where man performs his most rebellious act. He exchanges the glory of an incorruptible God for an image shaped after his own corruptible frame, some flitting bird, a four-footed beast, or some creepy crawler. The sovereign wonder of God is depicted as some slimy worm (Rom. 1:23). The lowest form of idolatry is depicted. Not only creature worship (ὁμοιώμα εἰκών) but image worship (ὁμοιώματι εἰκόνος) is employed.

Interestingly enough, there are some who point to the idolatrous condition of the heathen as evidence of their search for a way to God. Idolatry is viewed as piety and reverence yet to be perfected. Nothing could be further from the truth. These are not gropings for God. They are evidence of rebellion against God. "The idolatrous systems of the world," says Watts, "are actually states of man's departure from God and expression of his desire for other gods rather than the true, living God."[27]

To understand better the severity with which God views idolatrous worship, one need only review the Old Testament denunciations of the evil practice. Idolatry is hardly a search for God. Forsaking God who made him, the idolater sacrifices to demons, not God (Deut. 32:17). Israel's adoption of idolatrous Canaanite practices is considered a snare and a pollution, and is roundly condemned by God (Ps. 106:36-39).

Paul's point is clear. The apparently innocent heathen are far from innocent. They have received a clear revelation from God through conscience and creation. The revelation inwardly experienced, outwardly witnessed, and clearly understood has been repressed. That repression is evidenced in the degradation of man's thoughts, emotions, and actions. No matter how isolated a man may be from the revelation of God's righteousness in the gospel of Jesus Christ, that man is entirely without excuse. The wrath of God is on him because of his ungodliness and unrighteousness, not because of his lack of faith in Christ.

DESTRUCTION RESULTING FROM MAN'S REBELLION

God might be charged with injustice, were He to send people to hell on the basis of their failure to respond to revelation they have never received. It has been shown that the basis of His judgment is not on unrevealed truth but on the clear revelation received and rejected by those who are condemned. McQuilkin expresses it well: "They are not condemned for rejecting a Saviour of whom they have never heard. They are condemned for sinning against the light they have."[28]

Paul's argument in Romans not only outlines the basis of God's judgment but shows that God does not *send* people to destruction. He simply *lets them go* on that self-designed course.

Like some terrible refrain, the desperate sentence is thrice repeated, "God gave them over (παρέδωκεν αὐτοὺς ὁ Θεὸς). There is a stress on the constative aorist verb, God *did* give them up. God's action is judicial. Since these who have suppressed the truth are determined on self-destruction, justice decrees that it be so. It is as if God responded, "Let them go!"

It is probably best not to view three stages in the giving over or abandonment by God. Robertson is undoubtedly correct in seeing "a repetition of the same withdrawal."[29] These are not three phases but three aspects of God's release of the ungodly to their own devastating destiny.

It is not within the scope of this article to deal with the details recorded in man's self-designed destruction. However, it is important to note the extent of God's threefold release. God gave them over in the lusts of their hearts (Rom. 1:24-25), to degrading passions (1:26-27), and to a depraved mind (1:28-32). The destruction is all-inclusive. In direct contrast to God's great commandment, "YOU SHALL LOVE THE LORD YOUR GOD WITH ALL YOUR HEART, AND WITH ALL YOUR SOUL, AND WITH ALL YOUR MIND" (Matt. 22:37), man here is left with a darkened *heart*, degraded *soul*, and depraved *mind*.

One of the most sordid lists in all of Scripture follows like a whole lineup of devastating character witnesses against the accused (Rom. 1:29-31). Paul concludes this section of his argument by reminding the reader that, although they know the ordinance of God, these who are abandoned to destruction and a death well deserved not only participate in all the ungodly atrocities listed, but they give hearty approval to that sordid behavior (Rom. 1:32). These are not innocent acts of the misinformed. The action is willful. God's judgment is certainly as warranted as it is sure. He does not send people to hell; He lets them go. The judgment, of course, is for God to make, not other men, no matter how righteous they may seem (Rom. 2:1-3).

Nonetheless it is abundantly clear that God *has* judged the unevangelized billions of the world. His judgment is just. It is based on revelation clearly received and willfully refused by the defendant. His sentence is fair. It is a release by God for man to pursue his own destruction and eternal death. The world's untold billions are lost!

Contrary to the restricted views that Paul is simply describing "the moral condition of the pagan world when he wrote" the letter to the Romans,[30] or that "Paul presents in

Romans 1:18-32 a theological interpretation of the religious history of the nations as it took place after the dispersion of the people from Babylon as recorded in Genesis 11:1-9,"[31] the extent of Paul's arguments are clearly of a broader scope. He is speaking of mankind universally. The word "Gentiles" or "nations" (ἔθνοι) does not occur. The force of Paul's presentation is that "all the world may become accountable to God" (Rom. 3:19). Furthermore his remarks are not limited to a historical account. The truth of Romans spans the entire age. The stark contrast between man's sin and God's salvation are as pertinent today as the day the letter was penned.

The conclusion is clear. The untold billions are lost. They are desperately lost! There is no way for well-meaning Christians or conscientious unbelievers to bridge the gap between a righteous God and a reprobate mankind. Only the God-man, Jesus Christ, can reach across the gulf between a perfect God and a perverse human race. If the unevangelized billions are truly lost, one burning question remains. How will they hear the unique message of hope? Human agents must be mobilized by the Lord to cross the frontiers that stand as barriers to gospel penetration. God has so willed it. As Kane points out, "There is not a single line in the book of Acts to suggest that God can save a human being without employing a human agent. On the contrary there are several examples of God's going to great lengths to secure the active cooperation of one or another of His servants."[32]

Even when an unevangelized heathen appears to show an initial response in line with the revelation afforded him, as in the case of Cornelius in Acts 10, the Lord employs one of His servants to bring the fuller revelation of Jesus Christ necessary for salvation. Packer summed it up well: "We must never forget that it is God who saves. It is God who brings men and women under the sound of the gospel, and it is God who brings them to faith in Christ. . . ."[33] It may also be stressed that it is God who imparts His vision to His servants of a desperate, dying world and in His grace involves those servants in the exciting enterprise of carrying the message of eternal life in Christ to that world.

Will the untold billions remain untold? A world in crisis needs the Word of Christ. Responsive and responsible agents are needed to serve as ambassadors of the King in that exciting enterprise called world missions—an enterprise dedicated to the untold billions!

NOTES

1. Ross S. Bennett, ed., *Our World* (Washington, D.C.: National Geographic Society, 1979), p. 20.
2. Carl Haub and Douglas W. Heisler, comps., "1980 World Population Data Sheet" (Washington, D.C.: Population Reference Bureau, 1980).
3. Walbert Bühlmann, *The Coming of the Third Church* (Maryknoll, N.Y.: Orbis, 1977), p. 143.
4. C. Peter Wagner, *Stop the World, I Want to Get On* (Glendale, Calif.: Gospel Light, 1974), p. 5.
5. P. J. Johnstone, *Operation World* (Bromley, England: STL, 1978).
6. Donald A. McGavran, ed., *Eye of the Storm* (Waco, Tex.: Word, 1972), p. 233.
7. Ralph P. Winter, "The Grounds for a New Thrust in World Mission," in *Evangelical Missions Tomorrow,* ed. Wade Coggins and Edwin Frizen (South Pasadena, Calif.: Wm. Carey Library, 1977), pp. 1-26.
8. Edward R. Dayton, *That Everyone May Hear* (Monrovia, Calif.: MARC, 1979), p. 19.
9. Roger C. Palms, "Three Billion People—Shall They Hear?" *World Evangelization* 20(September 1980):2.
10. C. Peter Wagner and Edward R. Dayton, eds., *Unreached Peoples '79* (Elgin, Ill.: David C. Cook, 1978).
11. Barbara I. Grimes, ed., *Ethnologue* (Huntington Beach, Calif.: Wycliffe Bible Translators, 1974).
12. George Cowan, *The Word That Kindles* (Chappaqua, N.Y.: Christian Herald, 1979), p. 12.
13. Ralph D. Winter, "The Highest Priority: Cross-Cultural Evangelism," in *Let the Earth Hear His Voice,* ed. J. D. Douglas (Minneapolis: World Wide, 1975), p. 229.
14. Arthur P. Johnston, "Focus Comment," *Trinity World Forum* 1(Fall 1975):3.
15. E. O. James, *Christianity and Other Religions* (Philadelphia: J. B. Lippincott, 1968), pp. 29, 173.
16. R. Pannikan, *The Unknown Christ of Hinduism* (London: Darton, Longman & Todd, 1868), pp. 51, 137.
17. Clark Pinnock, "Why Is Jesus the Only Way?" *Eternity,* December 1976, p. 32.
18. S. D. F. Salmond, *The Christian Doctrine of Immortality* (Edinburgh: T. & T. Clark, 1895), p. 672.
19. J. Herbert Kane, *Understanding Christian Missions* (Grand Rapids: Baker, 1974), p. 135.
20. Pinnock, p. 32.
21. R. C. H. Lenski, *The Interpretation of St. Paul's Epistle to the Romans* (Minneapolis: Augsburg, 1936), p. 92.
22. John Calvin, *Calvin's Commentaries,* trans. Russ Mackenzie (Grand Rapids: Eerdmans, 1960), 8:30.
23. Thomas Chalmers, *Lectures on the Epistles of Paul the Apostle* (New York: Robert Carter & Brothers, 1855), p. 24.
24. Richard W. DeHaan, *The Word on Trial* (Grand Rapids: Zondervan, 1970), p. 14.

25. Donald Grey Barnhouse, *Man's Ruin* (Grand Rapids: Eerdmans, 1952), p. 243.
26. Gleason L. Archer, *The Epistle to the Romans: A Study Manual* (Grand Rapids: Baker, 1959), p. 11.
27. Malcolm H. Watts, "The Case of the Heathen," *Bible League Quarterly* (July-September 1978) p. 149.
28. Robert C. McQuilkin, *The Message of Romans* (Grand Rapids: Zondervan, 1947), p. 29.
29. Archibald T. Robertson, *Word Pictures in the New Testament,* 6 vols. (Nashville: Broadman, 1931), 4:338.
30. James Denny, "St. Paul's Epistle to the Romans," in *The Expositor's Greek Testament,* 5 vols. (Grand Rapids: Eerdmans, 1974), 2:593.
31. George W. Peters, *A Biblical Theology of Missions* (Chicago: Moody, 1972), p. 89.
32. Kane, p. 102.
33. J. I. Packer, *Evangelism and the Sovereignty of God* (London: Inter-Varsity, 1961), p. 27.

21

Missions in a Religiously Pluralistic World

George W. Peters

Religious pluralism is nothing new. Throughout the millennia of history various religions have functioned in the world. The Bible refers to numerous gods and systems of worship in various cultures of the ancient Near East. These religions—which are historic realities of tremendous significance—cause no little perplexity to the student of the Bible and to the missionary. The latter is confronted by this reality in its most vivid complexity, and he experiences it as a life-determining and community-governing force.

Of course, religious pluralism is no longer something overseas and beyond the boundaries of this nation. Several million adherents of non-Christian religions are fellow citizens in the United States. They have become neighbors on the same street where Christians live. Christians share with them the same post office and postman, the same bank, the same grocery store, the same playground. Yet they attend their temples and worship their god or gods in the very cities where Christians attend church and worship the only true God.

George W. Peters
Th.B., A.B., Tabor College; A.B., University of Saskatchewan; B.D., St. Andrews College; Ph.D., Hartford Seminary Foundation
Professor Emeritus of World Missions
Dallas Theological Seminary

THE NEW IMAGE

Religious pluralism has become a universal phenomenon and is becoming an accepted pattern of life. This new pattern of life has raised some searching questions in the minds of many people. One question is this: Are "the heathen" actually as pagan as either mission reports or one's own imagination has projected them to appear and to which Christians have liberally and sympathetically responded in missions and charity? Since non-Christian religions are no longer isolated from North America and other parts of the "civilized world" by great distances, a new image arises. Newbigin mentions five change factors which are affecting the thinking of many people.

> Students from every part of the world and from every religious community jostle one another on the campuses of Western universities, share the same studies, the same books, the same discussions of world affairs. The great international and inter-governmental organizations, both the United Nations itself and also its many specialist agencies, provide a sphere in which some of the ablest men of all religions are constantly co-operating in seeking the solution of the pressing problems of mankind. In UNESCO there is an organization which deliberately seeks to create the means for a common spiritual basis for the life of mankind. In a multitude of international conferences, for all sorts of commercial, scientific, and cultural purposes, men and women from all over the world meet as equals in a milieu in which any suggestion that absolute truth belongs to one of the many strands of human religious life seems simply absurd. And finally, for those who do not share in any of these opportunities for inter-cultural meeting, there is the ceaselessly growing flood of tourists bringing ordinary men and women of every land into direct contact with each other, not to mention the movements of migrants, refugees, people forced by pressure of population to seek work in other lands.
> It is not surprising if, in the face of these new experiences, some of the traditional supports for the missionary enterprise began to shake. For it must be frankly admitted that—whatever might be said from the pulpit about the true basis of missions in the Gospel itself—the motives with which they have been supported have been mixed.[1]

The "poor heathen" out there made a tremendous appeal to the conscience and the sense of sympathy and responsibility in many people. The urge of compassion became a strong motivating power.

A second penetrating question is addressed to the church and missions: Are "the heathen" actually as destitute of spiritual light and truths as Christians have believed them to be? Evaluating the noblest elements of their religions and entering into the religious experiences of some of their poets, philosophers, "theologians," and "saints," can one deny or even question the presence of Christ and the reality of the ministry of the Holy Spirit in their midst? Has not God disclosed Himself to them? Are they not meeting Him in their experiences? Is not Christ the Lord of history who at no time and place has left Himself without a witness (John 1:9; Acts 14:17; Rom. 1:18-20; 2:7, 10, 14-15)? And does He not operate in historical processes in order that "in the dispensation of the fulness of times he might gather together in one all things in Christ, both which are in heaven, and which are on earth; even in him" (Eph. 1:10 KJV)?* These questions cannot be dismissed lightly.

A number of years ago, Arno C. Gaebelein published a book of considerable import. The title—*Christianity or Religion?*—was a message in itself.[2] Then Samuel G. Craig wrote a book entitled *Christianity Rightly So Called.*[3] W. H. Griffith Thomas narrowed the circle when he entitled his publication *Christianity Is Christ.*[4] Thus the tunnel narrowed. From the wide entrance of religion it narrowed to Christianity, then to Christianity "rightly so-called," and then from Christianity to Christ. This narrowing and focusing on the person of Jesus Christ is of utmost importance. The widest circle thus is that of religion.

THE SIGNIFICANCE OF RELIGION

No one should think lightly of religion. It is not only a universal human phenomenon; it is also the most meaningful and most sacred possession of mankind. Humanity makes mockery of the thought that man has matured beyond religion and that modern man is advancing toward a postreligious world. But the world is more religious today than ever before.

---

*All scripture quotations in this article, except those noted otherwise, are from the King James Version.

Four observations can be made in relation to religion, including Christianity as a system of religion, beliefs, and practices.

ALL RELIGIONS HAVE PRACTICES THAT APPEAR TO BE ALIKE

Bavinck has written about the similarities in religious practice between Christians and followers of non-Christian religions.

> A Christian who is accustomed to pray cannot help recognizing that the Moslem whom he sees praying is doing something similar. And seeing a Hindu bowing down before his god stirs the Christian, because he himself has learned to bow his head before the God who appears to us in Jesus Christ. Indeed, he cannot deny that our Christian faith and those other religions have something in common, that there are certain similarities between them.[5]

Similar things can be said about the vocabulary among religions. There seemingly is a religious vocabulary which is quite universal.

ALL RELIGIONS HAVE A UNIQUE FUNCTION TO PERFORM

Religions are purposive and meaningful. They are uniquely sacred and filled with awe, fear, reverence, and expectations. They are to serve life and to produce effects. While for people of the non-Western world all of life is sacred and all of culture is religion-permeated, it still remains a fact that religion is sacred and has a specific function to perform. Malinowski states that the African distinguishes well between folklore (and legend) on the one hand and myth on the other hand.[6] Modern man, however, thinks of the former as secular and entertaining and of the latter as sacred. In case of extremity he resorts to the mythology and practices of religion. His expectations from religion are real and demanding. He expects religion to perform and to produce results.

ALL RELIGIONS HAVE STRUCTURE

Just as there is no unstructured society, so there is no unstructured religion. The peculiar thing is that basically all religions are structured very similarly, including Judaism and Christianity.

First is the outer ring which includes the total ethos or religio-cultural atmosphere and world view with its traditional presuppositions and philosophy, whether formulated or not, which determines or at least influences the life-style of the devotees or adherents and related societies. *Second* are the personnel or functionaries (such as priests, or other officiating personnel and people of religious influences); institutions such as sacrifices, holy days, holy places and pilgrimages, and special observances; and practices such as prayer, fasting, almsgiving, etc. Beneath this second level is a *third* layer consisting of the codes of behavior, the written and unwritten rules and regulations which constitute the ethic and general beliefs of the religions. The innermost heart of the *fourth* circle consists of a specific core of beliefs which forms the soul of the total religion. In some of the primitive religions, such as Shamanism of Siberia and the religions of many of China's tribespeople, this innermost core is difficult to discover because it is a mystery kept as a sacred trust and is known only to the initiated shaman. In some Australian tribespeople only men above a certain age level are allowed to know the inner core of teaching. But, however this may be, religion has a structure and the structures are surprisingly similar.

ALL RELIGIONS ARE EXPERIENCE-ORIENTED

A strong psychological aspect or "soulishness" exists in religion. This is universal. No religion could survive as a mere doctrinal system, ethical code, or practice-oriented system if it did not reach into man's inner being with deep and impressive psychological imprints. Carried to the extreme, this results in mysticism and/or ecstaticism, which sweeps man along in prolonged experiences. Without some kind of experience, religion would soon die a natural death. This more than anything else makes man cling to religion. And it has accurately been said that man is incurably religious.

These are some of the things all religions have in common. Are all religions, therefore, also alike? Do they all represent truth? How is it then that Christians claim total uniqueness for the gospel of Jesus Christ, the heart and core of Christianity? Indeed, Christians make for Christianity "rightly so-called" the most astounding claims. These claims, however, are not always fully incarnated, utilized, or even recognized and expressed by the Christian church. And of course, Christians do not claim to have discovered them nor has the genius of Christianity invented them. Followers of Christ humbly confess that these unique claims come to mankind as God's gracious disclosures or revelation. They come from men who were devoted followers of Jesus Christ—and who received the truth by revelation through the Holy Spirit. These are not Western ideas. Therefore, no credit comes to believers today. They are merely passing on what they have received from others and what they have experienced as truth and reality.

Therefore, Christians witness to the following truths:

1. Christianity claims to be the religion of absolute fulfillment, bringing wholeness and completion to the human personality in all sanctified aspirations, hopes, and potentials.

2. Christianity asserts absoluteness in religious authority, contending for total control over man's mind, conscience, conduct, and relationships in all spheres of life.

3. Christianity claims completeness and finality as a revelation of God's person, work, and purpose; it cannot be supplemented or complemented by other religions.

4. Christianity claims universality in scope and rule, and promises to supplant all other religions in the world. It will make Christ the sole Savior and sovereign Lord of all history.

Sincerely one may ask, Are not such claims devastating in one's relationship to non-Christian religions? Can a person be as categorical as all that? In a world that strives for unity, harmony, tolerance, and peace, such questions are legitimate. It seems evident, however, that the Bible leaves no choice. There is such a thing as "holy intolerance" that is more wholesome to mankind than "unholy tolerance." Yet Christians should be as open as truth permits them to be and as charitable as the Bible bids them to be.

Theories to Build Natural Bridges

Theories have abounded in man's search to build natural bridges from the gospel to non-Christian religions. Elsewhere I have referred to eight such theories.[7] Gensichen, of Heidelberg University, analyzes four theories,[8] and Braaten, of the Lutheran School of Theology at Chicago, wrestles with three theories presented by John Hick, Karl Barth, and Karl Rahner.[9] If the vastness of the field is an indication of the depth of the issue, then there is little hope of finding a human solution.

To think, however, of all religions as alike, interrelated, and originating from the same source and leading to the same conclusions and destiny is a serious mistake. That approach betrays either intellectual distortion, if not dishonesty, or presuppositions that are neither biblical, historical, nor acceptable to the conscience attuned to truth and the eternal. *The revelational concept of God and the Father of Jesus Christ as revealed in the Trinity, the creation of the world with its history and purpose, and the biblical doctrine of man as created in the image of God, fallen into sin and his redemption in Christ, simply cannot be fitted into the ethnic religions of the world.* Revelational religion in its fundamental concepts remains unique, no matter how much of value, ethical precepts, social cohesiveness, beauty, and elements of truth may be discovered in or ascribed to non-Christian religions. The gulf cannot be spanned. There is a "total otherness" in revelational Christianity "rightly so-called" and in the gospel of the Lord Jesus Christ. It simply is incomparable.

Christianity is and remains the "nonmixer," as Hammer has called it.[10] Christianity possesses a "total uniqueness." There is a fundamental "discontinuity," to use Kraemer's term,[11] a "total uniqueness" in Christianity, which refuses to be acculturated. To the contrary, it *confronts* culture and demands a verdict.

THE PRESENT-DAY DEBATE

In recent years an attractive theory has captured many minds and constitutes the heart of a far-reaching debate. It may be stated in two propositions: (a) Jesus Christ is Lord. As the Lord of all history, He is present in all history. There is no history beyond Him and outside of Him. (b) As Lord of history and in history, Jesus Christ can be met by men of faith in living experiences whatever their outward religious allegiance may be and whether they recognize Him as Savior and Lord or not.

Consequently, there is "the Unknown Christ of Hinduism" (Raimundo Panikkar), the "anonymous Christian" (Karl Rahner) and the "latent church" (J. C. Hoekendijk and Paul Tillich) in the world of non-Christian religions. Though these men represent extreme views, it is a fact that they express widely held positions.

From the natural point of view these two propositions appeal to the human mind and natural sympathy. One could almost wish they were true and could be proved. Therefore, they must be more closely evaluated.

THE BIBLE AND HISTORY

It is the clear doctrine of the Bible that God is the Creator of this universe and all that is in it. The New Testament adds the emphasis that such creation was in and by Christ Jesus (John 1:3; Col. 1:16-17; Heb. 1:2). It also affirms that Jesus is Lord of lords and King of kings, on whom all depends and who holds all authority in heaven and on earth (Matt. 28:18-20; Rom. 14:9; 1 Cor. 12:3; Phil. 2:9-11; Col. 1:16-18; Heb. 1:2-3; Rev. 19:11-16). The Bible leaves no room for doubting the creatorship of God, the saviorhood of Jesus Christ, and the lordship of Christ. As such, Christ is *the ultimate source* of all things, the *hope* of all things, the *purpose* of all things, the *meaning* of all things, and the *destiny* of all things. The material universe and human history are neither meaningless nor purposeless. They have a goal toward which they are being guided. This is confirmed by the Scriptures.

THE FATEFUL SURRENDER

To give such an unconditional affirmation, however, would require a twofold surrender. First, one would need to surrender the teaching of *Heilsgeschichte* (sacred history) as a unique history within the history of all mankind and accept the position that all history is alike and sacred. Thus the qualitative distinctness of the history of Israel as it began in Abraham and continued throughout the times of the Old Testament must be yielded. The faith in the uniqueness of Old Testament revelation in the history of religions would need to be relinquished. What Christians have considered as a sacred and qualitatively unique stream of revelation in the midst of the religious streams of the world would cease to claim qualitative distinctiveness. While there still may be quantitative differences, the claims to qualitative distinctiveness would need to be surrendered, and all history acknowledged as one.

A second surrender would be the biblical truth that a second force is operative in this world and uniquely so in the history of mankind and not least in the realm of religion. Christians would need to yield the doctrine that this force is an outflow of a person known in the Bible as Satan, the devil, "the dragon, that old serpent" (Rev. 20:2). The Bible, however, does not present a unified sacred history. There are parallel lines of serious interactions and bitter conflicts between Christ and Satan, though of course Christ is and will be the Victor.

To ascribe present evil to the bestiality of man because of his supposed evolutionary background or to structures, institutions, establishments, and traditions is too superficial from the biblical point of view. The Bible sees as the ultimate source of evil in the world a person — Satan — who is also known as "the god of this world" (2 Cor. 4:4) and "the prince of the power of the air" (Eph. 2:2). The Bible concretizes evil by informing believers that "we wrestle not against flesh and blood, but against principalities, against powers, against the rulers of the darkness of this world, against spiritual wickedness in high places" (Eph. 6:12). The Bible warns Christians against the strategies, the cunning devices, the clever schemes of the devil (Eph. 6:11). And the Bible states that he is deceiving the nations and leading them astray (Rev. 20:3). The world system (Col. 2:8, 20) binds and blinds the world of mankind and threatens to destroy it (Gal. 4:3).

These are not empty words. They speak of stark reality. And human history is the most convincing commentary on these truths. The last two world wars and all the horrifying bloodsheds that are continuing into the present are merely a prolongation and intensification of the "conflict of the ages." And they will not stop until finally the Prince of peace comes and bids them cease.

THE INVASION OF HUMAN HISTORY

An invasion of human history by evil forces has taken place, and this invasion affects every aspect of life. Can one be assured that the religions of mankind are exempt from this invasion with its evil influences and effects? Is religion insulated against demonic influences? Are religions too sacred for satanic invasion? Paul seemingly did not think so (Rom. 1:18-25; 1 Cor. 10:14, 19-21), and history would not validate such a position. As one cannot claim such insulation for Christianity as a religious system, such insulation cannot be claimed for the other ethnic and living religions. Of course, reforms have occurred in some of these religions, and evil aspects and some inhuman practices have been eliminated in the course of the past centuries.

Two tendencies, however, are evident in non-Christian religions. The first is that their "perfecting" at the same time results in greater cohesiveness and they become an increasingly closed system. The second tendency is that they become increasingly immune and adverse to the gospel of Jesus Christ. They grow more self-contained and more resistant. If Christ were in all of history and all of history were of Christ, including the world's living religions, then these religions would be moving toward Christ. But such is not the case. Instead, there is a misleading, deceiving, opposing, immunizing, and resisting force at work that adopts and absorbs Christian elements while at the same time it resists and opposes Christ as the only Savior and sovereign Lord.

THE REALITY OF RELIGIOUS EXPERIENCES

The situation differs little when the second proposition is considered and one studies the religious experiences of "men of faith" in the world's religions. This is not to deny that man encounters deep religious experiences. They are realities and cannot be disregarded or explained away. They may even be ecstatic, mystic, rapturous, absorbing, ennobling, and personality-transforming. Their psychological phenomena and immediate aftereffects may closely resemble types of "Christian conversions" in many respects. It is not unusual to find such experiences accompanied by rapturous glory, insensibility to the world, ecstaticism, tongues phenomena, utterances and visions, or lostness in meditation. They are real to the individual involved and may become life-determining for the devotee, as was the case with Gautama Buddha and numerous others. The many documented cases presented by William James cannot be dismissed lightly.[12] They deserve serious consideration. There are transreligious experiences of great similarity wherever religion is taken seriously and motivation is sufficient and sustained.

Christians who believe in the lordship of Christ, in the cosmic operations of the Holy Spirit, and in a certain commonness and unity of mankind, and who are interested in finding as much truth as possible, can earnestly enquire into the source, nature, and meaning of such experiences. Whence are they? Where do they lead? What is their meaning?

The *possibility* of such is in itself an indication of the grace of God. It may well be that this possibility could be ascribed to the religious nature of man. However, were it not for the grace of God, sin would no doubt soon destroy such possibilities and man would become a religionless creature, incapable of any religious experiences. It is difficult to fathom the depth and awfulness of sin in its destructive powers.

It may also well be that the *search* for such experiences finds its source in the cosmic operation of the Holy Spirit, which seems to be touching every human life (John 1:9). A restlessness and yearning in the heart of man is the result. One certainly cannot overlook such scenes as were witnessed in India in January and February of 1977 near the city of Allahabad, India. In five weeks fifty million Hindu pilgrims from all over India converged on the place where the Yamuna River meets the Ganges River. The occasion was the Jar Festival (the Kumbh Mela). At tremendous expense and personal hardship, these pilgrims came to bathe in the waters of the Ganges, hoping thus to be cleansed completely and forever from all their sins and to be assured of eternal bliss after death. Their goal is to be released from the wheel of transmigration or reincarnation. This underlying motivation, thirst, and yearning was not merely human or demonic. The cosmic operations of the Holy Spirit preserve men in a savable condition, and it is possible that from time to time the slumbering yearning becomes an intense search for spiritual reality. However, as man so readily ignores or misuses God's natural gifts (Acts 14:17; Rom. 2:4-5), is he more prepared to accept God's gracious spiritual gifts and acknowledge them in humble gratitude? History seems to be pointing in a different direction.

It can hardly be established historically that the rapturous experiences of men and women in non-Christian religions have caused them to be more open to the message of the gospel of Christ. Instead, it is more accurate to state that such experiences have insulated them to the penetration of the message and immunized them against the gospel of Christ. Nor is it conceivable that so-called "men of faith" (i.e. religious people) met an unrecognized Savior and Lord in their depth experiences and then became more closed to Him when He was presented to them in the gospel. Men more often turn from Him or even against Him. Of course, it is fully acknowledged that God works in mysterious ways, but does He work in self-contradictory ways? Does He work in experiences that alienate people from Him and immunize them against the gospel of Christ and the gift of God in Christ Jesus? To say the least, this is rather peculiar and self-contradictory.

Regarding so-called "men of faith" in non-Christian religions, two facts need to be emphasized. First, there seems to be a mystic-realistic relationship between saving faith and hearing the Word of God. Faith is born out of hearing the Word. Paul wrote that "faith cometh by *hearing,* and hearing by the word of God" (Rom. 10:17, italics added). Similarly he questioned the Galatians, "Received ye the Spirit by the works of the law, or by the *hearing* of faith?" (Gal. 3:2, italics added). This is in keeping with the words of Christ. "No man can come to me, except the Father which hath sent me draw him. . . . It is written in the prophets, and they shall be all taught of God. Every man therefore that hath *heard,* and hath *learned* of the Father, cometh unto me" (John 6:44-45, italics added). These passages relate saving faith to hearing the Word of God similar to the way James and Peter relate the new birth to the Word of God (James 1:18; 1 Pet. 1:23). Does one therefore have a right to speak of "men of faith" *apart* from the Word of God? Abraham "staggered not at the *promise* of God . . . being fully persuaded that, what [God] had *promised,* he was able also to perform" (Rom 4:20-21, italics added). The Word of God was the source of Abraham's faith. Although the psychological basis and processes may be similar, could there be a qualitative distinction between the religious experiences of men in non-Christian religions and the experiences of men who hear the Word of God?

Another point to keep in mind is the fact that the object of faith, not the "man of faith," is significant. Abraham believed *God* and that was "counted unto him for righteousness" (Rom. 4:3). Faith may be the channel, but the nature of the inflow is not determined by the channel but by the source to which it relates. Therefore, the Bible is insistent and totally consistent in affirming that life-bringing faith must be related to Jesus Christ who is Life, outside of whom there is no life (1 John 5:11-12). Salvation is possible only by receiving Him (John 1:12; Acts 4:12). And "whosoever believeth in Him should not perish, but have everlasting life" (John 3:16). The object of faith becomes the decisive and determining factor.

CONCLUSION

Categorically one may affirm that all history is *not* of Christ, and Christ is *not* in all history. Nor is Christ in all religious experiences or necessarily encountered by "men of faith." Satan, too, is busy in history and present in religious systems and experiences (2 Thess. 2:7-12; 2 Tim. 3:5-8; 1 John 4:1-3; Rev. 13:1, 2, 8, 11-15). These words cannot be erased from the Bible or history. They are horrifyingly factual. One dare not go beyond biblical criteria.

Does this make Christ less than Lord? No! Instead, it proves Him to be Lord as much as He proved His lordship on the cross (Col. 2:15). "In the dispensation of the fulness of times" God will "gather together in one all things in Christ, both which are in heaven, and which are on earth; even in Him" (Eph. 1:10). For some undisclosed or veiled reason, however, He permits history to take a course beyond human comprehension, assuring man only that His is the victory. In this the Christian rests with confidence!

NOTES

1. Lesslie Newbigin, *Trinitarian Faith and Today's Mission* (Richmond, Va.: John Knox, 1964), p. 14.
2. Arno C. Gaebelein, *Christianity or Religion?* (New York: Our Hope, 1927).
3. Samuel G. Craig, *Christianity Rightly So Called* (Philadelphia: Presbyterian & Reformed, 1946).
4. W. H. Griffith Thomas, *Christianity Is Christ* (London: Longmans, Green, & Co., 1919).
5. J. H. Bavinck, *The Church Between Temple and Mosque* (Grand Rapids: Eerdmans, 1966), p. 13.
6. Branislaw Malinowski, *Myth In Primitive Psychology* (Westport, Conn.: Negro U., 1926). p. 91.
7. George W. Peters, *A Biblical Theology of Missions* (Chicago: Moody, 1972), pp. 320-21.
8. Hans-Werner Gensichen, "Dialogue with Non-Christian Religions," in *The Future of the Christian World Mission*, eds. William J. Danker and Wi Jo Kang (Grand Rapids: Eerdmans, 1971), pp. 33-35.
9. Carl F. Braaten, *The Flaming Center* (Philadelphia: Fortress, 1977), pp. 93-118.
10. Raymond Hammer, *Japan's Religious Ferment* (New York: Oxford U. 1962), p. 91.
11. Hendrick Kraemer, *The Christian Message in a Non-Christian World* (Grand Rapids: Kregel, 1956), p. 351.
12. William James, *The Varieties of Religious Experiences* (New York: Longmans, Green, & Co., 1902).

General Index

Abraham, and the law, 107
Abrahamic covenant
  believer's relationship to, 215-16
  and circumcision, 45-46
  and the imprecatory psalms, 122, 124-25
  and the olive tree, 44
Accommodation, and inspiration, 7-8
Amillenarians
  and Israel, 42
  view of the church, 40
  view of the Millennium, 52-67
Angels, in the Millennium, 56-57
Apologetics
  apostolic testimony, 72-73
  as confirmed testimony, 70-71
  and glory to God, 75
  Johannine, 68-80
  last will and testament, 72-73
  purpose of, 74-76
  results of, 76-77
  and salvation, 75-76
  scope of, 78-79
  as sealed testimony, 72
  and "signs," 68, 71
  and supernatural, 70
  as sworn testimony, 71-72
  as testimony, 69
  and truth, 74-75
  and unbelief, 77
  and "witness," 68, 71
Apostolic church, and sign gifts, 136, 138
Arminians, and unlimited redemption, 22-23
Atonement, limited and unlimited, 22-39
Augustine
  and first resurrection, 58
  and imprecatory psalms, 120

  and inerrancy, 7-8
  and the 1,000 years, 62
Authority
  and marital roles, 202-5
  of the Bible, 223

Balaam, 122
Balance
  in local church, 192, 196
  in marital roles, 199, 205
Bible
  authority of, 223
  and history, 254-59
  and Holy Spirit, 223-24
  inerrancy of, 3-12, 223
  inspiration of, 4-5, 223
  and miracles, 18-20
  and special revelation, 225-26
Body of Christ
  and the local church, 192-94
  unity of, 193

Call of God, 32
  to Jeremiah, 127-29
  to people today, 133
Calvin, John
  and Chalcedon, 103
  and the imprecatory psalms, 120
Calvinists, and limited redemption, 22-23
Chalcedon Council
  anniversary of, 93-103
  and Calvin, 103
  and Christology, 93-103
  and definition of faith, 101-3
  and *homoousion* doctrine, 99
  and *Myth-of-God-Incarnate* debate, 94-98
  and Nicene Creed, 98-100
Charismatic movement, 135

versus salvation, 158, 161-62
Feminism, 207-21
and Abrahamic covenant, 215-16
  and biblical interpretation, 212, 217-18
  and hermeneutics, 213-19
  and inspiration, 211-12, 218-19
  and marital roles, 198, 200-201
  and Paul, 207-21
  and subordination, 201-2
  and women in the church, 207-19
Forgiveness of sins
  and justification, 163-64
  and the law, 112

Gentiles, and Israel, 42-43
God
  call of, 32, 127-29, 133
  fellowship with, 160-62, 167
  holiness of, 109-10
  jealousy of, 150
  as light, 156-57, 159-60, 167
  and miracles, 15-17
  reality of, 240
  strength of, 130-32
  truthfulness of, 4-5
  wrath of, 241-42
Godliness, and Puritanism, 87-90
Great Commission, and limited atonement, 27-28

Heathen
  lost condition of, 233-46
  religions of, 249-60
Heilsgeschichte, 254
Hermeneutics
  and feminism, 213-19
  and Holy Spirit, 224
History
  and Bible, 254-59
  and Christianity, 254-56, 259
Holy Spirit
  and Bible, 223-24, 229
  cosmic operations of, 256-57
  and hermeneutics, 224
Homoousion, doctrine of, 99
"Hour of testing"
  meaning of, 177
  posttribulational view, 169, 177-80

pretribulational view, 169, 177-80
  purpose of, 179
  scope of, 178-79
Hume, and miracles, 14
Husbands. *See* Marital roles

Idolatry, and God's judgment, 242
Imprecatory psalms, 115-25
  and Abrahamic covenant, 122, 124-25
  attitude of author in, 123-24
  and Augustine, 120
  and Calvin, 120
  definition of, 116
  and ethics, 117
  identification of, 116-17
  problem of, 117-18
  purpose of, 121-22
  solutions to, 118-23
  and vengeance, 116-20
Inerrancy
  and accommodation, 7-8
  and Augustine, 7-8
  and Docetism, 9-11
  and Ebionism, 9-11
  and errancy, 5-6, 11
  and God's truthfulness, 4-5
  and inspiration, 3
  and subjectivism, 5-6
Inspiration, 3-5
  and accommodation, 7-8
  and feminism, 211-12
  and imprecatory psalms, 120-21
  and Jeremiah, 132
Israel
  and Abrahamic covenant, 44
  and amillenarians, 42
  and Balaam, 122
  and church, 40-50
  and Gentiles, 42-43
  of God, 41
  and the law, 109-14
  millennial representatives, 56
  and New Covenant, 47-49
  and New Jerusalem, 50
  and postmillenarians, 42
  and premillenarians, 42

James, epistle of
  and the Christian walk, 145

Index of Scripture

20:4	53, 56-57, 59-61, 72, 170, 179	20:11-15	55, 125
20:4-6	52-56, 61-62, 64-65	20:12	31
20:5	61, 63-64	20:14	64
20:7-15	55	20:15	54
20:9	61	22:17	37